POWS AND THE GREAT WAR

THE LEGACY OF THE GREAT WAR
A Series sponsored by the Historical de la Grande Guerre Péronne-Somme

General Editor
JAY WINTER

Previously published titles in the series

Antoine Prost
IN THE WAKE OF WAR
'Les Anciens Combattants' and French Society

Patrick Fridenson
THE FRENCH HOME FRONT 1914-1918

Stéphane Audoin-Rouzeau
MEN AT WAR 1914-1918

Gerald D. Feldman
ARMY, INDUSTRY, AND LABOR IN GERMANY 1914-1918

Rosa Maria Bracco
MERCHANTS OF HOPE

Adrian Gregory
THE SILENCE OF MEMORY
Armistice Day 1919-1646

Ute Daniel
THE WAR FROM WITHIN
German Working-Class Women in the First World War

Annette Becker
WAR AND FAITH
The Religious Imagination in France, 1914-1930

David W. Lloyd
BATTLEFIELD TOURISM
Pilgrimage and the Commemoration of the Great War
in Britain, Australia and Canada, 1919-1939

Alex King
MEMORIALS OF THE GREAT WAR IN BRITAIN
The Symbolism and Politics of Remembrance

Margaret H. Darrow
FRENCH WOMEN AND THE FIRST WORLD WAR
War Stories of the Home Front

POWS AND THE GREAT WAR
Captivity on the Eastern Front

ALON RACHAMIMOV

Oxford ● New York

For Tami, Amit and Iddo

First published in 2002 by
Berg
Editorial offices:
150 Cowley Road Oxford, OX4 1JJ, UK
838 Broadway, Third Floor, New York, NY 10003-4812, USA

Berg is the imprint of Oxford International Publishers Ltd.

Library of Congress Cataloging-in-Publication Data

Rachamimov, Alon.
  POWs and the Great War : Captivity on the Eastern Front / Alon
Rachamimov.
      p. cm. -- (The legacy of the Great War)
Includes bibliographical references and index.
    1. World War, 1914-1918--Prisoners and prisons, Russian.
2. Austro-Hungarian Monarchy. Heer--History--20th century.
3. Prisoners of war--Austria--History--20th century. 4. Prisoners of
war--Hungary--History--20th century. I. Title. II. Series.
    D627.R8 R33 2002
    940.4'7247—dc21

                                                    2002000016

British Library Cataloguing-in-Publication Data

A catalogue record for this book is available from the British Library.

ISBN 1 85973 573 8 (Cloth)
         1 85973 578 9 (Paper)

Typeset by JS Typesetting, Wellingborough, Northants.
Printed in the United Kingdom by MPG Books, Cornwall.

Contents

List of Figures, Tables and Charts   vii

Acknowledgements   ix

List of Abbreviations   xii

Introduction   1
Clio's Veil   1
Historiographic Contexts   4

1   **Becoming Prisoners of War**   31
    The Creation of the Austro-Hungarian POW Problem   31
    Austro-Hungarian POWs in Russia: A Quantitative
       Overview   34
    Becoming POWs: The View from Below   44

2   **The Hague Convention and the Treatment of POWs:**
    Mission and Omissions   67
    Prisoner of War Camps in World War I and the 'Barbaric'
       Twentieth Century   67
    The Legal Framework   69
    The 'Prototype' Thesis   78

3   **The Treatment of POWs in Russia**   87
    Prisoner of War Camps and other Places of Internment   88
    Living Conditions in POW Camps   97
    Prisoners of War as Labor   107
    Propaganda and Recruitment Among the Prisoners   115
    The Treatment of POWs and the Perception of
       World War I   122

Contents

4   **In Search of the 'Good and Loyal Prisoner': The Austro-Hungarian Censorship and the POWs**   133

Patriotism in a Multi-National State   133

The Austro-Hungarian POW Censorship   135

Austro-Hungarian POWs, the Censorship and the Issue of Loyalty   145

5   **The Emperor's Clothes: The Austro-Hungarian POW Relief Effort**   161

POW Relief in World War I: The Uniqueness of the Eastern Front   161

The Austro-Hungarian POW Material Relief   164

The Austro-Hungarian Nurses   172

6   **Imperial Identities and Personal Concerns: The Perspective of the Prisoners**   191

Repatriation and the Repatriation System (*Heimkehrwesen*)   191

Prisoner of War Letters and their Usefulness as a Historical Source   196

The Relief Effort: The Prisoners' Perspective   197

Epilogue: Captivity in the Collective Remembrance of the Great War – The Emergence of a Commemorative Pecking Order   221

Bibliography   231

Index   251

Figures, Tables and Charts

Figure 0.1: cover of In *Feindeshand*. Source: In *Feindeshand* 2

Figure 1.1: Losses Reported by the Austro-Hungarian 10th Infantry Division between 10–25 September 1915. Source: Kriegsarchiv, Vienna 36

Figure 1.2: POWs resting on their way to the Russian rear. Source: *Za Svobodu* 49

Figure 1.3: Assembly Camp Darnitsa near Kiev. Source: *Za Svobodu* 56

Figure 3.1: Rank-and-file POWs eating 'Russian style' from a collective bowl. Source: Kriegsarchiv, Vienna 98

Figure 3.2: Class schedule from the officer camp of Krasnoyarsk. Source: Military Archives Freiburg im Breisgau, Germany 100

Figure 3.3: Memorandum written by officers in Irkutsk complaining of overcrowding with accompanying diagrams. Source: Russian State Military-Historical Archive (RGVIA) 102

Figure 3.4: POW officers delousing their beds in the camp of Rasdolnoe. Color illustration in the camp journal. Source: Military Archives Freiburg im Breisgau, Germany 106

Figure 4.1: Prisoners writing their first letter from captivity. Source: *Za Svobodu* 136

Figure 4.2: Letter written by POW officer (and future historian) Hans Kohn to his friend Robert Weltsch (future editor of the Zionist Newspaper *Die Welt*). The letter was intercepted by the censorship due to its Zionist content. Written on 7 October 1917. Source: Kriegsarchiv, Vienna 143

Figure 4.3: Deciphered postcard from Khabarovsk (the Russian Far East) 19 December 1914 144

Figure 4.4: Two wedding photographs showing POWs with their new Russian wives. Source: Kriegsarchiv, Vienna 152

Figure 5.1: Distribution of aid at the Khabarovsk camp September 1916. Source: War Archives, Vienna 166

Figures, Tables and Charts

Figure 5.2: 'Is the sun finally coming into our lives?' The visit of Elsa Brändström in an infirmary barrack. Source: *In Feindeshand*   170

Figure 5.3: Prisoners in Chinese clothing from Tientsin. Source: Elsa Brändström, Unter Kriegsgefangenen in Rußland und Sibirien, 1914–1920   171

Figure 5.4: POWs in the camp of Chita displaying worn clothes to the Red Cross delegation. Source: Kriegsarchiv, Vienna   177

Figures 5.5: Nora Kinsky in nurse's uniform. Source: Kinsky, *Russisches Tagebuch*   184

Figure 5.6: Nora Kinsky distributing money. Source: Kinsky, *Russisches Tagebuch*   184

Table 1.1: POWs held by Primary Entente Belligerents   39

Table 1.2: POWs held by Central Powers   41

Table 3.1: Buildings Used to House POWs: Summer and Fall 1915   90

Table 4.1: The Personnel of the GZNB Censorship – 21 January 1916   140

Table 6.1: POWs Attitude Toward the Relief Effort: December 1916–November 1917   200

Table 6.2: Distribution of Complaint Letters: January– November 1917   205

Chart 4.1: The Mail Sorting Process at the GZNB   141

Acknowledgments

It is a great pleasure to thank those who helped me along the way with their advice, suggestions, critique, admonitions, financial support and caring encouragement. It is clear that this book would have been very different – or more likely would not have existed at all – without this help.

My adviser and teacher, Professor István Deák, guided this project from its embryonic stages, allowing me to benefit from his immense knowledge of Central European History. The members of my dissertation committee at Columbia University contributed to this project in their unique ways: Professor Volker Berghahn helped me immeasurably in urging me to think about methodology and the 'big picture'. Professor Dennis Showalter, the president of the Society for Military History, won me over with his erudition, encyclopedic knowledge, kind words and sports metaphors. Professor Mark von Hagen and Professor Claire Nolte challenged me with their vast knowledge of Russian and Czech History. At Columbia, I wish also to thank Professors Michael Stanislawski, Fritz Stern and John Micgiel, and the staff of the History Department, the Institute on East Central Europe and Butler Library especially Mr Bob Scott. The Harriman Institute has generously supported my archival research in Russia with a Pepsico fellowship and the History Department has twice awarded me a Brebner travel grant enabling me to present my work at academic conferences.

In Austria, I owe special gratitude to the Austrian Exchange Service (ÖAD) for its financial support during my stay in Vienna and to Mr Ernst Aichinger its representative in New York City. Professor Horst Haselsteiner encouraged me during my meandering travels in the Austrian archives, restoring my confidence over lunches of scampi and wine. Dr Rudi Jeřábek offered invaluable suggestions in the archives and introduced me to contemporary Austrian alpine music. Ms. Louise Hecht was, and still is, a wonderful friend and teacher. I wish to thank also Drs Erwin Schmidl, Tirza Lemberger,

Acknowledgments

Rainer Egger, Hannes Leidinger and Verena Moritz, as well as the whole staff of the Austrian State Archives. Thanks are also in order to Dr Christoph Tepperberg, the Director of the *Kriegsarchiv* for generously allowing me to use the photographic material contained in this book.

In Russia I would like to express my appreciation to Drs Sergei Listikov and Evgenii Sergeev and to the staff of the Russian State Military Historical Archive (RGVIA). Thanks are also due to the staff of the Institute of Universal History at the Russian Academy of Sciences for organizing the first conference on World War I captivity and facilitating my research in the archives.

In Germany I benefitted from a German Academic Exchange Service (DAAD) stipend. I would like to thank my adviser there, Dr Wolfram Wette, and the staff of the German Military Archives in Freiburg im Breisgau. I would like also to thank historian Dr Reinhard Nachtigal.

Many colleagues and friends supported me at various stages of this journey. It is a joy to be able to acknowledge them: Professor Maria Bucur, Professor Alon Confino, Dr Mark Cornwall, Professor Gerald H. Davis, Professor Peter Fritzsche, Dr Eagle Glassheim, Professor Nili Gold, Professor Charles Ingrao, Professor Alon Kadish, Dr Christian Nielsen, Professor Peter Pastor, Professor David Rousseau, Professor Gary Shanafelt, Professor Emmanuel Sivan, Professor Daniel Unowsky, Professor Nancy Wingfield, Professor Robert Wistrich and Professor Moshe Zimmermann. I would like to thank in particular Drs Shelly Dattner and Susanna Neumann for their encouragement and advice. It meant a great deal to me.

Hamon todot to the History Department at Tel Aviv University and especially its former chairperson, Professor Miri Eliav-Feldon, for offering me a place to teach and work upon the completion of my doctoral studies. You made me feel very welcome.

I would like to express my thanks to Ms Kathryn Earle, the Editorial and Managing Director of Berg Publishers, and all the people at Berg who helped publish this book. My thanks and enormous admiration go to Professor Jay Winter, the General Editor of the Legacy of the Great War Series, and one of the foremost authorities on World War I.

I would like to thank two committees for honoring this book with distinguished prizes, even before its publication: The Talmon Prize awarded by the Israeli Academy of Sciences and the Hebrew University in Jerusalem and the Fraenkel Prize, bestowed by the Institute of Contemporary History and the Wiener Library in London to young historians completing a first major study.

I would like to express my thanks and love to my parents Hannah and Rami Rahamimoff, my brother Nimrod, my sister Tammy and my father-in-law Dan Spira. The Klein clan of New Jersey has been kind and caring during our years in New York; my love to Vera, Reuben, Sonia, Ron, Jennifer and all the Klein kids. The late Imre Klein passionately talked to me about Central European history; he would have probably given me a few pointers about this book too.

Finally, my greatest appreciation and thanks go to my wife Tami and my son Amit. Tami has read more versions of this book than I care to admit and dealt with the moods that regretfully accompany working on such a big project. She spent many long hours preparing the graphic work found in the following pages. Amit brought me constant joy in the past seven years. I thank him for being so lively, happy and alert.

Abbreviations

AdR	Archiv der Republik (Archive of the Republic-Austria)
AHY	Austrian History Yearbook
Akt.	Akte/n (File/s)
AOK	Armeeoberkommando (Army High Command-Austria-Hungary)
BA/MA	Bundesarchiv/Militärarchiv (Military Archives-Freiburg im Breisgau, Germany)
d.	delo (file)
f.	fond (collection)
IR	Infantrieregiment (Infantry Regiment)
Kart.	Karton (Carton)
k.u.k.	kaiserlich und königlich (Imperial and Royal)
GZNB	Gemeinsames Zentralnachweisbureau des Roten Kreuzes-Auskunftstelle für Kriegsgefangene (Central Information Bureau of the Red Cross-Austria-Hungary; POW Censorship)
KA	Kriegsarchiv (War Archive – Austria)
KÜA	Kriegsüberwachungsamt (War Supervisory Office, Austria)
KM	Kriegsministerium (War Ministry, Austria-Hungary)
NA	The National Archives of the United States
l.,ll.	list, listy (folio, folios)
op.	opis (inventory)
ÖstA	Österreichisches Staatsarchiv (Austrian State Archive)
ÖUlK	Österreichisch-Ungarns letzter Krieg 1914–1918
RGVIA	Rossiiskii gosudarstvennyi voenno-istoricheskii arkhiv (Russian State Military Historical Archives-Moscow)

Introduction

Clio's Veil

'War literature is gradually becoming enormous', wrote Professor Hans Weiland, the honorary chairman of the Austrian Federal Association of Former POWs (*die Bundesvereinigung der ehemaligen österreichischen Kriegsgefangenen* or B.e.ö.K.) in 1931.

> There are diaries by field marshals and leading diplomats, artillery men and munitions' workers . . . We listen to generals and soldiers, poets and humble storytellers describing what they thought, felt, did, and believed . . . But there is a World War appendage, which had been pushed back, already during the war but also after it, which remained almost unnoticed: war captivity, the fate of the neutralized fighters, the living dead. It is as though Clio herself is afraid to write down such a painful part of human history, afraid to lift the veil that covers people and fates about whom no one speaks gladly.[1]

The conviction that throughout Europe POWs have been ignored, pushed aside and denied a proper place among veterans led to the publication in 1931, in Vienna, of *In Feindeshand*, the most extensive compilation of personal recollections about World War I captivity ever to be brought together. Containing 477 separate contributions, a statistical appendix and hundreds of photographs, maps and illustrations, *In Feindeshand* aimed 'to present for the first time to the public' the story of 'around ten million Europeans who became captive during the World War, among them 1,300,000 Germans.'[2] According to the co-editor of the book, Dr Leopold Kern, the publication of *In Feindeshand* was crucial not only because of the torrent of memoirs about other war experiences, but also because 'with each passing year, the prisoners, those living sources for the study of captivity, become fewer and fewer; because relevant sources are lost through absent-mindedness and destruction, and because memory fades and interest disappears.'[3]

Figure 0.1 cover of *In Feindeshand*.

Source: *In Feindeshand*

By publishing *In Feindeshand*, Weiland and Kern hoped to convince (at the very least) the German-speaking public that captivity was a significant part of the war, and should consequently be given a proper place in its collective remembrance.[4] Nonetheless, despite the ubiquity of ex-prisoners in post World War I Europe (one out of every eight veterans to re-enter civilian society after the war had been a POW), despite the activities of ex-POWs organizations and despite the publication of scores of POW memoirs, the story of captivity never became part of what had been termed the Memory (or the Idea) of the Great War.[5] In this respect, the publication of *In*

Feindeshand in 1931, the establishment of the *Archiv und Museum der Kriegsgefangenschaft* (also in Vienna) and even the founding of a Blue Cross organization to deal specifically with POW matters did not change the marginality of war captivity.

Seven decades after the publication of *In Feindeshand* World War I is becoming once more a subject of considerable scholarly and popular interest. With the chronological end of the twentieth century in mind, a number of prominent historians turned their attention to the event that in the opinion of many constituted the 'primordial catastrophe' (*Urkatastrophe*) of the twentieth century, namely World War I. Roger Chickering, Niall Ferguson, Martin Gilbert, Holger Herwig, John Keegan, Hew Strachan, Manfried Rauchensteiner and Jay Winter have all published during the 1990s comprehensive studies of the First World War with a number of these works enjoying broad popular appeal.[6] Still, despite these significant recent additions to the historiography of World War I, the story of captivity remained at best what literary historian Samuel Hynes called a 'side show story'. Among the twenty-three separate contributions to *World War I: A History* not one focuses on prisoners of war, and only Niall Ferguson's book contains a section on the millions of captive soldiers. Michael Howard's point is certainly well taken that 'There has, to put it mildly, been no lack of books on the First World War during the past half century, but if we reckon them all up they only tell us a great deal about very little of it.'[7]

Why should that be the case? After all, there were millions of ex-World War I prisoners of war living in post-World War I Europe, some of whom would later achieve great fame or notoriety. Otto Bauer, Bela Kun, Ernst Reuter and Josip Broz Tito were all POWs during World War I, as were the influential historians Henri Pirenne and Hans Kohn and the immensely popular Czech satirist Jaroslav Hašek. Captivity continued to have an emotional grip for countless others with POW associations holding reunions well into the 1960s and newsletters informing members about deaths, relocations and newly-published memoirs. The absence of studies on World War I captivity is particularly remarkable in connection with the eastern front and with Austria-Hungary. Out of an estimated eight-and-a-half million men taken captive during the First World War, about six million were captured on the eastern front where warfare had been mobile and frontlines longer than anywhere else. One could justifiably make the argument that captivity was one of the quintessential war experiences for soldiers serving in the Russian and Austro-Hungarian armies: about 2.8 million Russian soldiers became prisoners of war during the war, almost exactly the same number as the estimated 2.77 million Austro-Hungarians. In the case of the Habsburg Monarchy the number of POWs was especially noteworthy because prisoners accounted for more than one third of the total number of men mobilized in the years 1914–18.

On one level the purpose of this study is simple: to fill a considerable empirical gap in the historiography of World War I, particularly in the historiography of the eastern front. By relying on archival sources from Austria, Germany, Russia and the US, this work examines fundamental aspects of the experience of prisoners of war on the eastern front, primarily Austro-Hungarian POWs in Russia: the process of becoming prisoners, treatment in captivity, the activity of international philanthropic societies (primarily the Red Cross) and the intricate relationship between captive soldiers and the home country. Throughout history these themes have been the *sine qua non* of narratives about captivity (military and otherwise), reflecting what psychologist Amia Lieblich called 'age old human myths about the Fall and Return'.[8]

World War I captivity ought to be researched because it constituted one of the most widespread and important experiences of the war. Yet, captivity can also serve as a fascinating case study for a number of current academic discussions. Throughout this work I attempt to demonstrate that the study of POWs can illuminate in a very unique way much broader issues such as the formation of collective identities and loyalties, the writing of history from the perspective of non-elite groups or the legacy of World War I on human rights in the twentieth century. In the following pages I will survey what has been written so far about World War I captivity and place this present study within a larger theoretical perspective.

Historiographic Contexts

The story of World War I captivity encompasses eight years, from the very first days of fighting in August 1914 until the repatriation of the last group of POWs from the port of Vladivostok in the summer of 1922. Most of the prisoners who survived the ordeal (and an estimated 750,000 out of 8,500,000 prisoners died in enemy custody) spent on average three to four years in captivity before returning home in the years 1918–19. About 430,000 prisoners from Austria-Hungary, Germany and Turkey found themselves in Siberia and

Turkestan during the Russian Civil War and were transported back only in the years 1921-22. As in other wars in the twentieth century, World War I POWs were the last group of veterans to return to civilian life, constituting a fresh reminder of a past that many of their compatriots had already begun to put behind them.

The military historian, Richard Holmes, is probably correct in arguing that a certain degree of disillusionment is inevitable for all returning veterans, soldiers as well as POWs.[9] Peacetime civilian society rarely offers moments of intense self awareness that accompany the threat of death at the front. It rarely provides for close non-familial affective relationships akin to wartime 'camaraderie'.[10] And it rarely exposes a person to exotic places, strange events and unusual people which are often part and parcel of the soldierly experience.[11] Thus, although 'home' is invariably the ultimate place of yearning, it is often an idealized version of home purged of frictions and stifling routines. For returning POWs this disillusionment was in certain respects more acute than for other veterans: they were away for a longer period of time, the details of life in captivity were less-known to civilians and, as Jonathan Vance pointed out, there was far less sympathy for POWs than for other groups of veterans.[12]

With a few notable exceptions, the great majority of people who wrote about World War I captivity during the interwar period were either ex-POWs themselves or officials who had been involved in some capacity in POW affairs. Although ideologically these writers traversed the whole gamut between pacifism and bellicose nationalism, they did nonetheless share a common objective – to make captivity less foreign and unknown.

The interwar literature dealing with captivity in Russia could be divided into three broad groups.[13]

The first group consists of works written by various officials involved in POW affairs. The most important text in this group was by far Elsa Brändström's *Among Prisoners of War in Russia and Siberia* which was published first in Germany in 1920 under the title *Unter Kriegsgefangenen in Russland und Sibirien 1914-1920*.[14] Based on Brändström's highly successful Swedish lecture tour at the beginning of that year, the book described in detail the living conditions of Austro-Hungarian and German POWs in Russia and the activities of various relief agencies on their behalf. As the daughter of the Swedish Ambassador in Petrograd, Brändström coordinated the POW relief in Russia for five-and-a-half years, under the auspices of the Swedish Red Cross, traveling widely throughout Russia and visiting many individual POW camps. Her hands-on involvement in the organization of relief and her extensive connections placed her in a position to provide both a grass-roots and a bird's-eye view of captivity. Furthermore, Brändström's belief that she 'was the only neutral who witnessed the fate of the prisoners of war in Russia and Siberia from beginning to end' convinced her that her duty was to 'rouse public opinion to the necessity of new legislation for dealing with prisoners of war.'[15] Thus, at the center of Brändström's book is an assessment of the treatment of prisoners of war in Russia and a plea for international humanitarian cooperation. Like her diplomatic colleagues at the American Embassy in Russia, Brändström often found herself baffled by contradictory impulses within various Russian administrations and by the discrepancy between the official policy of abiding by the Hague Convention and the reality she witnessed in camps. She therefore preferred to focus on the material and psychological adversity encountered by the prisoners and the various attempts to aid them. In this respect *Among Prisoners of War in Russia and Siberia* is an authoritative, sober portrayal of the plight of prisoners, and of the great difficulties in organizing an effective relief effort. The fact that Brändström often used 'national characterizations' (for example 'The good-nature of the Russian is proverbial . . . [although] there is something childlike, unbalanced and unaccountable in his nature'; 'the natural charm of the Austrian' and so forth) as explanatory devices when concrete information was unavailable does not detract from the solidity of her work. Her main concern was by no means to prove certain 'national traits' or to construct a European hierarchy of civility.

In addition to Elsa Brändström, a number of other Red Cross nurses published accounts of their work with the prisoners.[16] Like Brändström these were almost all patrician women whose primary concern was examining the living conditions in the camps. However, in contrast to Brändström, who as a delegate from a neutral country stayed in Russia throughout World War I and most of the Civil War, the other nurses visited Russia only on three to four months' stints as representatives of the Austrian, Hungarian and German Red Cross Societies. The fact that, in the midst of a fierce war, official enemy envoys were permitted to inspect hundreds of internment facilities is unusual in twentieth century history; a testimony to the aristocratic threads that connected these three warring empires. Indeed the list of names reads like a 'who's who' of central European aristocracy: Princess Kunigunde von Croy-Dülmen, Countess Nora Kinsky, Countess Anna Revertera, Countess Helene von Rosty-Forgách, Countess Alexandrine von Uexküll, Baroness Käthe von Mihalotzy and others. With the exception of Nora Kinsky, who stayed as a simple nurse in Astrakhan in the years 1917–18 to be near her interned brother Zdenko, the other nurses usually lacked an in-depth knowledge of the circumstances of captivity and relied at times on crude national stereotypes (especially Anna Revertera). Still, these accounts constitute a distinct and fascinating body of literature, relevant to the study of philanthropy, gender and class during warfare.

The works of three Austro-Hungarian high-ranking officials – Ernst von Streeruwitz, Heinrich Freiherr von Raabl-Werner and General Max Ronge – provide useful factual information about captivity while opening a window into how POWs were perceived by the civilian and military leadership of the Dual Monarchy.[17] Ernst von Streeru-witz, a Christian Social industrialist from western Bohemia whose political career would climax in his short tenure as Austrian Chanc-ellor in 1928, headed the political section of Department 10.Kgf. (or 10.Kgf/Abt.) of the Austro-Hungarian War Ministry. This department was in charge of coordinating the activities of POW offices in the Army, Foreign Office, Red Cross, Censorship and the Emperor's Military Bureau, and consequently synthesized an enormous amount of information into specific reports about different aspects of captivity.[18] These reports as well as Streeruwitz's private wartime notes became the basis for his unpublished manuscript *Kriegs-gefangene im Weltkrieg* which he deposited in the Viennese *Heeres-geschichtliches Museum* in October 1928. Parts of this manuscript were later published in *In Feindeshand* and in Streeruwitz's 1937 memoirs *Springflut über Österreich*. As in the case of the nurses' narratives, the treatment of POWs in Russia occupied a central role in his writings, but as expected a much greater place was given to the activity of the Dual Monarchy on behalf of its captured soldiers. In his writings Streeruwitz advanced a thesis consisting of four interlocking arguments: in the years 1914–18 Austro-Hungarian POWs suffered great misery principally because the Russians disre-garded the Hague Convention; the Austro-Hungarian government opted for the high moral ground and did not retaliate against Russian POWs in the Dual Monarchy despite pressure from the Austro-Hungarian Army High Command (AOK); the only way to alleviate the misery of Austro-Hungarian prisoners was by sending relief to

Russia; however, this relief was not sufficient due to the great shortages at home and the large number of prisoners in Russia, 'but the maximum was done under the given conditions'.[19] Consequently, argued Streeruwitz, the Austro-Hungarian authorities and by extension the Austro-Hungarian state were regarded with unfair hostility by the POWs and their families. This 'official' reading of captivity resonated also in the writings of Streeruwitz's colleague in 10.Kgf/Abt, Heinrich von Raabl-Werner. Although Raabl-Werner published sparsely and did not rise into subsequent prominence in postwar Austrian politics as Streeruwitz did, he was nonetheless the only Austrian official to handle POW affairs continuously between the years 1914–22. During the first years of the First Republic he advised the Austrian State Committee on POWs and Civil Internees, and served as the Head of the Bureau for POW Affairs (*Amtsleiter des Kriegsgefangenenamtes*) until the repatriation of the last prisoners.[20] Raabl-Werner functioned as the ultimate reference for factual information for writers like Elsa Brändström, and it was he who calculated the final number of Austro-Hungarian POWs in Russia at 2,111,146 (a number that even he admitted was absurdly precise). In contrast to Streeruwitz who often used pathos to accentuate his assertions, Raabl-Werner was ever the *Beamte* relying on a matter-of-fact style and analytic approach; his 'Austria-Hungary's Official POW Relief' is prefaced by the statement: 'This study is based on archival material from the Viennese Archives and consequently can . . . claim full authenticity.'[21] Raabl-Werner's writings were well within the 'official' Austro-Hungarian interpretation but not as explicitly (nor in so racist a tone) anti-Russian as Streeruwitz's work. He was perfectly willing to admit that Austro-Hungarian authorities themselves made grave errors during the war, which sometimes resulted in unnecessary misery for the families of POWs. Yet, in the final analysis, he still held the view that the Russians were the ones who were chiefly responsible for POW suffering. A third high-level official who wrote about the prisoners was Colonel General (*Generaloberst*) Max Ronge, head of the Intelligence Bureau in the Austro-Hungarian General Staff (and the successor of the notorious Colonel Redl). In 1918 General Ronge was responsible for weeding out Bolshevik and anti-Habsburg sentiments among returning POWs and instituting a repatriation system which would 're-educate' the *Heimkehrer* and ascertain loyalty. His memoirs published in 1933 provide a fascinating glimpse into the attitudes of the Habsburg military leadership towards the POWs, particularly during the latter part of the war.

The second group of interwar sources consists of narratives written by ex-POWs and published in the form of essays, memoirs, diaries or captivity fiction.[22] These texts were written almost exclusively by POW officers, the great majority of whom came from a bourgeois and educated background. The military chaplain Karl Drexel, for example, was a well-known Catholic priest from the alpine province of Vorarlberg even before the war, Roman Dyboski taught at the Jagiellonian University in Cracow (and later became its rector) and Avigdor Hameiri was a rising expressionist poet on the nascent Hebrew literary scene. Out of the 477 contributions in the collaborative effort, *In Feindeshand*, probably less than thirty texts were written by rank-and-file POWs. The preponderance of officers among the POW memoirists stands in sharp contrast to their actual share among the prisoners: according to the official Austro-Hungarian statistics 54,146 officers were taken captive by the Russians during World War I or a mere 2.5 percent of the total number of POWs.

These texts adhered usually to a uniform plot structure (a sequence of seven 'narrative event-scenarios' in Robert Doyle's terminology) which commenced with the pre-captivity period, continued with the protagonist's capture, his removal from the front, his daily-life in captivity, his repatriation and finally reflections on the time lost.[23] The second of these seven stages, 'Capture', was a blown-up description of how the narrator became a prisoner, usually presented in such a way as to absolve him from personal disgrace. Combat injuries became the ultimate indication of having performed one's duty and, when these were absent, other exculpatory factors were emphasized. The Austrian surgeon, Professor Burghard Breitner (later President of the Austrian Red Cross Society), named his memoirs *Unverwundet Gefangen* to indicate the ignoble nature of his capture and his inability to justify himself completely. Prisoner-of-war memoirists invariably strove to prove that their capture was not due to their own failings as men, soldiers and patriots. A World War I POW memoir seemed as an apologia that appealed for understanding and absolution from the reading public. This contrasted with front-line narratives, especially Western-front texts, which cast a critical look at their own societies and demanded explanations (or scapegoats) for the discrepancy between pre-war expectations and front-line realities. Thus, POW memoirs lacked the edge and the urgency of other narratives and conceded priority in the commemorative pecking order.[24]

Among the narratives written by ex-POWs in Russia, the most important was the collaborative work *In Feindeshand* published in two volumes in Vienna in 1931.[25] As mentioned above, the editors of *In Feindeshand*, Leopold Kern and Hans Weiland, regarded the work as part of a broad campaign to make captivity an integral part of the collective remembrance of the Great War, and established in addition a museum for captivity as well as a Blue Cross society for POW affairs. Although the great majority of the contributors to *In Feindeshand* were German speakers from the former lands of the Habsburg monarchy, the work itself was tinged with a pan-European spirit and a mood of 'we were all victims of the War'. Hans Weiland entertained the hope that presenting the story of the prisoners of the Great War might serve as an uplifting example for contemporaneous Europeans about people of various backgrounds who could actually live together: 'Germans with Russians, Italians, French, English . . . all kinds of occupations, parties, world-views and religions; Catholics, Protestants, Anglicans, Calvinists (Hungarians), Orthodox, Jews, Mohammedans and Buddhists.'[26] Accordingly, the cover of *In Feindeshand* shows a circular chain whose links contain miniature portraits representing various nationalities: the German POW connected to the Russian, the Austro-Hungarian to the Italian, the Australian to the Turk and so forth (see Figure 0.1). Despite, the idyllic phrases and the grand hopes, the work focused almost exclusively on captivity in Russia, proceeding along a traditional captivity plot structure (Doyle's seven narrative event scenarios) and providing the first comprehensive statistical appendix of World War I captivity.

In addition to *In Feindeshand* and to the abundance of published officer memoirs – the most important of which are footnoted below – three additional works by ex-POWs should be mentioned. The first two works belong to a category designated by the literary historian Paul Fussell as 'fiction-memoirs' – works whose primary concern is not 'accurate recall' but rather 'recovering moments' while making a bigger point.[27] The first of these 'fiction-memoirs' is Edwin Erich Dwinger's best-selling trilogy, which was published in Germany in the years 1929–31. The first two volumes of the trilogy, *The Army behind Barbed Wire* (*Die Armee hinter Stacheldraht*) and *Between White and Red* (*Zwischen Weiß und Rot*) recounted respectively Dwinger's experiences as a POW ensign in Russian captivity and as a volunteer officer fighting with White Cossack forces in Siberia in the years 1919–20.[28] As a son of a Prussian father and a Russian mother, Dwinger spoke both German and Russian fluently and was

quite immersed in the culture of both countries. In his portrayal of
the life of rank-and-file POWs in Russia (and Dwinger indeed spent
the first two years of captivity among the men), Dwinger attempted
to present a sympathetic view of the 'true' Russia and appeal for
German-Russian understanding based on reliable information about
the respective peoples. Following the same plot-lines of *All Quiet
on the Western Front* (where the brutalities and deprivations of their
wartime experience affect a group of friends), Dwinger produced
the most widely read account in German about World War I captivity,
and one of the most affecting works to present the experiences
'from below'. In this sense, Dwinger attempted to link captivity
literature with the themes and sensibilities of western front literature.
Differently put, Dwinger endeavored to transform captivity from a
'sideshow' to an integral part of the story of the Great War.[29]

The second important 'fiction-memoir' was Avigdor Hameiri's
pacifist work in Hebrew, *Be-gehenom shel Mata* (Hell on Earth),
which constituted the second volume of his wartime memoirs (the
first was *Ha-Shiga'on Ha-Gadol* (*The Great Madness*).[30] Hameiri
(born Feuerstein) dedicated a substantial part of his life's work to
arguing against the evils of war, producing altogether two autobio-
graphical novels, one play, twenty-seven short stories and fifty poems
centering on the eastern front and on captivity. Besides having the
distinction of being – in Avner Holtzman's words – 'the first best-
seller written in the Hebrew language', Hameiri's memoirs provide
a fascinating example of the myriad of identities and loyalties
competing for the attention of a late-imperial Habsburg subject.
Being simultaneously a Hungarian patriot, a Zionist, a Habsburg
officer, a cosmopolitan writer, a young man and a prisoner, Hameiri
confronted in affecting style the push and pull of various identities.
His brief and exceptionally scathing descriptions of homosexual
relationships among the prisoners are one of the only sources to deal
directly with the issue of love and sexuality among POWs.

However, the work which illuminates questions of sexual identity
most notably is Hermann Pörzgen's *Theater ohne Frau*, which
focuses on the theatrical productions of German-speaking POWs in
Russia.[31] A significant part of the work is devoted to the men who
portrayed women on stage (accompanied by luscious 'glamorous'
pictures) and how their admiration extended in many cases well
beyond the confines of the stage. This adulation of the woman
impersonator in camps attests to the theater's role in creating a safe
arena where erotic tensions and definitions of masculinity could be

explored. Pörzgen's work (as well as the short section on the POW theater in *In Feindeshand*) does not seem to support the thesis of literary critic Marjorie Garber regarding the strong misogynist qualities of the POW all-male theater.[32]

The third group of works published during the interwar years focused on anti-Habsburg and Bolshevik military formations recruited from the POW population in Russia and revolved around the issues of nationalism, patriotism and class loyalties. The great majority of these works focused on specific groups of prisoners (such as Czech Legionnaires, volunteers to South Slav units or the Bolshevik Internationalists) and usually approached the material from a partisan point of view.[33] The Czech Legion attracted the most attention mainly because of its victorious confrontation with the nascent Red Army in the spring of 1918 and its self-proclaimed 'anabasis' – with its classical mythical allusions – through Siberia during the years 1918–20.[34] Works about the Legion published in Czech during the First Czechoslovak Republic reflected generally a strong nationalist sentiment. With the exception of literature written by Czech communists, the Legion was regularly portrayed as the scion of the Hussite soldierly spirit of the fourteenth and fifteenth centuries, an interpretation created and promoted by the president of the republic, T. G. Masaryk. In scholarly monographs such as those by Šteidler and Kudela, through commemorative books as for example the four-volume history *For Liberty* (*Za Svobudu*), through personal reminiscences of leading figures such as Masaryk, Gajda and Vondrák to sanitized textbooks for school children, Legionnaires came to assume a legendary place as co-founders of the Czechoslovak state (alongside the leaders of the émigré 'Mafia' Masaryk, Beneš and Štefánik).[35]

However, captivity itself seldom occupied a prominent role in these narratives. it was either the conduct of Czech soldiers prior to their capture by the Russian army – especially a few prominent cases of ostensible mass desertion (for example Infantry Regiments 28 and 36) – or the story of the volunteers after they had left internment facilities that figured prominently. Only rarely was it even mentioned that the great majority of Czech POWs preferred to languish in camps rather than volunteer.[36] It was the mythologized, heroic and – as Nancy Wingfield aptly put it – the 'official historic memory' that was rehearsed and venerated in interwar Czechoslovakia.[37]

German-language works about the Czech Legion tended to underplay the heroic qualities of Czech volunteers, while highlighting

some of the more controversial actions of the Legion and its leadership. Thus, for example, the most celebrated victory of the Legion
– the battle of Zborov on 2 July 1917 – was presented as an outcome
of the disloyal and questionable behavior of the Legion's opponents,
the Czech soldiers of the Habsburg 35th and 75th Infantry Regiments.
It is ironic that both Czech and German nationalist historiography
agreed that the Czech soldiers of the Habsburg army were by and
large disloyal to the Habsburg monarchy.[38] The German historian
Margarete Klante, who wrote extensively about the Czech Legion
during the late 1920s and throughout the 1930s, saw the Legion
primarily as an anti-German and anti-Bolshevik tool of the Entente
powers. She and other German writers emphasized the atrocities
committed in Siberia by Czech Legionnaires and the controversial
decisions taken by the leadership of the Legion (for example, to hand
over Admiral Kolchak to the Bolsheviks for execution).[39]

In the same vein, the interwar literature about South Slav volunteers
and the prisoners fighting with the Red Army approached the subject
with an unmistakable political ax to grind. As in the case of the Czech
Legion in post-1918 Czechoslovakia, the soldiers of the Serbian
Volunteer Corps were extolled in interwar Yugoslavia. According to
Ivo Banac, their relatively insignificant military achievements while
fighting with the Serbian army on the Salonika front, acquired a
prominent symbolic place 'in the semi-official literature of interwar
Yugoslavia'.[40] Interestingly, it was the Czech historian, Milada Paulová,
who published the standard work about South Slav volunteers in
Zagreb in 1925, and who emphatically asserted that 'the volunteers
elevated the prestige of Serbia and with their own blood testified to
a doubting Europe that the Yugoslavs from the Austro-Hungarian
Monarchy demanded unification with Serbia.'[41] However, the frequent
dissention among South Slav volunteers, the overwhelming Serb
makeup of the rank-and-file (in contrast to the officer corps) and the
fact that the great majority of Serb, Croat and Slovene POWs in Russia
did not volunteer received only minor attention.

As mentioned above, the question of POW susceptibility to
socialist and Bolshevik ideas became a major concern of the Austro-
Hungarian leadership following the February revolution in 1917. The
participation of Magyar and German prisoners of war in Red Army
units during the Russian Civil War and the captivity background of
many commissars in the short-lived Hungarian Soviet Republic of
1919 (including its leader Bela Kun) gave support to the thesis
regarding the profound effects that the revolutionary changes in

Russia had at the very least on Magyar prisoners. Soviet historiography tended to emphasize the genuine class solidarity of POW Internationalists and estimated their number at 50,000 (of which 60–70 per cent were Hungarian speakers). In contrast, Hungarian historiography of the interwar years tended to downplay the number of POW volunteers and their communist convictions (while emphasizing their Jewish background), and suggested that malnutrition and abysmal camp conditions were the main driving forces.[42] There is dialectic irony in the fact that Soviet historiography preferred to emphasize an 'idealistic' explanation whereas Hungarian nationalist historiography opted for a 'materialist' explanation.

Interwar historiography about Russian captivity grappled with a number of distinct themes and focal points. For the most part it was fueled by the eagerness of ex-POWs to relate their story to a mostly-indifferent public. Alongside these texts were 'semi-official' studies that looked at questions of politicization and collective loyalties, usually within an accepted interpretive framework and at times bordering on hagiography.

From World War II until the late 1970s one sees a significant reduction both in the number of works about Russian captivity and in the scope of their subject matter. Gone completely were works focusing on humanitarian issues or on the experience of captivity *per se*. To a certain extent this development is understandable, taking into consideration the advancing age of POW memoirists and the more recent atrocities of World War II, which made World War I humanitarian concerns appear antiquated and irrelevant. The main focus shifted to political issues and more specifically to the participation of prisoners of war in various fighting formations during the years 1917–20.

As might be expected, works published in the Soviet bloc continued to devote considerable attention to the history of the internationalist volunteers.[43] In the years following the Twentieth Congress of the Communist Party in 1956 (at which Khrushchev revealed among other things the execution of Bela Kun and other leading Internationalists in the late 1930s) a new batch of works about the internationalist units began to see publication primarily in the USSR, Hungary and East Germany. The emphasis in this literature was on the organizational framework of the internationalist political sections (often examining them in microscopic detail), the military action of internationalists alongside the Red Guards and the Red Army and the role of a few well-known figures. Although seldom deviating from official party guidelines, these works did attempt at times to explain why relatively few POWs joined the Bolsheviks and why it was so difficult to make political commitments in such a volatile environment. As Russian political scientist Robert Ezerov argued recently, this in itself was a significant revision of Stalinist historiography.[44] Czechoslovakia during the 1950s saw the publication of a number of critical works about the role of the Czech Legion in revolutionary Russia, the most significant of which was Vlastimil Vávra's 1958 *Klamná cesta: Příprava a vznik protisovětského vystoupení* čs. *legií (The Wrong Road: The Preparation and Development of the Anti-Soviet Uprising of the Czechoslovak Legion)*. Vavra, alongside Karel Pichlík and Jaroslav Křížek returned to the subject during the Prague Spring, focusing this time on the complex forces influencing the role of the Legion such as Czech national aspirations, Austro-Hungarian politics, Russian revolutionary conditions and the policies of the entente. Pichlík's *Zahraniční odboj, 1914–1918, bez legend (Revolt Abroad, 1914–1918, Without Legends)* and the collaborative volume *Červenobílá a ruda (RedWhite and Red)* still remain very valuable syntheses.[45] The unique role of Yugoslavia among communist countries found expression in works praising simultaneously the South Slav Internationalists and South Slav entente volunteers. Ivan Očak, the leading scholar on the subject, introduced a canonical historical narrative on South Slav POWs which underscored their singular achievements and 'was very critical in the evaluation of the literature on the subject, of whatever provenance'.[46]

Works written during that period in the West – specifically, in Austria, France, West Germany and the US – did not differ in their choice of subject matter from their counterparts in eastern Europe. They had, however, the advantage of being able to examine political questions outside a framework of official historiography, but were nonetheless hampered by limited access to relevant archival sources. Particularly valuable among these works were the monographs written by Inge Przybilovski and Otto Wassermair in Austria, John Bradley in France, Gerburg Thunig-Nittner in West Germany and Ivan Völgyes and Rudolph Tökes in the United States.[47]

Since the early 1980s a number of historians (primarily working in the West) began to look at Russian captivity through the prism of social history. The first one to do so was Gerald H. Davis who published his ground-breaking article 'The Life of Prisoners of War in Russia, 1914–1921' in 1983.[48] In this article, Davis combined the humanitarian emphasis of interwar literature with the political

concerns of post- World War II historiography. By relying on diplomatic material, Danish Red Cross records and published memoirs,
Davis surveyed some of the most fundamental aspects in the life of
POWs in Russia (for example confinement, work, illness). Moreover,
Davis juxtaposed political questions and humanitarian issues in a way
that consistently reminds the reader that the political behavior of
the prisoners was not divorced from the realities of captivity. Davis
wrote three additional important articles regarding the Red Cross,
sports in captivity and a microhistorical study of the POW camp of
Krasnoyarsk. The main shortcomings of Davis's work lie in the fact
that he paid relatively little attention to the differences between
officers and men in captivity, which I argue are crucial to understanding the overall treatment of POWs in Russia (Chapter 3 below);
that he relied heavily on the 'official' Austro-Hungarian version of
captivity, rarely reflecting critically on the various biases and
subtexts contained within it; and that he continued to present the
opinions and behaviors of the rank-and-file POWs as either motivated
by material needs or influenced by manipulation from above.
Consequently, the great majority of the prisoners seldom appear as
three-dimensional subjects capable of acting and reacting.

In addition to Davis, important contributions have been made by
Hannes Leidinger regarding ex-POWs in Austrian society and politics
in the years 1917–20, Reinhard Nachtigal and Yulia Kudrina concerning the activities of the Red Cross, Verena Moritz about the POW
labor and its significance to the Russian economy, Yücel Yanikdağ
about Ottoman prisoners of war in Russia and by Nancy Wingfield
with regard to the memory of the battle of Zborov in interwar
Czechoslovakia.[49] Likewise, solid research continued to be done
about issues of politicization and militarization among the POW
population, most significantly by Peter Pastor, Ivo Banac, Arnold
Krammer and again Verena Moritz.[50]

While drawing on the research and insights of previous scholars and
contributing to the questions and concerns outlined above, this study
seeks to place the study of captivity in a broader historiographical
scope.

First, by using many rank-and-file narratives – including over 3,000
letters written by POWs – this study forms part of what has been
called alternately 'history from below,' 'grass-roots history,' or
Alltagsgeschichte.[51] Although, each of these approaches is slightly
different (due to differences in time, place of origin, academic

environment and political agendas) they all share the goal of rescuing the experiences of the bulk of the population from what E. P. Thompson called 'the enormous condescension of posterity'.[52] The emphasis here is on 'experiences' and on how reality is subjectively perceived and interpreted by non-elite groups. In contrast to social scientists of the 1960s and 1970s who aimed at structural analysis and objective results, *Alltags* historians draw their inspiration from Clifford Geertz – and his call for 'thick description' – and look for a multiplicity of voices. Thus, in the past two decades a significant amount of work has been done in Britain, the US and Germany, of which the studies of Carlo Ginzburg, Sheila Fitzpatrick, Christopher Browning, Alf Lüdtke and John Keegan have proved very influential. However, grass-roots historians found it difficult at times to explain the wider significance of their work; put differently, the basic critique raised against this approach has revolved around the question 'what is attained by listening to a plethora of voices, beside a confusing cacophony?' In Chapters 1, 2, 3 and 6 of this work I examine three important debates where the methodology of 'history from below' provides unique and illuminating insights: the controversy regarding mass desertions on the eastern front (Chapter 1), the discussion about POW camps as 'prototypes' of Soviet gulags and Nazi concentration camps (Chapter 2 and 3) and the question of political attitudes and loyalties among Habsburg POWs (Chapter 6).

Second, this work is also a part of the much broader debate regarding the human rights implications of World War I. George Kennan, Thomas Nipperdey and others, saw the war as the *Urkatastrophe* of this century and suggested a direct trajectory between World War I and subsequent atrocities.[53] The thesis concerning the Great War as the event where Europe abandoned the ideals of progress (it was a 'hideous embarrassment to the Meliorist myth' in Paul Fussell's distinctive language)[54] is a widely held one. According to one of the most recent formulation of this interpretation – Omer Bartov's *Murder in our Midst* – World War I unleashed the murderous potential inherent in modernity itself and set into motion a process of 'industrial killing' that is still very much with us today (as evidenced by the examples of Rwanda and Bosnia). By analysing the treatment of POWs in Russia in the context of contemporaneous legal conventions I seek to re-examine this hypothesis and suggest why and in what way it should be qualified.

Third, this study also seeks to contribute to the burgeoning field of memory studies. The explosion in recent years in works about 'collective memory' – or, as more appropriately termed by J. Winter and E. Sivan 'collective remembrance', – attests to the widespread interest in understanding why and how certain memories are preserved by societies, while others are discarded.[55] Thus, from the early 1990s a significant amount of literature has been published about commemorations, 'sites of memory' (for example, museums and monuments) and the 'invention of tradition', which highlighted the constructed and at times manipulative character of collective remembrance. Some of the most important works in the field of memory studies have been done on World War I, most notably by George Mosse, Antoine Prost and Jay Winter. The epilogue of this work attempts to explain why World War I captivity never became part of the 'collective remembrance' of the war despite being such a common phenomenon.

Fourth, The historiography of World War I has been dominated so far by works focusing on the western front. By looking at what was above all an eastern front phenomenon, this book contributes to a small but growing number of works examining other aspects and other theaters of the war. Following in the footsteps of Norman Stone, Dennis Showalter, Manfried Rauchensteiner and Holger Herwig, I seek to demonstrate how different the warfare was in the east and why certain generalizations about the war (for example, that it was 'static') should be qualified.[56] Moreover, by focusing on the millions of prisoners who found themselves displaced by the war, this dissertation draws attention to the significant population movement which occurred in eastern Europe during World War I. Besides the prisoners of war, millions of civilian refugees (German, Polish, Ukrainian, Lithuanian and Jewish) either fled the fighting zone or were forcibly removed from the area by the Russian army. These refugees swelled the Russian and Austrian interior, living often in abysmal squalor. Mark von Hagen, David Rechter, Peter Gattrell and Vejas Gabriel Liulevicius have recently examined various aspects of this population dislocation.[57]

Finally, this book is part of an expanding body of literature examining nationalism and patriotism. Since the early 1980s historians, sociologists, anthropologists and political scientists have attempted to understand what creates and sustains the bond between individuals and large, abstract entities (imagined or otherwise). Still, despite many studies examining attachments to nations and nation states, relatively few have looked at the links between individuals and multi-national states. By analyzing the attitudes of Austro-

Hungarian POWs toward their home state (as well as the expectations of the Habsburg leadership vis-à-vis its captive soldiers), I aim to show that the recruited citizenry of the Dual Monarchy had expectations similar to those of citizens of nation states such as France and Germany.[58]

In addition to the sources described above, this work makes comprehensive use of archival material from Austria, Germany, Russia and the US, most of which has rarely, if ever, been used before.[59] The different types of archival and published sources provide an excellent opportunity to scrutinize captivity from different perspectives. As will be clear in the following pages, I do not think that looking at things 'from below' precludes examining issues also 'from above'. Rather, the two approaches can be and in many cases are complementary. The expectations and opinions of elite and non-elite groups should be examined both separately and in their interactions. In the same vein, statistics, charts and graphs can go together well with artwork, poems, photos, reminiscences and narrative analysis; all of which are included in the following pages.

Throughout this work names follow the spelling of the source. Diacritical marks were not always provided by the writers or do not always appear in official documents. Although it seems some of the names have been altered by the officials we cannot be sure of that. The best procedure therefore is to follow the given spelling rather than attempt to correct it according to today's conventions.

Notes

1. Hans Weiland, 'zum Geleite', in Hans Weiland and Leopold Kern (eds) *In Feindeshand: Die Gefangenschaft im Weltkriege in Einzeldarstellungen*, Vienna: Bundesvereinigung der ehemaligen österreichischen Kriegs-gefangenen, 1931), vol.1, p. 9.
2. The first figure – 10 million POWs – is an exaggeration. Most textbooks estimate the number of POWs during World War I in the area of 7.5–8.5 million POWs. The figure of 1.3 million German POWs pertains to all German-speaking POWs not just to those who were German citizens. See detailed discussion in Chapter 1 about the problems of assessing the number of POWs.

3. *In Feindeshand*, vol. 1, p. 32.

4. There was considerable debate in the 1990s regarding the meaning and applicability of the term 'collective memory'. In the context of this work I use the terms 'public memory' and 'collective memory' according to Michael Schudson's definition (who in turn is influenced by Maurice Halbwachs's ideas about collective memory). According to Schudson 'collective memory' refers to:

1 The fact that an individual memory is socially organized or socially mediated.

2 Socially produced artifacts that are the memory repositories (libraries, museums, monuments etc.) of past experiences.

3 Images of the past held by individuals who themselves did not exper- ience it but learned of it through cultural artifacts.

Jay Winter and Emmanuel Sivan present the view that 'memory' is 'collective' only in a metaphoric sense. It is individuals who do the remem- bering even if their memories are 'socially framed'. They suggest therefore the term 'collective remembrance' as a good alternative that doesn't involve anthropomorphism. See Michael Schudson, 'Dynamics of Distortion in Collective Memory', in Daniel Schacter (ed.), *Memory Distortion: How Minds, Brains and Societies Reconstruct the Past*, Cambridge: Harvard University Press, 1995, p. 348; see also Jay Winter and Emmanuel Sivan, 'Setting the Framework', in Jay Winter and Emmanuel Sivan (eds), *War and Remembrance in the Twentieth-Century*, Cambridge: Cambridge University Press, 1999; Pierre Nora, in Lawrence D. Kritzman (ed.), Arthur Goldhammer (trans.), *Realms Of Memory: Rethinking The French Past*, English edition, New York: Columbia University Press, 1996; Maurice Halbwachs, (ed.) *On Collective Memory*, Chicago: University Of Chicago Press, 1992.

5. George Mosse used the term 'Memory' alongside the term 'Myth'. In Mosse's terminology the 'Myth of the War Experience' is designed to mask the reality of war in the service of nationalist forces; Paul Fussell uses both 'memory' and 'Idea' as synonyms. To confuse things even further Samuel Hynes uses the term 'myth' but without the pejorative connotations of Mosse. For Hynes a myth is just a simplified version of what had actually happened designed to highlight a certain meaning. George Mosse, *Fallen Soldiers: Reshaping the Memory of the World Wars*, Oxford: Oxford Univeristy Press, 1990; Paul Fussell, *The Great War and Modern Memory*, Oxford: Oxford University Press, 1975; Samuel Hynes, *The Soldiers's Tale: Bearing Witness to Modern War*, New York: Penguin Books, 1997; Jay Winter, *Sites of Memory, Sites of Mourning: The Great War in European Cultural History*, Cambridge University Press, 1995.

6. Niall Ferguson, *The Pity of War: Explaining World War I*, New York: Basic Books, 1999; John Keegan, *The First World War*, New York: Alfred Knopf, 1999; Roger Chickering, *Imperial Germany and the Great War, 1914–1918*, Cambridge: Cambridge University Press, 1998; *The Oxford*

Introduction

Illustrated History of the First World War, ed. Hew Strachan, Oxford: Oxford University Press, 1998; Holger Herwig, *The First World War: Germany and Austria-Hungary 1914–1918*, London: Arnold, 1997; Jay Winter and Blaine Baggett, *1914–1918: The Great War and the Shaping of 20th Century*, London: BBC Books, 1996 this book accompanies the eight part PBS and BBC series; Martin Gilbert, *The First World War: A Complete History*, New York: Henry Holt and Company, 1994; Manfried Rauchensteiner, *Der Tod des Doppeladlers: Österreich-Ungarn und der Erste Weltkrieg*, Graz, Vienna, Cologne: Styria Verlag, 1993.

7. Michael Howard, '"Lighting the Torch", a review of Hew Strachan's The First World War, Vol.1 To Arms', *The Times Literary Supplement*, 20 July 2001, p. 28.

8. Amia Lieblich, *Seasons of Captivity: The Inner World of POWs*, New York: NYU Press, 1994, p. 11.

9. Richard Holmes, *Acts of War: The Behavior of Men in Battle*, New York: The Free Press, 1989, chapter 7.

10. 'Group cohesion' in contemporary military discourse or *Gemeinschaft* in the sociological terminology of Ferdinand Tönnies. See also George Mosse, *Fallen Soldiers*.

11. On that see W.G. Runciman, *Relative Deprivation and Social Justice*, London: Routledge & Kegan Paul, 1966.

12. Jonathan Vance, *Objects of Concern: Canadian Prisoners of War through the Twentieth Century*, Vancouver: University of British Columbia Press, 1994, p. 18. Moreover, the countries to which Austro-Hungarian, German, Turkish and Russian POWs returned in the years 1918-22 were fundamentally different from the ones that had originally sent them to war.

13. This division is based on the identity of the writer (official/nurse/statesman/POW), the kind of the text (memoir/fiction/history) and the main concern of the narrative (humanitarian/political). This classification is meant broadly to sort out various narratives written about captivity. It is not meant to be an exhaustive typology and there is some overlapping between the groups.

14. Elsa Brändström, *Unter Kriegsgefangenen in Russland und Sibirien 1914-1920*, Berlin: Koehler & Ameland, 1920. The revised English edition appeared in 1929 under the title *Among Prisoners of War in Russia and Siberia*, London: Hutchinson, 1929. All quotations in this book are from this edition. Elsa Brändström's papers were given after the war to the German War Archives and are kept today in the *Miltärarchiv* in Freiburg im Breigau (collection number Msg. 200) alongside other documents dealing with World War I captivity. Unfortunately, most of the sources listed in a 1937 inventory are missing (my estimate is that only 10 per cent of the original documents are still there). On Elsa Brändström see *Elsa Brändström-Dank*, Hrsg. Hanna Lieker Wentzlau, Berlin, 1938, and Alon Rachamimov, 'Elsa Brändström' in Jonathan Vance (ed.), *The Historical Encyclopedia of Prisoners of War and Internment*, Santa Barbara CA: ABC Clio, 2000.

15. Elsa Brändström, *Among Prisoners of War in Russia and Siberia*, p. 5.

16. Magdalene von Walsleben, *Die deutsche Schwester in Sibirien*, Berlin: Furche Verlag, 1919; Gräfin Anna Revertera, 'Als österreichische Rotkreuzschwester in Rußland,' *Süddeutsche Monatshefte*, September 1923, pp. 251-81; Revertera, 'Als Rotkreuzschwester in Rußland und Sibirien', *In Feindeshand* vol. 2, pp. 244-51; Käthe von Mihalotzy, 'Eine Reise durch Kriegsgefangenenlager in Rußland und Turkestan. Aus dem Tagebuch einer Delegierten des österreichischen Roten Kreuzes', *In Feindeshand*, vol. 2, pp. 249-58; Anne-Marie Wenzel, *Deutsche Kraft in Fesseln: Fünf Jahre Schwesterdienst in Sibirien*, Potsdam, 1931; Alexandrine von Üxküll, *Aus einem Schwesterleben*, 2. Auflage, Stuttgart, 1956; Nora Gräfin Kinsky, *Russisches Tagebuch 1916-1918*, Stuttgart: Seewald Verlag, 1976.

17. Ernst Ritter von Streeruwitz, *Kriegsgefangene im Weltkrieg 1914-1918*, unpublished manuscript at the Heeresegeschichtliches Museum in Vienna deposited 1928; Streeruwitz, 'Der Umsturz in Rußland und die Kriegsgefangenen', *In Feindeshand*, Vienna, 1931, vol. 1, pp. 269-71; Streeruwitz, *Springflut über Österreich: Erinnerungen, Erlebnisse und Gedanken aus bewegter Zeit 1914-1929*, Vienna and Leipzig: Bernina Verlag, 1937; Heinrich Freiherr von Raabl-Werner, 'Österreich-Ungarns offizielle Kriegsgefangenenfürsorge', *In Feindeshand*, vol. 2, pp. 324-31; Raabl-Werner, 'Der Einfluß der Propaganda unter den Kriegsgefangenen in Rußland auf den Zusammenbruch Österreich-Ungarns', *Militärwissenschaftliche und-technische Mitteilungen*, vol. 59, Vienna, 1928, p. 782; Max Ronge, *Kriegs-und Industriespionage: 12 Jahre Kundschaftdienst*, Vienna and Leipzig, 1933.

18. Ernst von Streeruwitz, *Kriegsgefangene im Weltkrieg*, Band I. 1-5, 67-70.

19. *Kriegsgefangene im Weltkrieg*, Band I, p. II.

20. See the minutes of the various committees in the Austrian State Archives/Archiv der Republik-KGF V4, Schachtel 175.

21. Heinrich Freiherr von Raabl-Werner, 'Österreich-Ungarns offizielle Kriegsgefangenenfürsorge', *In Feindeshand*, vol. 2, p. 324.

22. The following is a sample of some of the more interesting memoirs published during the interwar period: Burghard Breitner, *Unverwundet gefangen: Aus meinem sibirischen Tagebuch*, Vienna, 1921; Karl Drexel, *Feldkurat in Sibirien* 1914-1920 2nd edition, Innsbruck and Leipzig, 1940; Edwin Erich Dwinger, *Die Armee hinter Stacheldraht*, Berlin: E. Diederichs, 1929; Roman Dybosky, *Seven Years in Russia and Siberia*, translated by Marion Moore Coleman, originally published in Polish in 1922, Cheshire CT, 1970; Georg Hahn, *Kriegsgefangenen in Russland*, Mainz: Verlag der Volkszeitung, 1926; Avigdor Hameiri, *Begehenom shel Mata* (Hell on Earth) 3rd edition, Tel Aviv: Dvir, 1946; Mehmet Arif Ölçen, *Vetluga Memoir: A Turkish Prisoner of War in Russia, 1916-1918*, translated and edited by Gary Leiser, Gainesville FL: University Press of Florida, 1995 ; Hereward

Introduction

Price, *Boche and Bolshevik*, London, 1919; Herbert Volck, *Die Wölfe: 33,000 Kilometer Kriegsabenteuer in Asien*, Berlin: Ullstein & Co., 1918.
23. Robert C. Doyle, *Voices from Captivity: Interpreting the American POW Narrative*, Lawrence KS: University Press of Kansas, 1994, chapter 4 and appendix 1.
24. See also epilogue below.
25. See note number 1.
26. *In Feindeshand*, p. 17.
27. See Fussell's analysis of Robert Graves's *Good-bye to All That*. Paul Fussell, *The Great War in Modern Memory*, Oxford: Oxford University Press, 1975, pp. 203-20. See also Avner Holtzman, *Avigdor Hameiri ve-Sifrut ha-Milchama* (Avigdor Hemeiri and War Literature), in Hebrew, Tel Aviv: Merkaz Koved, 1986, pp. 10-12.
28. See note 20 above; the English version is Edwin Erich Dwinger, *The Army Behind Barbed Wire: A Siberian Diary*, translated by Ian Morrow, London: George Allen & Unwin, 1930, and Erich Dwinger *Between White and Red*, translated by Marion Saunders, New York: Charles Scribner's Sons, 1932.
29. During the 1930s Dwinger may have played also an important role in preparing minds in the Nazi regime for the idea of mass murder. Apparently, based on his experiences among the White forces during the Russian Civil War, Dwinger was appointed as the top Nazi expert on Russian mass murder techniques (and indeed some pages of *Between White and Red* are shockingly similar to descriptions of the activities of the *Einsatzgruppen*). This hypothesis needs to be investigated more rigorously and in much greater detail, something that is outside the scope of this present study.
30. See above note 22.
31. Hermann Pörzgen, *Theater ohne Frau: Das Bühnenleben der Kriegsgefangenen Deutschen 1914-1920*, Königsberg and Berlin: Ost-Europa Verlag, 1933.
32. Marjorie Garber, *Vested Interests: Cross Dressing and Cultural Anxiety*, New York: HarperCollins, 1992, pp. 59-66.
33. The following are the key works published during the interwar period: *Von Wolga bis Amur: Die Tschechische Legion und der russische Bürgerkrieg*, Königsberg and Berlin: Ost-Europa Verlag, 1931; Margarete Klante, *Die Geschichte der Tschechischen Legion in Rußland*, Berlin: Ost-Europa, 1929; Milada Paulová, *Jugoslavenski odbor: Povijest jugoslavenske emigracije za svjetskog rata od 1914-1918*, Zagreb, 1925; *Za svobodu: obrázková Kronika Českloslovenského hnutí na Rusi 1914-1920*, four vols, Prague, 1924; Josef Kudela, *Prehled vývoje čsl. revolucního hnutí na Rusi*, Prague, 1923; František Steidler, *Československé hnutí na Rusi*, Prague: Nákl. Památníku Odboje, 1922.
34. Although there were Czech, Slovak and South Slav volunteers in the Czech Legion, it was from the very beginning an overwhelmingly Czech-speaking military formation. Indeed, it was named the *Česká družina*

23

(Czech Company) in the years 1914–16. Only in June 1916 would it become a *Československá brigáda* and later a *Československá legie* when the idea for an independent postwar Czecho-Slovakia/Czechoslovakia gained supporters. The lack of clarity about the Legion's name and 'true' national profile is emblematic of the same problems experienced by the Czechoslovak state in the years 1918–38.

35. The anniversary of the battle of Zborov in 1917, 2 July, was designated as Army Day in interwar Czechoslovakia assuming an importance second only to that of independence day on the secular calendar of the country. See: Nancy Wingfield, 'Commemorations of the Battle of Zborov: Gender and Politics in the Construction of Official Historic Memory in Czechoslovakia', work in progress. I thank Professor Wingfield for providing me with a copy of this paper.

36. See below, Chapter 3.

37. Nancy Wingfield, 'Commemorations of the Battle of Zborov'.

38. This thesis will be tackled and problematized in Chapter 1 below and a different conclusion regarding the motivation of soldiers will be presented.

39. See note 30 above.

40. Ivo Banac, 'South Slav Prisoners of War in Revolutionary Russia', in *Essays on World War I: Origins and Prisoners of War*, eds Samuel Williamson and Peter Pastor, New York: Columbia University Press, 1983, p. 121.

41. Ibid.

42. Discussed in Peter Pastor, 'Hungarian POWs in Russia during the Revolution and Civil War', in *Essays on World War I: Origins and Prisoners of War*, pp. 149–62; See the Hungarian language works: *Hadifogoly magyarok története* (History of Hungarian Prisoners of War), Budapest, 1930; Jenö Lévai, *Fehér cártol-vörös Leninig: Magyar hadifoglyok szerepe a nagy orosz átalakulásban* (From White Tsar to Red Lenin: The Role of Hungarian Prisoners of War in the Great Transformation), Budapest, 1932; György Szamuely, *A Kommunisták Magyarországi Pártjának elökészítése*, (Preparations for a Hungarian Communist Party), Sarlo és Kalapács, vol. X, p. 4.

43. See in Russia: I. M. Krivoguz and I. S. Polyanskii, *Germanskie i avstriiskie voennoplennye-internatsionalisty*, Moscow, 1967; M. Birman ed. *Internatsionalisty v boiakh za vlast' Sovietov*, Moscow, 1965; V.A. Kondrat'ev, 'Iz istorii bor'by nemetskikh voennoplennych- internatsionalistov za ustanovlenie sovetskoi vlasti v Sibiri i na Dal'nem Vostoke v 1917–1920 gg', *Noiabr'skaia revoliutsia v Germania*, Moscow, 1960.

In Hungary: Zsigmond Pál Pach and A.P. Okladnikov, *Magyar Internacionalisták Szibériában és a Távol-Keleten*, (Hungarian Internationalists in Siberia and in the Far East), Budapest, 1978; Józsa Antal, *Háboru hadifogság forradalom: Magyar internacionalista hadifoglyok az 1917-es oroszországi forradalmakban*, (War, Captivity, Revolution: Hungarian Internationalist Prisoners of War in the Russian Revolution of 1917), Budapest, 1970.

Introduction

In East Germany: Rudolf Dix, *Deutsche Internationalisten in der Großen Sozialistischen Oktoberrevolution*, East Berlin, 1987; Sonja Striegnitz, *Deutsche Internationalisten in Sowjetrußland 1917-1918, proletarische Solidarität im Kampf um die Sowjetmacht*, East Berlin, 1979; Sonja Striegnitz, 'Die aktive Teilnahme ehemaliger deutscher Kriegsgefangener an der Oktoberrevolution 1917 und an den Kämpfen des Bürgerkrieges 1918-1922', *Zeitschrift für Geschichtwissenschaft* 8(1) (1960).

44. Robert Ezerov, 'Die sowjetische Historiographie und die deutschen und österreichischen Kriegsgefangenen-Internationalisten', *Zeitgeschichte*, 25(11-12) (1998), pp. 343-7.

45. Vlastimil Vávra, *Klamná cesta: Příprava a vznik protisovětského vystoupení* čs. legií, Prague,1958, see also Vávra's publications in the journal *Historie a vojenství* (HV; History and Warfare) during the 1950s and early 1960: 'Z Masarykovy kontrarevoluční činnosti v Ruska' ('From Masaryk's Counter-Revolutionary Activity in Russia'), *HV* 1954 (1); 'Americký imperiliasmus v pozadí čs. intervence na Sibiři' ('American Imperialism in the background of the Czechoslovak Intervention in Siberia'), *HV* 1954 (4); 'K počátkům intervence čs. legií v Rusku (léto 1918)' ('Regarding the beginnings of the intervention of the Czechoslovak Legion in Russia in the year 1918'), HV 1959 (4); 'Příprava protisovětské intervence na severu Rusko', ('The preparation of the anti-Soviet interventions in northern Russia'), HV 1963 (1). Regarding literature about the Czech Legion written during the Prague Spring see Karel Pichlík *Zahraniční odboj, 1914-1918, bez legend*, Prague, 1968, Karel Pichlík, Vlastimil Vávra and Jaroslav Křížek, *Červenobílá a ruda:vojáci ve valce a revoluce 1914-1918* (Prague,1967). See also the recent contribution of Vávra: Vlastimil Vávra, 'Formování České družiny', *Historie a Vojenství*, 1/1990, 107-18.

46. The quote is from Ivo Banac, 'South Slav Prisoners of War in Revolutionary Russia', in *Essays on World War I: Origins and Prisoners of War*, p. 122. Ivan Očak, *Jugosloveni u Oktobru* (Yugoslavs in October) Belgrade, 1967 and 'O Jugoslavenima u bjeolgardeskim jedinicama u Rusiji 1918-1920', ('About Yugoslav and White Guard Units in Russia 1918-1920'), *Časopis za suvremenu povijest* 1(1974), pp. 39-56; see also Bogumil Hrabak, 'Jugoslovenski sovjeti u Rusiji i Ukrajini 1919-1921 godine', ('Yugoslav Soviets in Russia and the Ukraine, 1919-1921'), *Tokovi revolucije* (1967), pp. 3-55; Nikola Popovič, *Jugoslovenski dobrovoljci u Rusiji, 1914-1918* (Yugoslav Volunteers in Russia 1914-1918), Belgrade: Udruzenje dobrovoljaca, 1977.

47. Ivan Völgyes, 'Hungarian Prisoners of War in Russia', *Cahiers du monde russe et Soviétique*, 14 (1973), pp. 54-85; Gerburg Thunig-Nittner, *Die tschechoslowakische Legion in Rußland: Ihre Geschichte und Bedeutung bei der Entstehung der 1. Tschechoslowakischen Republik*, Wiesbaden: Harrasonitz, 1970; Otto Wassermair, *Die Meutereien der Heimkehrer aus russischer Kriegsgefangenschaft bei den Ersatzkörpern der k.u.k. Armee im Jahre 1918*, (Ph.D. dissertation, University of Vienna, 1968); J. F. N Bradley, *La Legion tchecoslovaque en Russie 1914-1920*, Paris, 1968,

appeared in English - with a large number of typographic errors and
misspellings - in the Eastern European Monographs series: *The Czechoslovak
Legion in Russia 1914–1920*, Boulder and New York: Columbia University
Press, 1991; Rudolf Tökes, *Béla Kun and the Hungarian Soviet Republic:
The Origins and Role of the Communist Party of Hungary in the Revol-
utions of 1918–1919*, New York: Praeger, 1967; Inge Przybilovski, *Die
Rückführung der österreich-ungarischen Kriegsgefangenen aus dem
Osten in den letzten Monaten der k.u.k Monarchie*, (Ph.D. dissertation,
University of Vienna, 1965); see also the relevant sections in Richard
Plaschka, Arnold Suppan and Horst Haselsteiner, *Innere Front. Militär-
assistenz, Widerstand und Umsturz in der Donaumonarchie*, two vols,
Vienna: Verlag für Geschichte und Politik, 1974, and in Z. A. B. Zeman, *The
Break-Up of the Habsburg Empire 1914–1918, A Study in National and
Social Revolution*, London: Oxford University Press, 1961. The latter is
especially useful about the Czech case but rather uneven about everything
else.

48. Gerald H. Davis, 'The Life of Prisoners of War in Russia, 1914–1921',
in Samuel Williams and Peter Pastor (eds) *Essays on World War I: Origins
and Prisoners of War*, New York: Columbia University Press, 1983, pp. 162–
96; see also Davis's other articles: Gerald H. Davis, 'National Red Cross
Societies and Prisoners of War in Russia 1914–1918,' *Journal of Contemporary History*, vol. 28 (1993), pp. 31–52; 'Prisoner of War Camps as Social
Communities: Krasnoyarsk 1914–1921', *Eastern European Quarterly*, 21
(1987), pp. 147–163; Gerald H. Davis, 'Deutsche Kriegsgefangene im Ersten
Weltkrieg in Rußland', *Militärgeschichtliche Mitteilungen*, 1 (1982), pp. 37–
49.

49. Hannes Leidinger, 'Gefangenschaft und Heimkehr: Gedanken zu
Voraussetzungen und Perspektiven eines neuen Forschungsbereiches',
Zeitgeschichte, 25 (1998), pp. 333–42; Hannes Leidinger and Verena Moritz,
'Österreich-Ungarn und die Heimkehrer aus russischer Kriegsgefangenschaft
im Jahr 1918', *Österreich in Geschichte und Literatur*, 6 (1997), pp. 385–
403; Yulia Kudrina, 'Das Dänische Rote Kreuz in den Jahren des Ersten
Weltkrieges', *Zeitgeschichte*, 25 (1998), pp. 375–9; Reinhard Nachtigal, 'Die
dänisch österreichisch ungarischen Rotkreuzdelegierten in Rußland 1915–
1918: Die Visitation der Kriegsgefangenen der Mittelmächte durch Fürsorgeschwestern des österreichischen und ungarischen Roten Kreuzes,' *Zeitgeschichte*, 25 (1998), pp. 366–74; Reinhard Nachtigal 'Kriegsgefangene der
Habsburgermonarchie in Russland', *Österreich in Geschichte und Literatur*,
45a (1996), pp. 248–62; Yücel Yanikdağ, 'Ottoman Prisoners of War in Russia
1914–1922', *Journal of Contemporary History*, 34 (1999), pp. 69–85;
Nancy Wingfield, 'Commemorations of the Battle of Zborov: Gender and
Politics in the Construction of Official Historic Memory in Czechoslovakia';
Marina Rossi, *I prigionieri dello Zar: soldati italiani dell'esercito austro-
ungarico nei lager della Russia 1914–1918*, Milan: Murgia, 1997; see also
my contributions based on this work: Alon Rachamimov, 'Imperial Loyalties

and Private Concerns: Nation, Class and State in the Correspondence of Austro-Hungarian POWs in Russia 1916-1918', *Austrian History Yearbook*, 31 (2000), pp. 87-105; Alon Rachamimov, 'Alltagssorgen und politische Erwartungen: Eine Analyse von Kriegsgefangenenkorrespondenzen in den Beständen des Österreichischen Staatsarchiv', *Zeitgeschichte*, 25 (1998), pp. 348-56.

50. Peter Pastor, 'Hungarian POWs in Russia during the Revolution and Civil War', in *Essays on World War I: Origins and Prisoners of War*, pp. 149-62; Arnold Krammer, 'Soviet Propaganda among German and Austro-Hungarian Prisoners of War in Russia, 1917-1921', in *Essays on World War I: Origins and Prisoners of War*, pp. 239-64;Verena Moritz 'Die österreichische-ungarischen Kriegsgefangenen in der russischen Wirtschaft 1914 bis Oktober 1917', *Zeitgeschichte*, 25 (1998), pp. 380-9; Josef Kalvoda, Czech and Slovak Prisoners of War in Russia during the War and Revolution, in *Essays on World War I: Origins and Prisoners of War*, pp. 215-38.

51. On 'history from below' (and on military history 'from below'), on *Alltagsgeschichte* and 'Subaltern Studies' see: Samuel Hynes, *The Soldiers' Tale: Bearing Witness to Modern War*, New York: Penguin, 1997; Alf Lüdtke (ed.) *The History of Everyday Life: Reconstructing Historical Experience and Ways of Life*, translated by William Templer, Princeton: Princeton University Press, 1995; Leonard Smith, *Between Mutiny and Obedience: The case of the French Fifth Infantry Division during World War I*, Princeton, 1994; Sheila Fitzpatrick, *Stalin's Peasants: Resistance and Survival in the Russian Village after Collectivization*, New York and Oxford: Oxford University Press, 1994; *Der Krieg des kleinen Mannes*, edited by Wolfram Wette, Munich, 1992; Jim Sharpe, 'History from Below', in Peter Burke (ed.) *New Perspectives on Historical Writing*, University Park PA, 1989, pp. 24-41; Ranajit Guha and Gayatri Chakravorty Spivak (eds) *Selected Subaltern Studies* New York, 1988; Richard Holmes, *Acts of War: The Behavior of Men in Battle*, New York: The Free Press, 1986; John Keegan, *The Face of Battle: A Study of Agincourt, Waterloo and the Somme*, London: Penguin, 1976; E. P. Thompson 'History from Below', *Times Literary Supplement*, 7 April 1966.

52. Thompson, ibid.

53. Thomas Nipperdey, *Deutsche Geschichte, Vol.2 1866-1918, Machtstaat vor der Demokratie*, p. 758.

54. Paul Fussel, *The Great War and Modern Memory*, p. 8.

55. See above note 4 for a discussion of the term 'collective remembrance' and citations.

56. Holger Herwig, *The First World War: Germany and Austria-Hungary 1914-1918*, London: Arnold, 1997; Manfried Rauchensteiner, *Der Tod des Doppeladlers: Österreich-Ungarn und der erste Weltkrieg*, Graz, Vienna, Cologne: Verlag Styria, 1993; Dennis Showalter, *Tannenberg: Clash of Empires*, Hamden CT, 1991; Rudolph Jeřábek, 'The Eastern Front 1914-1918', in Mark Cornwall (ed.) *The Last Years of Austria-Hungary: Essays*

in Political and Military History 1908–1918, Exeter: University of Exeter Press, 1990, pp. 101–16; Norman Stone, *The Eastern Front 1914–1917*, New York: Charles Scribner's Sons, 1975.

57. Vejas Gabriel Liulevicius, *War Land on the Eastern Front: Culture, National Identity and German Occupation in World I*, Cambridge: Cambridge University Press, 2000; Peter Gattrell, *A Whole Empire Walking*, Bloomington: Indiana University Press, 1999; David Rechter, 'Galicia in Vienna: Jewish Refugees in the First World War', *Austrian History Yearbook*, 28 (1997), pp. 113–30; Mark von Hagen, 'The Great War and the Mobilization of Ethnicity in the Russian Empire', in Jack Snyder and Barnett Rubin (eds) *Post Soviet Political Order: Conflict and State Building*, New York: Routledge, 1998, pp. 34–57.

58. The most influential recent theoretical works about nationalism have been: John Breuilly, *Nationalism and the State*, 2nd edition, Chicago, 1994, originally published in 1982; Partha Chatterjee, *The Nation and its Fragments: Colonial and Post-Colonial Histories*, Princeton: Princeton University Press, 1993; Bendict Anderson, *Imagined Communities: Reflections on the Origins and Spread of Nationalism*, revised edition, London and New York: Cornell University Press, 1991, originally published in 1983; Eric Hobsbawm, *Nations and Nationalism since 1780: Programme, Myth, Reality*, Cambridge: Cambridge University Press, 1990; Anthony Smith, *The Ethnic Origins of Nations*, Oxford: Blackwell, 1986; Ernst Gellner, *Nations and Nationalism*, Ithaca and New York: Cornell University Press, 1983.

Some of the best known monographs about particular countries are: Alon Confino, *The Nation as a Local Metaphor: Württemberg, Imperial Germany and National Memory 1871–1918*, Chapel Hill and London, 1997; Linda Colley, *The Britons: Forging of the Nation 1707–1837*, New Haven and London: Yale University Press, 1992; Celia Applegate, *A Nation of Provincials: The German Idea of Heimat*, Berkeley, 1990; Eugen Weber, *Peasants into Frenchmen: The Modernization of Rural France, 1870–1914*, Stanford, 1976. See the following works regarding Central Europe: Jan Molenda, 'The Formation of National Consciousness among Peasants and the Part they Played in Regaining Independence', *Acta Polonica Historica*, 63–4 (1991) pp. 121–48; Hillel Kieval, *The Making of Czech Jewry*, Oxford: Oxford University Press, 1988; Gary Cohen, *The Politics of Ethnic Survival*, Princeton: Princeton University Press, 1981.

59. In Austria I had the opportunity to work extensively with the files of the Central Information Bureau of the Red Cross (*gemeinsames Zentralnachweisbureau* or GZNB) where the POW censorship was located. This repository, which is a part of the Viennese *Kriegsarchiv*, contains tens of thousands of POW letters (or excerpts) either in the original language or in German translation. The growth of the POW censorship into an institution of substantial size and organization opens the door for studying the opinions and behaviors of non-elite groups. Chapters 4 and 6 examine theoretically and empirically the advantages and drawbacks of working with this material.

In addition, the *Kriegsarchiv* contains scores of unpublished memoirs written by POW officers and deposited after the war. See exact citation of archival holdings in the bibliography.

In Germany the most important and relevant sources are located in the *Bundesarchiv/Militärarchiv* in Freiburg im Breisgau. During the interwar period many documents pertaining to Russian captivity were collected under the label of the *Elsa Brändström Gedächtnis Archiv*. This repository still contains some of the private documents of the Swedish nurse as well as such unique sources as camp journals written clandestinely in the years 1915 and 1917 by Austro-Hungarian officers in the Far Eastern camp of Rasdolnoe. One of the journals – *S'Vogerl* from 1917 – contains short stories, essays and illustrations of exceptional quality. Unfortunately the *Brändström Gedächtnis Archiv* is only a fraction of its interwar size and many of the documents listed in a 1937 inventory have been lost. Like the *Kriegsarchiv* in Vienna, the *Militärarchiv* also contains unpublished memoirs of ex-POWs, most of which were written and deposited by officers. The *Militärarchiv* contains two extraordinary and unique sources: First, newsletters written during the war and Russian civil war by families of POWs. From 1916 and onwards these newsletters were printed a few times a year, presenting a detailed picture of the lives of German and Austro-Hungarian officers in captivity. Second, the *Militärarchiv* contains also the proceedings of the Association of East Siberian POWs (*Plennygemeinschaft Ostsibiriens*) which met well into the late 1950s.

In Russia I worked with the extensive collections of the Russian State Military Historical Archive (*Rossiiskii Gosudarstvennyi Voenno-Istoricheskii Archiv* or RGVIA). Particularly relevant proved the collections of the Turkestan Military District (Fond.1396), Priamur Military District (F.1558), Moscow Military District (F.1606), Kiev Military District (F.1759) the Stavka (F.2000 and 2003) and the Red Cross Society (F.12651 and F.16275).

Finally the collections of the Department of State now held by the US National Archives contain numerous reports about living conditions in POW camps in Russia. As the official representatives of Austro-Hungarian and German interests in Russia in the years 1914–17, State Department envoys traveled throughout Russia to inspect the treatment of military and civilian prisoners.

1

Becoming Prisoners of War

And what is exactly so shameful?
I arrived in captivity with my whole division. With its soldiers, with
its officers, with its commanders and even with its heavy artillery. Why
should I personally feel embarrassed? I did not understand them [the other
officers]. Is this a sign that their soul is more shaken than mine? A sign
that I have lost something of that noted feeling for the homeland?[1]

Avigdor Hameiri (Feuerstein)
Jewish-Hungarian Officer
Captured June 1916

The Creation of the Austro-Hungarian POW Problem

During World War I an estimated number of 2.77 million Austro-
Hungarian soldiers were captured by enemy forces.[2] This staggering
number constituted about one third of the total number of men
mobilized by Austria-Hungary during the war, and about 11 per cent
of the total male population of the Dual Monarchy.[3] Apart from
360,000 soldiers, taken by the Italian Army in November 1918,[4] the
great majority of these prisoners had been captured by the Russian
army, primarily in the years 1914–16. Overall, about two million
Austro-Hungarian soldiers fell into Russian hands during World War
I. The numbers of Austro-Hungarian prisoners in Russian hands
appear particularly striking when compared to Austria-Hungary's ally
on the eastern front, Imperial Germany: only 167,000 German
soldiers were captured by Russian forces during World War I,
although after the initial campaigns of 1914 the number of German
troops on the Russian front usually equaled or surpassed the number
of Austro-Hungarian troops.[5]

The magnitude of the POW problem seriously hampered the war
effort of the Habsburg monarchy, embarrassing the Army High
Command (*Armeeoberkommando* or AOK) and its Chief of Staff in
the years 1914–17, Field Marshal Franz Conrad von Hötzendorf. From

the very first months of the war, Conrad became convinced that soldiers from certain Habsburg nationalities (particularly Czech, Serb, Italian and Ukrainian) were disloyal to the monarchy and that the high number of prisoners of war was due in a large measure to desertion.[6] Thus, as early as November 1914 the AOK ordered a series of *ad hoc* measures aimed at preventing soldiers from deserting. Among these were: 'the death penalty without trial for desertion, for encouraging desertion or for any actions that lead others to neglect or reject their military duty';[7] mixing units from 'suspect' nationalities with troops considered 'loyal' (thus a Czech battalion, for example, would be sandwiched on the front between two Magyar battalions); integrating soldiers from 'suspect' areas into 'reliable' regiments rather than into their home regiment; holding the families of deserters accountable, which meant in practice confiscation of their property and monitoring of their actions. In Conrad's view the only way to combat desertion effectively was 'through the most careful supervision and through draconian measures'.[8]

The notion that many soldiers went over to the enemy willingly has been widely accepted in the historiography of the Austro-Hungarian war effort.[9] Works written in Austria and in other successor states usually cite a few well-known examples of desertion – particularly the Czech Infantry Regiments 28 and 36 – as indications of widespread disaffection among the troops. The Austrian military historian, Manfried Rauchensteiner, who in 1993 published the most detailed account of the war since the monumental 1930s Austrian 'official' history *Österreich-Ungarns Letzter Krieg* (ÖULK), forcefully reiterated this argument:

> A special problem was the increasing number of desertions among the Austro-Hungarian troops, which took place first and foremost among the Czech troops. There was no use denying them, they were just too evident and reached such a dimension that would not have been tolerated in any army . . . on the 20th of October 1914, six companies from the k.u.k. 36th Infantry Regiment (Jungbunzlau) deserted, again Czechs. And so it went on and on until during the last Carpathian offensive, parts of the Prague 28th 'house regiment' went over.[10]

Yet, there are ample reasons to examine more closely the notion of widespread desertions.

First, as Richard Plaschka has noted with regards to the Prague Infantry Regiment 28 (IR 28), even the best-known case of desertion had a 'prehistory' (*Vorgeschichte*), which included incompetent officers, abusive training methods and a collapse of morale, which had been reported long before the troops reached the front.[11] Thus, mentioning the mere fact that troops from a certain nationality went over to the Russians simply does not tell the whole story. It certainly does not tell us why they deserted and to what extent political convictions played any role in it.

Second, using a few cases of desertion as a litmus test for the loyalty of whole nationalities is a highly problematic procedure. After all, millions of Czech, Serb, Croat, Ukrainian, Italian, Romanian, Slovene, Slovak and Polish soldiers continued to serve in the Austro-Hungarian army until the final days of the war. In fact, the 360,000 soldiers captured by the Italian army in November 1918 (after the Dual Monarchy had already fractured into a host of successor states) were overwhelmingly from the very same nationalities long considered by the AOK as 'disloyal' to the state.[12]

Third, to desert during military action is an extremely difficult thing to do (and all of the well-known cases of 'desertion' occurred during fighting). There are so many intangibles involved in going over to the enemy that soldiers who do wish to desert – or pre-arrange surrender – can never be entirely sure whether they will actually be given quarters by the enemy. Military historian Richard Holmes, who wrote the most comprehensive synthesis on the behavior of front-line soldiers, estimated the chances of making it to the other side at no more than 50 per cent.[13]

Fourth, talking about disloyalty and desertion ignores the fact that many of the Austro-Hungarian prisoners of war in Russia were captured in the course of very large 'catches'. When, for example, the fortress of Przemyśl surrendered to the Russians in 22 March 1915, 119,000 soldiers were led into captivity by the Austro-Hungarian Major General (*Feldmarschalleutnant*) Hermann Kusmanek. A year later, during the Brusilov Offensive of June 1916, an entire section of the Austro-Hungarian front collapsed near Lutsk and an estimated 200,000 soldiers were captured by the Russians in merely three days. It is highly unlikely that soldiers caught in such circumstances had any control over the situation or any real possibility of agency, which are necessary conditions of a reasonable definition of desertion.

Thus, in order to determine to what degree disloyalty accounted for the extraordinary numbers of Austro-Hungarian POWs in Russia, we need to shift the discussion away from the oft-cited cases of certain Czech regiments and try to accomplish two things: first, look at the 'big picture' and deal with questions such as when and under what circumstances were most of the prisoners captured? What was the national distribution of the prisoners? Did certain nationalities indeed dominate the POW population? Second, to follow the process of becoming a prisoner as it appeared 'from below' through the eyes of the prisoners themselves; how did Austro-Hungarian soldiers describe and interpret their capture? Did they consider captivity such a desirable alternative to the front? How were the prisoners treated immediately upon their capture and during their removal from the front to the rear? To what degree were they subjected to torture, beatings and robbery?

To do so, I will first provide a quantitative overview of captivity by relying on archival material from Austria, Russia, Germany and the US, and by using existing published sources. Next I will examine the particulars of being taken prisoner by the Russian army during World War I, I will follow the prisoners during their first weeks in captivity: from the moment of their capture, through the foot marches and the train rides, to the large assembly camps in Kiev and Moscow. Finally, I will return to the initial question and offer an explanation as to why so many Austro-Hungarian POWs were captured by the Russian army.

Austro-Hungarian POWs in Russia: A Quantitative Overview

In July 1921 *Oberintendant* Heinrich von Raabl-Werner wrote a memorandum entitled 'The Total Number of POWs and Civil Internees'.[14] Raabl-Werner, who had held between 1914–18 various senior positions at the Department of POW Affairs (*Abteilung* 10.kgf) of the Austro-Hungarian War Supervisory Office (*Kriegsüberwachungsamt* or KÜA), was appointed after the war as the Director of the Office for POW Affairs in the newly-formed Austrian Republic. He was also a member of the State Commission for POWs set up by the Austrian Parliament to expedite the repatriation of the POWs trapped in Russia during the Civil War years (1918–20). As the last remaining POWs were leaving Vladivostok for Europe in the summer of 1921, Raabl-Werner attempted to offer exact figures regarding the numbers of Austro-Hungarian POWs in Russia.

However, this proved an extremely difficult task. The basic problem, according to Raabl-Werner, was that during the war 'it was impossible to obtain even half-reliable statistics', and therefore the total number of Austro-Hungarian POWs 'could only be roughly estimated'.[15] In Raabl-Werner's mind the responsibility for this uncertainty lay both with Austro-Hungarian and Russian registration practices but ultimately it should be attributed to the general confusion reigning at the front. On the Austro-Hungarian side the most serious obstacle to reliable statistics was the inability to differentiate between various categories of 'missing in action' (*Vermißte*) especially during what he euphemistically called 'battles of retreat'. Raabl-Werner gave the following hypothetical example: division X may have suffered a loss of 10,000 soldiers during a particular battle. Of these 10,000 soldiers, 2,000 would be immediately located at first-aid stations within the division's area of control. An additional 3,000 soldiers would be found eventually in various military hospitals or would be discovered to have joined non-divisional units during the retreat. What happened to the rest of the soldiers was anyone's guess: some may have been killed during battle (and buried in mass graves without proper identification as was customary during the early part of the war) while others may have been captured by the Russian army. However, for the sake of registration, the division had to report as 'missing' all the soldiers who could not be located in the days following the battle. Thus, division X probably would have reported close to 8,000 men 'missing' out of the 10,000 who were counted as 'losses'.[16]

The situation was not significantly better in offensives initiated by the Austro-Hungarian army: a *Verlustrapport* submitted by the Tenth Infantry Division during the September 1915 'Black and Yellow Offensive' (so-called because the German army did not join the Austro-Hungarian initiative) reported 2,275 soldiers 'missing' out of the 3,312 who were declared 'lost' (Figure 1.1). The number of confirmed prisoners of war was a mere twenty-nine. It is hardly surprising then that when the war ended the Austro-Hungarian War Ministry had still the names of 837,483 soldiers categorized as '*Vermißte*'.[17] Most of these were presumed dead although there was still hope that at least some of them would be found among the POWs trapped in Russia during the Civil War.

There were also severe shortcomings with the Russian registration process. First, official registration of prisoners of war did not begin in earnest until they were removed from the front to the huge assembly stations in Kiev (Darnitsa) and Moscow (Ugrishkaia and Kuzhukhovo). Until then Austro-Hungarian POWs were given temporary registration numbers that were valid for a specific convoy or a specific marching column. These numerous columns of prisoners

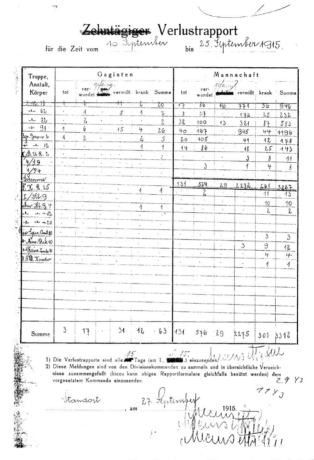

Figure 1.1: Losses Reported by the Austro-Hungarian 10th Infantry Division between September 10–25, 1915.

Source: Kriegsarchiv, Vienna

marched alongside millions of refugees, who had been evacuated or deported from the war zone by the Russian military, and who now clogged the roads adjacent to the front. Thus POWs walked tens and at times hundreds of miles, then were transported hundreds of miles by train before their status as 'prisoners of war' became official. It is open to speculation how many seriously injured Austro-Hungarian soldiers died after they had been captured but before they could be placed on the official POW lists.

Second, the Hague Convention did not specify clearly the exact information each soldier was required to give his captors: Article 9 stipulated that 'every prisoner of war is bound to give, if he is questioned on the subject, his true name and rank'.[18] Article 14, on the other hand, stated that an inquiry office should be established in belligerent countries with the ability to provide the following information: 'name, surname, age, place of origin, rank, unit, wounds, date and place of capture, internment wounding and death'.[19] Thus, there was a discrepancy between what a soldier was required to give and what was needed for proper identification. As a result, the lists of Austro-Hungarian POWs in Russia ran the whole gamut between very detailed and very rudimentary. Raabl-Werner complained that regimental and company numbers were regularly missing from the Russian lists, which 'was always a problem with very common names such as Schmidt Josef, Kovács János or Novotny Karl'.[20] It is conceivable, however, that Austro-Hungarian POWs themselves were reluctant in some cases to give their own regimental numbers because of the tendency of the Habsburg military authorities to label whole regiments as 'suspect' (on this see Chapter 4). The fact that the information provided in the POW lists was often insufficient for proper identification was exacerbated by overlapping between various lists. Consequently, it was never entirely clear if an oft-repeated name belonged to one, several or many people. Third, the Russian military authorities very seldom forwarded official death notices to the International Red Cross. During the war only 15,000 death certificates arrived in Austria-Hungary, although Department 10.kgf estimated the number of POW deaths in captivity at twenty-five to thirty times higher.[21] As a result it was impossible to reach an approximation of the number of Austro-Hungarian POWs in Russia through a simple method of adding the number of returnees and the number of deaths.

An alternative approach, suggested by Raabl-Werner and consequently used also by historians A. Klevanskii and Gerald Davis, is to indicate ranges.[22] Raabl-Werner took the lowest Russian figure of 1.76 million Austro-Hungarian POWs as the lower end of the range and added what he estimated as 'the number of POWs who died in Russian custody either in the battle zone itself or in front-line medical establishments'. Thus he reached a range of 2 million to 2.5 million men. The Soviet historian A. Klevanskii took the official data published in 1925 in *Rossia v mirovoi voine 1914–1918 goda* which listed 1,961,333 POWs in Russia (of them 160,000–180,000 German and

50,000 Turkish) and crossed referenced these numbers with infor-mation found in other Soviet and Western publications.[23] He reached thus a range of 2 million to 2.3 million POWs in Russia of which 1.75–2.05 million were from Austria-Hungary. The American hist-orian Gerald Davis (and following him Reinhard Nachtigal, Hannes Leidinger and Verena Moritz) relied on a few additional published sources and broadened the range to 1.6 million to 2.1 million POWs from Austria-Hungary.[24] Therefore, the official Austrian figure of 54,146 officers POWs and 2,056,955 rank-and-file POWs (a total of 2,111,141 POWs) seems to fall within the higher range of most estim-ates, but does not appear to be a gross exaggeration (see Table 1.1).[25]

Of the estimated two million Austro-Hungarian POWs in Russia at least half were taken captive during 'big catches', usually in the course of major battles. It should be emphasized that battles on the eastern front during World War I were inherently different from western-front battles. Whereas western-front battles such as Verdun, the Somme or Passchendaele were first and foremost attrition battles with negligible territorial advances, eastern front battles involved often rapid and significant movement of forces: the Russian army's first offensive in Galicia and Bukovina (August–September 1914) led to an advance of over 200 miles in seventeen days, the German and Austro-Hungarian offensive in Tarnów-Gorlice in May 1915 resulted in a push forward of a hundred miles in less than a month and in the famed Brusilov offensive of the summer of 1916, the Russian Eighth Army advanced forty miles in just three days against the Austro-Hungarian Fourth Army.

In the process of capturing vast areas, the belligerents on the eastern front regularly captured many enemy soldiers as well. An estimated number of 100,000 Austro-Hungarian soldiers were captured during the first Russian offensive, 119,000 Austro-Hungarian soldiers were taken captive when the fortress of Przemyśl surrend-ered, about 100,000 Austro-Hungarian POWs were taken during the ill-fated Black and Yellow offensive (26 August–13 October 1915) and an astounding 300,000–380,000 Austro-Hungarian soldiers were estimated captured during the Brusilov offensive.[26] Finally, because of extreme weather in the Carpathian Mountains, it was never determined how many prisoners were among the 793,000 men lost during the Austro-Hungarian Winter Offensive (23 January–30 April 1915). On one day alone, 27 February 1915, 40,000 men from the Austro-Hungarian Second and Third Armies were reported missing, 'either captured by the enemy or lost in the snow'.[27]

Table 1.1: POWs held by Primary Entente Belligerents ❖

		by Russia	by France	by Britain	by Italy	by Serbia	by Romania	Total in Entente Powers
German	Officers	2,082	5,057	3,910			54	11,300
	Men	165,000	424,100	324,000		5,840	12,900	985,700
	Total	167,000	429,200	328,900			12,950	997,000
	Others*	51,200	43,250			2,670	840	98,000
	Mortality,	16,000	25,200	10,000		500	3,100	55,800
	(%)	(9½%)	(5¾%)	(3½%)		(8½%)	(24%)	(5.6%)
Austro-Hungarian	Officers	54,146			5,154	1,500	250	61,100
	Men	2,057,000	9,000**		523,000	108,000	9,700	2,708,000
	Total	2,111,146			528,154	110,000	10,000	2,770,000
	Mortality,	385,000			35,000	30,000	3,000	453,000
	(%)	(18%)			(7%)	(27%)	(30%)	(16⅓%)
Turkish	Officers	950	25	822				1,800
	Men	50,000	1,500	41,700			350	93,600
	Total	51,000	1,525	42,500				95,500
	Mortality,	10,000	150	4,500				14,700
	(%)	(20%)	(11%)	(10½%)				(15⅓%)

Table 1.1: POWs held by Primary Entente Belligerents❖ (continued)

		by Russia	by France	by Britain	by Italy	by Serbia	by Romania	Total in Entente Powers
Bulgarian	Officers							
	Men	200	4,000			8,000***	6,450	18,700
	Total		500				800	1,300
	Mortality, (%)		(12½%)				(12½%)	(7%)
Total	Officers	57,178	5,090	4,732	5,154	1,700	300	74,389
	Men	2,272,000	439,000	365,700	523,000	122,000	30,000	3,871,611
	Total	2,330,000	509,100	370,500	528,154	123,700	30,300	3,946,000
	Mortality,	411,000	27,000	14,500	35,000	31,000	7,000	526,000
	(%)	(17¾%)	(5⅓%)	(4%)	(7%)	(25%)	(23%)	(12%)

❖ Does not include POWs from the Central Powers held by Japan, USA and Montenegro. The Total includes all POWs. Therefore the columns may not add up to the figures presented in the total. Despite their specificity, all numbers should be considered as approximations (see Chapter 1 section II)

* 'Others' in Germany signified those who did not return from captivity or MIA who could not be confirmed as dead.
** Transferred to France from Serbia and Italy.
*** Transferred to France and Italy.

Source: *In Feindeshand: Die Gefangenschaft im Weltkrieg in Einzeldarstellungen*, eds. Hans Weiland and Leopold Kern, 2 vols, (Vienna, 1931), statistical appendix.

Table 1.2: POWs held by Central Powers.

		by Germany	by Austria-Hungary	by Turkey	by Bulgaria	Total
Russian	officers	14,000	4,977	164		19,200
	men	1,420,000	1,264,000	15,000	17,600	2,700,000
	total	1,434,000	1,269,000	15,164		2,801,000
	mortality,	55,000	63,000	2,500	2,200	122,700
	(%)	(4%)	(5%)	(16%)	(12%)	(4⅓%)
French	officers	10,865	22	9		10,900
	men	524,500	630	119	1,742	526,800
	total	535,400	652	128		537,700
	mortality,	17,000			150	17,200
	(%)	(3⅕%)			(8½%)	(3½%)
British	officers	4,456	43	441		4,940
	men	355,900	115	35,600	1,546	392,600
	total	360,400	158	36,000		397,500
	mortality,	11,000		4,200	130	16,000
	(%)	(3%)		(12⅓%)	(8½%)	(4%)

Table 1.2: POWs held by Central Powers. *(continued)*

		by Germany	*by Austria-Hungary*	*by Turkey*	*by Bulgaria*	*Total*
Italian	officers	4,589	10,158			14,750
	men	128,300	359,400			488,000
	total	133,000	369,600		293	502,750
	mortality,	5,300	26,000			31,300
	(%)	(4%)	(7%)			(6%)
Serb	officers	4	1,031			1,040
	men	27,000	153,600			180,600
	total	27,004	154,631			181,640
	mortality,					
	(%)					
Romanian	officers	1,056	589	3		2,245
	men	41,600	52,200	2,039	12,100	106,000
	total	43,300	52,800	2,042		108,250
	mortality,		4,200		1,200	6,000
	(%)		(8%)		(10%)	(5½%)
Total	officers	37,000	18,000	605		55,605
	men	2,553,400	1,843,000	50,600		4508395
	total	2,590,400	1,861,000	51,200	61,500	4,564,000
	mortality,	90,000	121,000	6,700	7,600	225,000
	(%)	(3½%)	(6½%)	(13%)	(12½%)	(5%)

Source: *In Feindeshand: Die Gefangenschaft im Weltkrieg in Einzeldarstellungen*, eds. Hans Weiland and Leopold Kern, 2 vols. (Vienna, 1931), statistical appendix.

Thus, becoming POWs was for many soldiers a mass event in which individual actions carried very little weight. Panic was often the rule in these 'big catches' and descriptions of terrorized soldiers retreating wildly characterized the Habsburg army during some of these engagements. British historian Norman Stone estimated that during the Brusilov offensive Pflanzer-Baltin's Seventh Austro-Hungarian Army lost as many as 40,000 soldiers to captivity because of confused orders of retreat.[28] Soldiers fleeing across pontoon bridges on the river Styr were reported to have been impaled alive on their own fortifications due to extremely chaotic conditions.[29] Richard Holmes is probably correct in asserting that 'once a panic gets under way it develops a frenetic momentum of its own . . . and those involved seem to lose many of their human characteristics, and become animals given over to the hysteria of the herd'.[30] The 'raging reporter' from Prague, Egon Erwin Kisch, described in his wartime diaries such a flight on the Serbian front during the first days of the war:

> The flight had begun and swept us further on. A routed army – no, an unrestrained horde ran in senseless fright back to the border. Coach drivers whipped their horses, cannon drivers spurred and hit theirs, officers and men pushed forward and slithered between the wagon columns or trudged in road ditches. Groups made up of all kinds of troop formations were represented, those with brick-red cuffs on their shirts, those with dark green, light green, milky gray, Landwehr [reserves], army, artillery, medics, sappers.[31]

In conditions such as these the national identities of soldiers were of little relevance: Pflanzer-Baltin's Seventh Army was composed primarily of Magyar and Croat soldiers long considered by the Austro-Hungarian AOK as among the most loyal troops.[32] The irrelevance of national identities could further be illustrated by examining the estimated national distribution among Austro-Hungarian POWs in Russia. As with the overall number of POWs in Russia we only have approximate ranges. Nevertheless, even these approximations suggest that the national distribution of the POW population did not differ significantly from the relative share of each national group in the general population of Austria–Hungary: the number of German speakers among the prisoners is estimated at 500,000–700,000 (or 25–35 per cent of the overall number of Habsburg soldiers in Russia).[33] This was slightly higher than the percentage of German speakers in the Dual Monarchy (23.9 per cent according to the 1910 census). Similarly, it is estimated that between 500,000–600,000 POWs in Russia were Magyars (25–30 per cent of the POW population).[34] As with the case of the German speaking POWs this figure constituted a slightly higher share than the proportion of Magyars in the Habsburg Monarchy (20.2 per cent in 1910). Czech and Slovak POWs accounted for 200,000-300,000 POWs (10–15 per cent) which, surprisingly perhaps, was lower than their combined 16.4 per cent in the 1910 census (Czechs 12.6 per cent, Slovaks 3.8 per cent). Finally the standard estimate of South Slav POWs in Russia is 200,000, which again is lower than the 12.9 per cent share in the population of Austria-Hungary (including Bosnia-Herzegovina).

One might argue, as some Hungarian historians have done, that the fact that the AOK preferred to deploy troops from 'reliable' nationalities in critical fighting areas increased their chances of becoming POWs.[35] This is undoubtedly true but it only emphasizes the fundamental argument here namely that even 'loyalty beyond reproach' could not prevent massive numbers of Habsburg soldiers from falling into the hands of the Russian army. Soldiers from some nationalities might have harbored resentments against their home state and their commanding officers, and an increasing number might have been demoralized beyond caring, however very few had felt that they had any control over the circumstances of their capture. This could be exemplified very well by looking at capture narratives written by POWs during and after the war.

Becoming POWs: The View from Below

When prisoners of war tell their story of captivity they often describe the moment of their capture in great detail. They inform their audience about the terrain, the strength of the enemy, the weather, the behavior of commanders and comrades, the food and ammunition situation, the amount of sleep they had prior to their capture and many other particulars that appear relevant to their story. The Czech speaking POW, Ferdinand Kalous, taken captive at the end of November 1914, reported how he and a few of his comrades were left behind when the rest of their battalion retreated, how they hid 'for four days in a hole in the ground without straw, food and water' and how they were finally spared by a Russian captain who found them half frozen.[36] As a narration device it is clear why so much space is allocated to what is often in reality just a few minutes in a saga of years: the moment of capture is the crucial pivot of the whole plot; the moment in which the narrator assumes a new identity of a POW and the real beginning of his story. Yet, the abundance of detail has another important function in POW narratives: to exculpate the narrator in the eyes of his readers. It is through details that a prisoner seeks to refute (or preempt) accusations of personal failure, coward-ice or treason. An Austrian chaplain from Vorarlberg, Karl Drexel, poignantly described in his memoirs how officers who were captured together would construct an accepted version of what took place in order to diminish their personal responsibility.[37]

Thus, by using what anthropologist Clifford Geertz would later call 'thick description' POW narrators were able to weave together the physical and emotional dimensions of their capture.[38] By describ-ing concrete hardships and intertwining them with questions of accountability, fear, humiliation and honor, they attempt to explain their behavior and solicit understanding from the readers. The starting point of capture narratives is almost always a situation beyond the control of the protagonist. Johann Zakostelecky, a Czech-speaking *Kavallerist*, converted into an infantry soldier, informed his father how

> there were so many Russians attacking that twenty to twenty-five Russians came for every one of us . . . I cannot describe this scene with a pencil it must wait until I come home. From my company just me and three other men remained. We finally came to a forest and I ordered the men to retreat. I wanted to join them there myself, but, damn-it, someone grabbed me by the throat and a crowd of Russians was ready to jump all over me. My hands still tremble when I write about it.[39]

Václav Jansta described with some irritation how, as a Czech-speaking soldier, he was constantly transferred from one German-speaking unit to another. He finally saw action in the Carpathian mountains on 13 February 1915 only to be captured a day later: 'it was eleven o'clock at night when Russians were suddenly discovered in our trenches, we were already fast asleep, so they took us prisoner without any shot being fired. They took the whole front-line trench. There were about 1,200 of us and we made a fine-looking column.'[40] Even a conspicuously disgruntled soldier, such as Josef Holý, who rather amazingly admitted in writing to his wife that he 'had allowed himself to be captured', related a long story of how his frozen feet were not treated properly by the regimental doctor, which prevented him from wearing boots during the cold Carpathian winter. He had to resort therefore to wrapping his feet with sacks and tarrying behind his company. His commander called him a *Schwindler* and ordered Holý to run behind him at all times.

> But I was not so dumb and he was not so clever . . . we had to retreat again from the front trench. Since I could not run at all, I stayed behind the troops, compelled to hide in an empty barrack. I did not want to leave behind a wife and children . . . but now I am here [i.e. in Russia] and not alone; there are thousands of us with frozen feet and we are properly taken care of. Please don't worry yourselves my dear wife and dear kids because I am here in Russia; you know at the very least that I am still alive.[41]

Seen from below, captivity never appears to have been a matter of personal choice. Indeed, if one takes into consideration the rumors that circulated regarding the behavior of Russian troops (especially Cossacks) toward prisoners, it seems unlikely that a soldier would have allowed himself be captured had he felt he had a choice.[42] Stories, for example, about eye-gouging, tongue-removal and summary executions were common on both sides of the front.[43] The German-speaking officer, Hans Weiland, reported that when Cossack troops captured him he was absolutely sure that he would be murdered on the spot. Only the appearance of a non-Cossack Russian officer persuaded Weiland that he would indeed survive the ordeal. Austro-Hungarian soldiers were convinced that possession of Russian military equipment would result in immediate execution upon capture. *Oberleutnant* Hans Baumgartner described how one of his soldiers feverishly tossed out everything from his rucksack because he remembered he had a Russian canteen at his disposal.[44] Rumors gained from time to time some credence by the fact that captured enemy soldiers were indeed executed either in the heat of battle or deliberately as retribution for perceived mistreatment. The Turkish officer Mehmet Arif Ölçen related how fearful he was for his life upon capture due to the fact that Turkish troops had killed a captured Russian officer just a few days earlier. A letter in Yiddish, written by a Jewish Russian soldier and accidentally arriving at the offices of the Austro-Hungarian censorship in Vienna, acknowledged the fact that Russian troops did sporadically kill POWs, especially when their own troops suffered heavy losses. Thus, going over to the enemy was by no means a guaranteed method of surviving the war and soldiers were very much aware of it.

Nevertheless, despite occasional brutalities, Austro-Hungarian soldiers usually reported decent treatment immediately after capture. The main complaint common to soldiers of all Habsburg nationalities was robbery of their personal belongings. Although Article 4 of the Hague Convention specifically stipulated that only 'arms, horses and military papers' were to be taken from prisoners of war, the reality was that personal property was regularly seized upon search. Wounded POWs were often stripped of all their belongings including clothing. Hans Weiland who had nine bullet wounds and one bayonet stab discovered that all his personal belongings including his shoes disappeared in a Russian first-aid station. At times, POWs were ordered to hand over valuables. The Hebrew expressionist poet Avigdor Hameiri, who as a Hungarian officer had been taken captive during the Brusilov Offensive in 1916, described the following scene in his captivity memoirs:

> We have to step out of the trenches. The Russian soldier commands us to file out in an orderly fashion. Suddenly, not far from us, we see a second Russian soldier removing a gold medal from the uniform of one of the soldiers. The prisoner resists and is stabbed with the bayonet. The prisoner falls on the ground and the Russian soldier takes away his medal. I want to remove my own medal and hide it. A Russian NCO who sees my attempt comes over and requests my medal. 'Don't give it!', yells Pály, my orderly, 'don't give him nothing! It is forbidden to rob!'. He stands between me and the Russian NCO. Margalit [a fellow Jewish soldier] pushes my orderly away and tells the Russian soldier '*pozhaluista!*' The Russian soldier, who was already prepared to stab Pály walks over to me angrily and tears off my Gold medal. I help him. '*Pasibo*' he mutters to me, and grinding his teeth, he says to my orderly: '*Magyar zvier*' [Magyar animal].[45]

At other times, the removal of valuables was done through the means of a transaction. A German-speaking Russian doctor offered Karl Drexel the sizable sum of 120 Rubles for his Zeiss binoculars arguing that they would be taken from him in any case (which indeed they were). In other cases soldiers were offered tobacco for valuables or could exchange Austrian Crowns for Rubles in unfavorable rates. There are a few reports of Russian officers intervening to halt robberies and various transactions, however this seems to have been the exception rather than the rule.[46]

Apart from prevalent (and universally resented) robberies, Austro-Hungarian POWs generally reported proper treatment by the forces that had captured them. Some POWs even described amicable treatment, especially during the first year of the war: former front-line adversaries exchanged cigarettes, food and complaints about hardships of serving at the front (and about the scoundrels serving in the rear).[47] 'Front-line soldiers are comrades even when they are enemies', Hans Weiland was told by one of his Russian captors, and the reservist officer, Bruno Prochaska, described how officers captured in Przemyśl were 'treated in a highly-correct fashion, even chivalrous . . . while the rank-and-file fraternized'.[48] Even the interrogations of officers appear to have been conducted without violence, and, perhaps even more surprisingly, without the threats of violence. In fact, memoiristic accounts of these interrogations seem at times as exercises in civility: 'As the highest ranking officer', wrote *Oberleutnant* Hans Baumgartner:

> I was brought to the [Russian] Commandant, a very friendly old general, who attempted in vain to get information about military matters. After he recognized the futility of his efforts, he began to talk to me about private matters. He told me that he had lived in Vienna for a long time, we talked for forty-five minutes about Vienna and Austria. Finally, he let me go requesting that I write home immediately where my relatives are surely waiting for some news from me.[49]

This rather cordial treatment very quickly changed as prisoners were removed from the front towards the rear. 'The farther their march brought the prisoners from the front,' wrote the Swedish Red Cross nurse, Elsa Brändström, 'the stricter and more ruthless grew their treatment.'[50] POWs letters and memoirs vividly described the physical travails of marching to the Russian rear, the frustration of attempting to make sense of new conditions and incomprehensible regulations, and the gradual realization that one has acquired a new identity as a prisoner of war. Karl Drexel described a feeling akin to anesthesia overcoming him upon being marched to the rear: 'I can only remember darkness, the only thing I said to people I knew was "you are also here then".'[51] The feeling that one has plunged into a dark, unfamiliar and mysterious place permeates many POW narratives. In this sense, psychologist Amia Lieblich's comparison of POW stories to myths about the Fall and Return is a very apt one. The POW protagonist finds himself suddenly in a strange environment, struggles with various unfamiliar forces for an indefinite amount of time, while hoping to return eventually home and re-unite with loved ones.[52] This feeling of confusion is especially pronounced in the weeks and months after capture when, in the words of historian Robert Doyle, 'soldiers experience a process of transformation and initiation when they become prisoners of war'.[53] In the case of Austro-Hungarian POWs in Russia, this transformation and initiation process was divided into three distinct phases: the march toward the rear, the first train ride, and the sorting centers in Kiev and/or in Moscow.

March Toward the Rear

From the moment of their capture until arriving in a fixed internment place, Austro-Hungarian POWs could expect to spend between a month and three months on the road. In the case of seriously wounded prisoners this period often lengthened considerably depending on the time required for convalescence in a military hospital. Those, however, who were captured unharmed or those who were 'walking wounded' spent usually the first week or two marching toward a main train depot in the Russian rear. During the first nine months of the war, when the Russian army occupied much

Figure 1.2: POWs resting on their way to the Russian rear.

Source: Za Svobodu

of Galicia, and again after the Brusilov offensive in the summer of 1916, the marches were especially long and arduous. 'After my capture we marched two weeks on foot,' wrote the Hungarian speaking POW Istvan Mayer, 'we were fed only once a day, early in the morning, and then we had to march the whole day.'[54]

The Slovak language censorship group calculated that POWs marched on average 25 kilometers a day (15.6 miles) for an average of twelve days with some marches exceeding 45 kilometers a day (28 miles) and extending well over two weeks. Such distances might not appear at first glance very grueling, especially because contemporaneous soldiers were used to marching very long distances on foot. However, for underfed, tired, bewildered and often wounded prisoners these distances appeared at times extremely difficult to endure. Bohuš Hlaváč, a Czech speaking infantryman from southern Bohemia described the march to his family:

> We were prodded hungry from the Carpathians to Lemberg. We marched for nine days, each day making 25 Kilometers. Because of weakness we could hardly walk or step on our feet. They gave us something to eat only after two days and indeed only a small amount of soup and a piece of bread. Those of us who had some money could buy here and there a little piece of bread, but this was very expensive. How I and others who had no money fared you cannot even imagine.[55]

The burden of the marches was alleviated at times by what seems to have been lax vigilance on the part of Russian guards (except when guards were Cossacks). Thus, during overnight stops POWs reported being able to sneak undetected from the marching columns and scavenge for food. Those who could communicate with the local civilian population – in most cases speakers of Slavic languages and Jewish prisoners – had a definite advantage. 'In twos we went into villages begging for food', wrote the Czech speaker Karel Lisy, 'we received potatoes with bacon which we devoured as you could probably imagine. In one house I even received one morning three pots of coffee and potatoes with sour cream. This was really something for me.'[56] The most fortunate in this respect were Jewish POWs who consistently received assistance from co-religionists in Galicia and Russia. It is interesting to note that this widespread support on the part of Jewish congregations was very negatively perceived by the Austro-Hungarian censorship and characterized 'as offending the patriotic feelings of other POWs'.[57] One letter in particular was used by the censors as an indication of 'the unmilitary and unpatriotic [*unstaatlich*] opinions of this people'. The letter written in the spring of 1915 by Naftali Schwarz to his wife described the following Švejkian tale:

> We were captured on Wednesday; a week before Passover. We went from Lipowice and arrived on Friday evening in Jaroslav. I sneaked into town and went to Yankely Burech. He gave me half a cake, a piece of fish and sold me a loaf of bread. He didn't take from me even one Heller. When I came back to the place where we had been before I didn't find my regiment. I found though a lieutenant who was looking for a servant and I volunteered, I ripped my stars off and became an orderly. Thus, I went to Russia with all the officers.[58]

As will be discussed in Chapter 3, the practice of picking individual letters as indicative of the attitudes of Austro-Hungarian nationalities toward their home state was common during the first two years of the war. At times it resulted in confrontations within the Austro-Hungarian censorship between various language groups who produced diametrically opposed letters in support of 'their' view concerning the trustworthiness of different national groups.

The least fortunate among the marching prisoners were those wounded POWs whose injuries did not result in immediate hospitalization. Bereft of proper medical attention and without access to bandages and medication, their wounds often worsened and resulted, according to the Swedish Red Cross nurse Elsa Brändström, in amputations and deaths.[59] Ironically, those whose injuries were severe enough for them to be hospitalized received treatment which was on par with the treatment given to Russian soldiers. In practical terms this favored first and foremost POW officers who reported receiving decent treatment from Russian medical personnel: 'I landed in a field hospital with a Russian Colonel and a Captain from Bessarabia as roommates,' reminisced Hans Knöbl after the war, 'the Russian front-line officers were all excellent people, the Colonel even spoke a smattering of German.'[60] Even Elsa Brändström, a harsh critic of Russian military medical facilities, found mostly positive things to say about 'the kind and careful treatment' of Russian front-line doctors.[61] This however did not diminish the fact that field hospitals in Russia (and for that matter also in Austria-Hungary) suffered enormous shortages in beds, medications, bandages and qualified personnel.

Train Rides

After marching a fortnight in miserable conditions Austro-Hungarian POWs reached train stations on the Russian side of the prewar border in what was often a demoralized state. In addition to hunger and lack of sleep many prisoners suffered from what the Austrian physician Gustav Jungbauer described as a 'bloody, dysentery-like diarrhea, which completely exhausted them'.[62] Thus, they began a long trek by rail (which for some would end only in the Primorskaia region in the Russian far east) under inauspicious physical and psychological circumstances. The trains on which they embarked did nothing to alleviate this situation.

A typical Russian POW train consisted of forty to fifty modified boxcars called 'warm cars' or *teplushki*. Each *teplushka* was equipped with an iron stove in the middle of the car (hence the name) and with two or three rows of plank bunks on each side. In addition, there was a separate space for the guard with his own bunk, and a collective bucket for latrine use. Altogether, a POW *teplushka* contained typically thirty to forty-five men transported in extreme constriction (in contrast a Russian military *teplushka* held usually sixteen to twenty-eight men). Austro-Hungarian POWs spent during their period of captivity in Russia many weeks (and sometimes months) riding the railroad, and the *teplushka* with its stench, overcrowding and unsanitary conditions occupied a central place in their narratives. 'It was like a little state', mused POW Bruno Prochaska, 'with social classes and social questions. The upper class had the upper planks, which were the warmest and offered enough room to sit upright. The middle class occupied the middle banks with its half-decent warmth and comfort, while the lowest stratum of this world order froze like dogs. There were also, of course, social questions, but in contrast to the outside world, the ones in the *teplushka* could be solved: every eight days bunks would be switched and everybody was happy like in an ideal state.'[63]

Still, negotiating a sufficient space to sleep on the bunks was a very difficult thing to do in a *teplushka*. Crammed usually six to eight people per bunk, POWs could only sleep sideways with every abrupt movement having a ripple effect on one's neighbors. 'Everybody had either to face the right side or the left side, squeezed closely to each other. Turning over was a collective affair, any effort by an individual to carve out more space was warded off as anti-social behavior.'[64]

The cramped conditions, however, were more than just a matter of personal discomfort. They affected the health of the entire transport. The close proximity to other prisoners coupled with the inability to clean body and clothes created an ideal environment for infectious diseases. Typhus, carried by body lice, loomed especially large during *teplushka* rides. 'I did not get a bath or an exchange of linen between September 11 and December 9 [1915]', wrote Hereward Price, an English expatriate who served in the German Army during World War I and was captured by the Russians on the eastern front.

> And then the lice. I shall never forget the first one I discovered on my collar-band. The horror of the moment never diminished, familiarity only bred deeper disgust. Everyday we took off all our clothing and searched it; towards the end it was necessary to do so three or four times a day. We never found less than a hundred in a search. Verminousness [sic] breaks a man's spirit more completely than any other affliction; he loathes himself and from self-loathing quickly falls into despondency and despair . . . Considering that the whole transport was in the same condition with regard to lice as ourselves, it is a wonder that no disease broke out on the journey.[65]

To alleviate the rank odors suffusing the interior of a *teplushka*, the sliding doors of the car were often rolled open during morning hours. This offered some ventilation (albeit in exchange for warmth) and gave riding POWs a view of the Russian countryside. The constant movement of the train and the slowly changing panorama imparted according to POW Bruno Prochaska 'a sense of freedom' that compensated for 'the less than excessive comfort'.[66] Those POWs who would later be sent to internment places in Siberia and Turkestan (Russian Central Asia) imagined themselves at times as explorers surveying a strange and wild land, and waxed poetically about Russian vistas. Franz Krisper, for example, devoted more than one third of his 120-page manuscript to various impressions from train rides.[67] Future historian Hans Kohn, who as a Austro-Hungarian POW in Russia spent five years in Central Asia and the Russian Far East, felt that the only way 'one can really experience . . . the immensity of the Russian empire' is to travel by train.[68] Thus, from the perspective of prisoners, train rides were both exhilarating and terrifying; offering a sense of change, direction and freedom at the price of overcrowding, filth and possible disease.

The food supply was again a chronic problem during rail journeys. As with the case of the marches to the rear it was only intermittently provided by the Russian military. Moreover, the nature of the food (usually cabbage soup or *kasha*) and even more so the 'Russian style' in which it was given (one collective bucket and one or two collective spoons for ten to twelve men) seemed at first strange and revolting for many of the prisoners. 'A dirty tin pail was brought by two Russians', reported POW Gustav Jungbauer

> and in an air of largesse they let us understand that we have here a very good supper. We all stood around this strange pail and sniffed it. The smell was not very pleasant. It was Russian cabbage soup, which we all pushed away in abhorrence, despite our growling stomach. Our two eldest officers taught us however that hunger is the best cook. They first tasted cautiously this foreign stuff and after a few spoonfuls discovered that it was not so disgusting . . . we probably should not have mocked these two hungry old officers as they packed spoon load after spoon load into their mouths.[69]

When food was not supplied by the Russian military, POWs were supposed to receive a daily allowance of 25 kopecks per man or 75 kopecks per officer, and purchase food in train stations along the way. It is unclear to what degree this rule was indeed followed. Many letters of complaint about this issue – accompanied by accusations of embezzlement on the part of the Russian Train Commander – suggest that these allowances were only haphazardly distributed.

Assembly Stations

Trains from the front arrived ultimately at central assembly camps in Kiev and Moscow. There, for the first time, prisoners were officially registered by the Russian military authorities and sorted into groups according to various identity categories. It was this sorting-out process that determined to what region a prisoner would be sent and in what kind of camp he would be interned. Thus, what took place in the camps of Darnitsa outside Kiev, and Ugrishkaia and Kuzhukhovo in Moscow was of crucial importance to the prisoners.

The registration process itself was in theory simple: each prisoner gave the Russian authorities his name and rank, and usually a few other identifying characteristics such as date of birth, place of residence and regimental affiliation. The Russian military would then give a copy of this list to representatives of the International Red

Cross stationed in Kiev and Moscow, who would proceed to send the names back to Austria-Hungary. Simultaneously, each prisoner was permitted to write his family a postcard (or occasionally a letter) notifying them of his capture. However, as mentioned above, this system seldom functioned smoothly. Darnitsa, for example, could not handle the rapid influx of Austro-Hungarian prisoners. According to Russian figures, approximately half a million prisoners passed through Kiev between August 1914 and June 1915, and were housed in barracks, tents and at times just out in the open.[70] At any given day there were no fewer than 4,000 POWs in Darnitsa and some days three times as many. 'Darnitsa consisted of a huge court covered with filthy sand', wrote Avigdor Hameiri, 'in it were ramshackle wooden barracks and thousands of wretched, ragged prisoners, walking, lying in the sand, eating and scratching themselves. A veritable Babel-like mixture of noisy people.'[71] The registration confusion was further exacerbated by the fact that the Russian authorities had considerable difficulties communicating with the multi-lingual POW population and at first did not rely on the prisoners themselves to assist them in registration. Only in the fall of 1915 was a revamped system introduced whose main feature was a double check on each prisoner both by the Russian authorities and by POW non-commissioned officers. Still, even after the implementation of the new registration system, the Austro-Hungarian War Ministry had difficulties making sense of the lists sent from Russia. It was not uncommon therefore that families first heard about their son's capture via postcards and not through official channels.

Besides registration, POWs were sorted in Kiev and Moscow into various identity categories. These categories had less to do with determining exactly who had been captured than with prescribing treatment, allocating resources and employing prisoners as labor. Two of these categories – rank and nationality – were of particular importance and influenced all aspects of a prisoner's existence in captivity.

The most significant by far was the rank of the prisoner. The Hague Conventions of 1899 and 1907 stipulated that POW officers were to be treated on the same footing as officers of the army that had captured them. They were to be given superior lodgings, paid a monthly salary by the captor state and be exempted from any work. One of the great fortunes of Austro-Hungarian POW officers was that the officer provisions of Hague Conventions were generally respected by the Russians, at least until the Bolshevik revolution in

Figure 1.3: Assembly Camp Darnitsa near Kiev.

Source: Za Svobodu.

November 1917 (see below, Chapter 3). The Russian military authorities usually registered Austro-Hungarian cadets and ensigns as
officers much to the dismay of fellow officers from Germany. The
anti-Semitic German officer, Josef Rey, claimed that POW officers
from Imperial Germany refused to forge any contacts in captivity
with 'these Jewish quasi-officers from Austria-Hungary'.[72] According
to Heinrich von Raabl-Werner the share of ensigns and cadets was
indeed very high, amounting perhaps to 60 per cent of the official
figure of 54,146 Austro-Hungarian POW officers. Still, those captured
had to present some proof that they were indeed officers (or cadets):
Eugen Komirol of the 7th Honvéd Infantry Regiment claimed in a
formal petition that he had been promoted during the siege of
Przemyśl to the rank of *Kadettaspirant*. However, since he could
furnish no documentation to support this claim, his petition was
denied by the Russian authorities.[73]

The flip side of this preferential treatment was that Habsburg
officers were separated now completely from their men, which
in turn eliminated the last vestiges of authority they still held over

their soldiers.[74] Soldiers and officers would inhabit strikingly different worlds in captivity; they would live in separate camps, enjoy fundamentally different rights and be subject to very different restrictions. As Hans Kohn aptly described in his memoirs, the fact that he was fortunate enough to complete a reserve officer course just prior to his capture, meant that his five years in Russia were used for reading, mastering languages and observing the local population rather than spent in back-breaking labor.[75]

In Kiev and in Moscow POWs were sorted also according to nationality. Russian General Staff Order number 15247 from 22 October 1914 (Old Style) required that 'preferences would be given to Slav POWs and to prisoners from Alsace-Lorraine'.[76] Therefore, POWs from these groups 'are to be located and housed separately from German and Austrian POWs'. The order went on to specify that these POWs are to be given the best available lodgings, clothing and food, and enjoy a greater freedom of movement than their comrades. Finally, article 7 of the order, stipulated that Slav and Alsatian POWs 'are to be granted a right to join special military units and participate in future military operation against Germany and Austria-Hungary'.[77]

As a consequence of Order 15247 Russian military authorities began registering the nationality of prisoners in November 1914. It is important to note that there was no unified, consistent and coherent registration system for nationality, and that the classifications employed depended on local understanding of what was required and relevant. At the assembly camp of Ugrishkaia in Moscow, for example, the registration system distinguished between 'Slavs', 'Germans' (with no distinction between those from Austria and Germany), 'Italians', 'Romanians' and 'Hungarians'.[78] The American inspector, Herbert Peirce, received from the Omsk Military Commander a list of k.u.k. POWs which contained the following categories: 'Germans', 'Austrians', 'Slavs', 'Roumanians' [sic], 'Italians', 'Jews', 'Magyars', 'Hungarians', and 'other nations'.[79] What seems to have mattered most to Russian military authorities was whether a certain prisoner was a Slav or not. The little interest in identifying the specific nationality of Slav POWs supports the argument that the Russian Supreme Command was very ambivalent about using Austro-Hungarian POWs in anti-Habsburg national units (at least until the spring of 1917). Thus, although the idea to try and turn the prisoners against their home state was already on the table from the first months of the war, the necessary steps to implement it were not taken.

It was up to the prisoners themselves to declare their nationality and some of them changed their declaration. Both the Austrian and the Russian military archives contain copious reports of Habsburg POWs altering their declarations (or conversely pretending to be of one nationality but 'actually' belonging to another). The registers of the Turkestan Military District, for example, describe the story of Staff Captain Karl/Karel Gütling from Prague who had been taken captive in Przemyśl. According to an official inquiry, Gütling at first declared himself to be a Czech and expressed sympathy with Russia. However, with the Russian retreat from Galicia in 1915 he changed his colors 'and became a zealous German, terrorizing other Czechs . . . and telling them that they will be hanged when they return to Austria. He used the most hateful expressions against Russia and the Russian government.'[80] It is unclear how widespread this phenomenon was. A considerable number of Austro-Hungarian soldiers spoke more than one language, and, as recent literature on the subject suggests, national identities were not as fixed in pre- World War I Austria-Hungary as previously assumed.[81] It appears then that when there was an incentive to change one's nationality declaration, some POWs took advantage of it and 're-invented' themselves. The figures given to Herbert Peirce in Omsk indicate that a significant number of POWs preferred nationally ambiguous categories when presented with the option: out of 96,113 POWs interned in the military district of Omsk, 16,883 chose a citizenship category of 'Hungarians' rather than the explicitly ethnic 'Magyars', 'Roumanian' [sic], 'German', 'Slav' or 'Jewish'; in the same vein, no less than 9,503 POWs declared themselves to be 'Austrians' (rather than 'German', 'Slav' and so forth).

Thus, although nationality did matter in Russian captivity it was a less coherent sorting principle than rank. The advantages bestowed on certain national groups were much less palpable than the advantages given to officers, and quite removed from the recommendations of Order 15247. The decision, for example, to leave Slav POWs in European Russia – rather than send them to Turkestan and Siberia – was no guarantee for decent living conditions. In fact, neutral observers often commented that some camps in Siberia were unquestionably superior to their counterparts in Europe (on this see Chapter 3). In any case, the intensifying usage of POW labor from the fall of 1915 placed a growing premium on their value to the Russian economy rather than on their nationality. From 1916 and onwards an increasing number of Magyar and German prisoners found themselves in agricultural and industrial work in the European part of Russia.[82]

After being registered and sorted in Kiev and in Moscow, Austro-Hungarian POWs found themselves again in *teplushki* headed to camps scattered in the various regions of Russia. Many assumed, as POW Alexander Dworski had done, that the hectic and most difficult period of their captivity was now over and that they could 'now rest and settle down' in a normal routine. As will be shown below in chapter two, this expectation rarely materialized for rank-and-file prisoners. Still, the period of very rapid change, which had begun with their capture, was unmistakably over. Some would later assess the weeks following their capture as among the most significant in their lives, the period in which they had become *Voennoplennye* (POWs).

Finally, a few concluding words about the process of becoming POWs on the eastern front during World War I. From what has been said so far, it is clear that the thesis that widespread desertions accounted for the extraordinary numbers of Austro-Hungarian POWs in Russia cannot be accepted. On a macro level, the numbers do not bear out such a conclusion; the ostensibly 'disloyal' nationalities were not overly represented in Russia, and, in any case, extremely large numbers of prisoners were taken during large 'catches' where no room existed for individual choice and action. On a micro level, POW capture narratives portray in vivid detail how small and inconsequential individual soldiers felt on the battlefield. Even if one makes allowances for the fact the prisoners attempted to exculpate themselves in their narratives, one is still left with the striking impression that captivity came as a shot from the blue for those captured. There was just no way for individual soldiers to know whether they would be given quarter by the Russians, and no reason to assume that by deserting they would save their lives.

It appears much more plausible that an astonishing number of Austro-Hungarian soldiers became prisoners during World War I due to two sets of problems:

First, there were severe structural deficiencies handicapping the Habsburg military long before the first shot was fired in 1914. Among these were chronic lack of funding, insufficient training, very limited usage of the available manpower pool and paucity of up-to-date weapons.[83] These problems were endlessly debated and discussed before the war had begun and labeled in the parlance of the time 'the withering away of the army' (*Verdorren der Armee*).

Modern commentators have even suggested that the true function of the Habsburg army was to keep order at home rather than serve as a foreign policy tool.[84]

Second, during the first few months of the war the Austro-Hungarian AOK made a series of mobilization blunders that played a major role in decimation of the pre-war standing army. By the end of 1914, the casualty rate among the original infantry units was 82 per cent, and the responsibility to fight was passed to soldiers who had received even less training than their poorly-trained predecessors. In the words of István Deák: 'by 1915 the traditional Habsburg army had been transformed into a militia . . . led moreover by a grossly inadequate number of civilians in uniforms, rather than by career soldiers.'[85]

Notes

1. Avigdor Hameiri, *Be-Gehenom shel Mata: Reshimat Katzin Ivri be-Shevi Russia* (Hell on Earth: The Notes of a Hebrew Officer in Russian Captivity), revised edition, Tel-Aviv, 1946, originally published 1932, p. 15. All translations into English are my own, unless otherwise indicated.

2. For a full discussion regarding the number of Austro-Hungarian POWs see below. The figure of 2.77 million is taken from Hans Weiland and Leopold Kern (eds) *In Feindeshand: Die Gefangenschaft im Weltkriege in Einzeldarstellungen*. Statistical appendix at the end of the second volume.

3. Russia also lost a tremendous number of men to captivity. According to Evgenii Sergeev, roughly one out of every five Russians mobilized during the war became a prisoner of war. See his 'Russkie voennoplenye ve Germanii i Avstro-Vengerii v gody pervoi mirovoi voiny', *Novaia i novei-shaia istoria*, 4 (1996), p. 66.

4. The armistice was signed on 2 November 1918 after the Austro-Hungarian state had already disintegrated and after a series of successor states had been proclaimed. Nevertheless, the armistice agreement took effect only two days later, which enabled the Italian Army to launch one last 'offensive' and proclaim the victory of Vittorio Veneto. Of the 360,000 POWs taken captive during this 'offensive', about 30,000 died in captivity.

5. Germany usually positioned about two-thirds of its forces on the western front and about one-third on the eastern front. On average 1.3 million German soldiers served on the Russian front. Austria-Hungary

allocated most of its forces to the Russian front, but had to shoulder also the main effort on the Serbian and Italian fronts. Vejas Gabriel Liulevicius, *War Land on the Eastern Front: Culture, National Idenitity and German Occupation in World War I*, Cambridge: Cambridge University Press, 2000, p. 14; Holger Herwig, *The First World War: Germany and Austria-Hungary 1914-1918*, London: Arnold, 1997.

    6. Kelly McFall, 'Pledging Allegiance: Perceptions of Patriotism in the Habsburg Officer Corps, 1914-1918' paper presented at the conference of the American Association for the Advancement of Slavic Studies (AAASS) September, 1998. According To Graydon Tunstall, Conrad 'came to view isolated acts of desertion as portents of a far greater problem.' See Tunstall, 'Traitors or Scapegoats: The Desertion of Czech Soldiers to the Russians in World War I', paper presented at the (AAASS) September, 1998, p. 4. See also Tunstall's examination of perception of Conrad von Hötzendorf by Austrian post-World War I military historians. According to Tunstall, a 'Conrad mythos' and a 'hero cult' were created during and after the war by Conrad himself and by Emil Ratzenhofer, August Urbanski, Karl Nowak, Rudolf Kiszling and Glaise-Horstenau who glorified Conrad's actions and decisions, while blaming other factors for failures. See Graydon A. Tunstall, Jr., *Planning for War against Russia and Serbia: Austro-Hungarian and German Military Strategies, 1871-1914*, Social Science Monographs/War and Society in East Central Europe XXXI, (Boulder CO: Columbia University, 1993), Chapters 7-8. These arguments are more forcefully presented in Tunstall's article: 'The Habsburg Command Conspiracy: The Austrian Falsification of Historiography on the Outbreak of World War I', *Austrian History Yearbook*, 27 (1996), pp. 181-98.

    7. All quotes are from McFall.

    8. McFall.

    9. See above note 6. *Österreich-Ungarns Letzter Krieg* (ÖULK), the 'official' Austrian history of the war, which was written during the interwar period by a group of ex-Habsburg officers, trumpeted the cases of a few Czech infantry regiments (IR 11, IR 28, IR36, Landwehr Infantry Division 21) as indication of widespread anti-Habsburg feeling among Czech soldiers. Nationalist historians in the successor states have also relied on a few examples to identify widespread disaffection among the troops. See also recent syntheses by Holger Herwig and Manfried Rauchensteiner.

    10. Rauchensteiner, *Der Tod des Doppeladlers*, p. 205.

    11. Richard Plaschka, 'Zur Vorgeschichte des Überganges von Einheiten des Infantrieregiments Nr. 28 an der russischen Front 1915', *Österreich und Europa: Festschrift für Hugo Hantsch zum 70, Geburtstag*, (Graz: Verlag für Geschichte und Politik, 1965), pp. 455-64; See also Tunstall, 'Traitors or Scapegoats'.

    12. The forces captured in Vittorio Veneto consisted primarily of speakers of Czech, Slovak, Serbo-Croat, Polish, Romanian and Ukrainian see Holger

Herwig, *The First World War*, p. 438; István Deák, *Beyond Nationalism: A Social and Political History of the Habsburg Monarchy*, 1848-1918, New York and Oxford: Oxford University Press, 1990, p. 203.

13. Richard Holmes, *Acts of War: The Behavior of Men in Battle*, New York: The Free Press, 1985, p. 382; Niall Ferguson also deals with the murder of prisoners immediately after their capture in: *The Pity of War: Explaining World War I*, New York: Basic Books, 1998, pp. 369-71.

14. Kriegsarchiv (Austria), Nachlass Heinrich von Raabl-Werner, B/141:4.

15. Ibid.

16. Ibid.

17. Wilhelm Winkler, *Berufsstatistik der Kriegstoten der öst.-ung. Monarchie*, (Vienna: L. W. Seidel & Sohn, 1919), p. 1.

18. Convention (IV) Respecting the Laws and Customs of War on Land, The Hague, 18 October 1907. Annex to the Convention: Regulations Respecting the Laws and Customs of War on Land, Chapter II Prisoners of War, Article 9. The relevant articles about Prisoners of War appear in articles 4-20 of the annex. The regulations will henceforth be quoted as: 'The Hague Regulations: Article #'.

19. The Hague Regulations, Article, 14.

20. Raabl-Werner often provided diacritical marks for Hungarian-language names but seldom for Czech-language names. All names appear as they appeared in the original source. Nachlass Raabl-Werner B/141:4.

21. Ibid.

22. A. Klevanskii, 'Voyennoplennye tsentral'nykh derzhav v tsarskoi i revolyutsnoi Rossii', in M.Birman (ed.) *Internatsionalisty v boyakh za vlast' Sovetov*, Moscow, 1965, pp. 22-5; Gerald H. Davis, 'The Life of Prisoners of War in Russia, 1914-1921', in Samuel Williamson and Peter Pastor (eds) *Essays on World War I: Origins and Prisoners of War*, New York, 1983, p. 165 and note 1, p. 190. Niall Ferguson, *The Pity of War: Explaining World War I*, New York: Basic Books, 1998, Table 42 p. 369.

23. A. Klevanskii, Ibid.

24. Davis, note 1 and Hannes Leidinger and Verena Moritz, 'Österreich-Ungarn und die Heimkehrer aus russischer Kriegsgefangenschaft im Jahr 1918', *Österreich in Geschichte und Literatur*, 6 (1997), pp. 385-403; Reinhard Nachtigal, 'Kriegsgefangene der Habsburgermonarchie in Russland', *Österreich in Geschichte und Literatur*, 4-5a, (1996), pp. 248-62.

25. See Hans Weiland, 'zum Geleite', in Hans Weiland and Leopold Kern (eds) *In Feindeshand: Die Gefangenschaft im Weltkrieg in Einzeldarstellungen*, statistical appendix.

26. Herwig, pp. 136-8, 147, 209.

27. Herwig, pp. 136-7.

28. Stone, *The Eastern Front*, pp. 251-5.

29. Stone, *The Eastern Front*, p. 250, Herwig, 212.

30. Holmes, p. 228. Holmes is influenced by W. Trotter's *Instincts of the Herd in Peace and War*, New York: Macmillan, 1915.

31. For a fascinating description of a panicky retreat see the diary of the 'raging reporter' Egon Erwin Kisch, *Schreib das auf Kisch!: Das Kriegstagebuch von Egon Erwin Kisch*, Berlin: Reiss, 1930, p. 60.

32. When units from the 'disloyal' Czech IR.36 were taken prisoner in the spring of 1915 they were captured with a host of other regiments, including 'unquestionably reliable' Alpine area units.

33. Trying to fit such a large number of people into a few ethno-linguistic categories is a risky procedure. Among the POWs in Russia were many who did not fit neatly into one – or just one – of these categories: polyglots, speakers of languages not formally recognized in Austria-Hungary (such as Yiddish), those who defined themselves in ethno-religious rather than ethno-linguistic terms (such as Bosnian Muslims or Jews) or people whose collective identities were either local or fluid. Yet, it is important to remember that contemporaries (both officials and civilians) preoccupied themselves with such efforts (on this see in detail Chapter 4 below).The estimates are based on the following works: Elsa Brändström, *Among Prisoners of War in Russia and Siberia*, London: Hutchinson, 1929; Ivo Banac, 'South Slav Prisoners of War in Revolutionary Russia', in Samuel Williamson and Peter Pastor (eds) *Essays on World War I: Origins and Prisoners of War*, New York, 1983, pp. 121–48; Gerald H. Davis, 'Deutsche Kriegsgefangene im Ersten Weltkrieg in Rußland', *Militärgeschichtliche Mitteilungen*, 1 (1982), pp. 37–49; Josef Kalvoda, 'Czech and Slovak Prisoners of War in Russia during the War and Revolution', in *Essays on World War I: Origins and Prisoners of War*, pp. 215–38; Peter Pastor, 'Hungarian POWs in Russia during the Revolution and Civil War', in *Essays on World War I: Origins and Prisoners of War*, pp. 149–62; Hans Weiland, 'Kriegsgefangenschaft im Weltkriege', in *In Feindeshand: Die Gefangenschaft im Weltkrieg in Einzeldarstellungen*, pp. 41–2.

34. Regarding Austro-Hungarian population and nationality statistics see Robert Kann, *A History of the Habsburg Empire, 1526–1918*, Berkeley: University of California Press, 1974, Appendix 1. Nationality (*Nationalität*) was determined in Austria-Hungary by ethno-linguistic criteria, though with slightly different shading in each half of the monarchy: in the Austrian half the criterion of 'language of daily use' (*Umgangssprache*) was used which was not necessarily the same as 'mother language' the criterion used in Hungary. Certain languages, such as Yiddish, were not recognized while Serbs and Croats were counted as separate groups in Hungary and one group (Serbo-Croats) in Austria.

35. This also led to a higher rate of casualties among certain nationalities. Austro-Germans, Magyars, Slovenes and Croats lost a proportionally larger share, something which received considerable attention in the Hungarian language press. It was also constantly debated in the Hungarian Parliament. On that see István Deák, *Beyond Nationalism*, p. 193.

36. The names quoted throughout the text follow the source's spelling. Diacritical marks were not always used by the writers and it seems they

Germanized or Magyarized some of the names. Still, one cannot be sure of that and the best procedure is to follow the given spelling. 'Böhmische Zensurgruppe A, 7. Spezialbericht: einige Schilderungen über die Situation bei der Gefangennahme', KA/AOK(1914/1915)/GZNB/Kart.3726/Akt 630.

37. Karl Drexel, *Feldkurat in Sibirien 1914–1920*, (Innsbruck and Leipzig: F. Rauch, 1940), pp. 38–9.

38. Clifford Geertz, *The Interpretation of Cultures*, New York: Basic Books, 1973; Robert C. Doyle *Voices from Captivity*, p. 89.

39. 'Johann Zakostelecky, Omsk an Thomas Z. in Kralup 19. November 1914', KA/AOK(1914/1915)/Kart:3726/Akt:630 letter 7.

40. 'Václav Jansta Kozetin Russland an Václav Jansta, Nouzon b.Dymokur', KA/AOK(1914/1915)/ Kart:3726/Akt: 849/ letter 20.

41. Ibid., letter 26.

42. On 'taking no prisoners' on the western front see Niall Ferguson, *The Pity of War*, pp. 374–5.

43. Regarding rumors of mutilations see: KA/AOK/GZNB/Kart:3733/ Akt:2300. The renowned French historian, Marc Bloch, was also struck by the prevalence and potency of rumors on the front during World War I. One of his first forays into the analysis of mentalities was his 'Réflexions d'un historien sur les fausses nouvelles de la guerre', *Revue de synthèse historique* 33 (1921); see also Marc Bloch, *Memoirs of War 1914–1915*, trans. Carole Fink, Cambridge: Cambridge University Press, 1988.

44. Hans Baumgartner, *Kriegsgefangenschaft in Sibirien 1915–1921*, Kriegsarchiv, Nachlaß Baumgartner B-268, p. 15.

45. Hameiri, ibid., pp. 9–10.

46. See for example Rüdiger Stillfried's unpublished manuscript: *Meine Erinnerungen aus dem Kriege und der Kriegsgefangenschaft*, Kriegsarchiv, Nachlaß Stillfried B/863, p. 50.

47. Regarding similar behavior on the western front see Holmes, p. 382–3.

48. Prochaska, 'Die Kapitulation Przemysl: Erinnerungen eines Landsturm-offiziers', in Hans Weiland and Leopold Kern (eds) *In Feindeshand: Die Gefangenschaft im Weltkriege in Einzeldarstellungen*, two vols, Vienna, 1931, vol. 1, p. 72.

49. Hans Baumgartner, *Kriegsgefangenschaft in Sibirien 1915–1921*, Kriegarchiv (Vienna) Nachlaß Hans Baumgartner B/268, p. 22.

50. Brändström, p. 37; this was by no means unique to the eastern front; see also Holmes, p. 382.

51. Drexel, p. 28.

52. Lieblich, *Seasons of Captivity*, p. 11.

53. Doyle, p. 89.

54. 'Instradierungen der Kgf. Vom Kriegsschauplatz nach dem Osten', Kart: 3729/ Akt 1509, pp. 4–5.

55. KA/AOK(1914/1915)/Kart: 3726, Akt 849, letter 23.

56. Ibid., letter 5.

Becoming POWs

57. KA/AOK(1915)/Kart: 3729,Akt 1416 p. 3.
58. Ibid., p. 3.
59. Brändström, pp. 38-9.
60. Hans Knöbl, 'Im Duklapaß gefangen', in Hans Weiland and Leopold Kern (eds) *In Feindeshand: Die Gefangenschaft im Weltkriege in Einzeldarstellungen*,vol. 1, pp. 64-5.
61. Brändström, ibid., p. 36.
62. Gustav Jungabauer, 'Auf Transport', *In Feindeshand: Die Gefangenschaft im Weltkriege in Einzeldarstellungen*, vol. 1, p. 86.
63. Bruno Prochaska, 'Tjeploschka', *In Feindeshand: Die Gefangenschaft im Weltkriege in Einzeldarstellungen*, vol. 1 pp. 101-2.
64. Ibid., p. 101.
65. Hereward T. Price, *Boche and Bolshevik: Experiences of an Englishman in the German Army and in Russian Prisons*, London: John Murray, 1919, pp. 124-5.
66. Prochaska, ibid., p. 101.
67. Franz Krisper, *Manuskript über Kriegsgefangenschaft in Rußland 1915-1920*, Kriegsarchiv Nachlass B/854.
68. Hans Kohn, *Living in a World Revolution: My Encounters with History*, New York: Trident Press, 1964, Chapter 9 'Russia'.
69. Jungabuaer, 'Auf Transport', *In Feindeshand: Die Gefangenschaft im Weltkriege in Einzeldarstellungen*, vol. 1, p. 86.
70. According to Russian figures, the exact number of Austro-Hungarian POWs passing through Kiev between the beginning of the war and 14 June 1914 (Old Style) were 476,856 men and 8,546 officers. These numbers did not include those who were sick or injured. See *Russkoe Slovo*, 17 June 1915.
71. Hameiri, pp. 51-2.
72. Josef Rey, *Meine Erlebnisse während und nach der Kriegsgefangenschaft in Russland in der Zeit von 1915-1920*, Bundesarchiv/Militärarchiv (Freiburg im Breisgau), Msg. 1/2725 pp. 51-4.
73. RGVIA. F.1396/op.2/d/1957/p.166 (1).
74. As pointed out by historians István Deák and Manfried Rauchensteiner, the pre-war officer corps had been largely decimated during the first four months of the war, replaced by hastily trained reserve officers. These officers seldom managed to win the respect and loyalty of their men, and were handicapped by insufficient knowledge of the various languages of the multinational Habsburg monarchy. Thus, while the Austro-Hungarian High Command was increasing the heterogeneity of its regiments by mixing up 'loyal' and 'disloyal' national elements, the officers it designated to command this diversity were conspicuously ill-equipped to handle the job. The loss of respect turned into a loss of authority once Habsburg officers became prisoners in Russia. Avigdor Hameiri who had a very low opinion of the abilities of his fellow reserve officers, provided in his memoirs many

examples of how rank-and-file POWs showed contempt for their former superiors. In one shocking example, an officer who had been castrated by an explosion is taunted during a train ride by his former charges.

75. Hans Kohn, p. 99. 'A prisoner of war, at least if he is an officer, has an abundance of free time and the liberty to dispose of it according as he wishes. Paradoxically, he enjoys freedom . . . [he] is a master of his own time; he may spend it reading good books, in conversation, or in thought and reflection.' It is interesting to note that Kohn, a historian writing these lines in the early 1960s, did not qualify this statement to World War I. He must have been aware that the treatment of World War II POWs (both rank-and-file and officers) was very different.

76. RGVIA fond 1606/ op.2/ d.1063/pp. 17–17(ob).

77. RGVIA fond 1606/ op.2/ d.1063/pp. 17–17(ob).

78. RGVIA fond 1606/ op.2/ d.1063/p. 7.

79. The National Archives of the United States, file 763.72114 suffix 820.

80. RGVIA fond 1396/op.2/d.1992/pp. 46, 46ob, 47, 47ob, 48.

81. In one especially interesting case, a Polish-speaking Greek-Catholic POW wrote to his village priest requesting a letter stating that he was indeed 'Ukrainian', all the while apologizing that he cannot actually write the request in the Ukrainian language.

82. The prolonging of the war beyond pre-war estimates created acute manpower deficits in all belligerent countries. In Russia, the absence of 15 million men from the workforce exacerbated food shortages and severe production bottlenecks. Thus, the influx of circa two million prisoners of war furnished a manpower pool that various sectors in the Russian economy competed to use. To make a more efficient use of this labor force a system of occupation registration was introduced in the winter of 1915/1916 aiming to identify artisans, skilled workers and experienced farmers among the rank-and-file POWs (officers of course were exempt). However, as with the case of nationality registration, occupational identification did not necessarily affect living and working conditions. The tug-and-pull between various interest groups within Russia resulted often in allocation of 'heads' to employers rather than assigning prisoners to places where they could bring the most help. Still, those prisoners who found employment as artisans or skilled workers invariably enjoyed better pay and improved living conditions.

83. Holger Herwig, *The First World War: Germany, and Austria-Hungary 1914–1918*, London: Arnold. 1997, pp. 12–13. Austria-Hungary trained significantly fewer people for combat that Russia, Italy, Germany and France. In 1914 it could field fewer infantry battalions than in the war of 1866 despite a twofold increase of its population.

84. See for example Deák, p. and Herwig, p. 13 .

85. Deák, p. 193

2

The Hague Convention and the Treatment of POWs: Mission and Omissions

There is little tradition of disciplined and reasoned assessment of how the laws of war have operated in practice. Lawyers, academics and diplomats have often been better in interpreting the precise legal meaning of existing accords, or at devising new law, than they have been at assessing the performance of existing accords or at generalizations about the circumstances in which they can or cannot work. In short, the study of law needs to be integrated with the study of history.

Adam Roberts
Land Warfare: from Hague to Nuremberg

Prisoner of War Camps in World War I and the 'Barbaric' Twentieth Century

In the introduction to what has become the standard work on Austro-Hungarian POWs during World War I, Hungarian-American historian Peter Pastor raised a provocative thesis regarding the treatment of prisoners in Russia. Taking a cue from Alexander Solzhenitsyn, Pastor compared POW camps in Russia during World War I with 'the GULags of Stalin's time' and argued that they 'could be considered prototypes of those set up later by the communists . . . The *voenno-plennyi arkhipelag* (prisoner-of-war archipelago) was followed by the GULags of Russia and by the extermination camps of Hitler's Europe.'[1]

By linking Russian POW camps with Nazi and Soviet camps, Pastor created a genealogy of ideological oppression with World War I at its starting point. This argument in turn supports a very prevalent interpretation of twentieth-century history that sees World War I as 'the century's Ur-catastrophe'.[2] The renowned military historian, Basil Liddell Hart, wrote for example that the decline of civilized behaviour became steeper during world-wide war of 1914-1918 . . . historic buildings and other treasures of civilization were subject to destruction on the lightest plea of military necessity and the rules of war designed to protect the civil population were callously violated in many directions.[3]

According to one of the most forceful formulations of this interpretation – Omer Bartov's *Murder in our Midst* – World War I unleashed the murderous potential inherent in modernity itself and set into motion a process of 'industrial killing' which is still very much with us today (as is indicated by the cases of Rwanda and Yugoslavia).[4] The best monograph on German occupation policies in the Baltic area during World War I, Liulevicius's *War Land on the Eastern Front*, argues that

[T]he 'lessons' of the Eastern Front [during the First World War] were eventually taken up by the Nazi movement and fused with the vile energies of their anti-semitism, to produce their terrible new plan for the East, which they would launch with the coming of the Second World War.[5]

Thus, if Pastor's assertion is indeed correct and prisoners of war in Russia did experience treatment comparable to that of inmates in Nazi and Soviet camps, then World War I captivity should justifiably assume a more prominent role than assigned to it so far in the historiography of the twentieth century. After all, mass incarceration of human beings is one of the most potent issues of twentieth century history, which produced some of its most harrowing imagery. Conversely, if the comparison with subsequent atrocities is proven highly exaggerated (or downright erroneous), one must ask whether this also affects our understanding of the role and legacies of World War I in general. Whether in certain areas of conduct, the belligerents in World War I showed some restraint – and even a certain degree of civility – which hindered barbarism rather facilitating it. Did World War I provide examples of mass incarceration that did not completely dehumanize prisoners?

The aim of this and the following chapter is to assess the treatment of Austro-Hungarian POWs in Russia and to reflect on its wider implications. I will try to illuminate this significant subject from various angles and points of view: from 'above', from 'below', through contemporaneous eyes and in the light of subsequent assessments. My intention here is to make considered judgments while highlighting competing positions and interpretations. The analysis will follow a 'zooming in' methodology: first obtaining a bird's-eye-view of the problem and then examining individual details through the eyes of prisoners and other witnesses. The current chapter will focus on what contemporaries considered 'acceptable' treatment of prisoners, i.e. the international legal framework set down at the Hague Peace Conferences of 1899 and 1907 and ratified by all belligerents except Serbia and Montenegro.[6] This chapter will also deal in detail with the argument regarding Russia as a 'POW archipelago' and why Pastor thought it should be linked with the Soviet gulag system and Nazi extermination camps. I will supplement Pastor's critique with that of Reinhard Nachtigal, who has recently done two important case studies on the Murman Railway project and the Totskoe typhus epidemic, and who presents a milder version of the 'prototype thesis'.

The next chapter – The Treatment of Austro-Hungarian POWs in Russia – will be devoted to assessing the treatment of prisoners of war in Russia, relying on three main groups of sources: administrative documents from Russia, Austria-Hungary and Germany; inspection reports written by neutral observers primarily Danish, Swedish and American and personal accounts of prisoners in the form of letters, diaries and memoirs. The chapter will conclude by assessing the place of POW interment in World War I in the genealogy of mass incarceration in the twentieth century, should it really be considered as a prototype?

The Legal Framework

Cultural definitions of what is permissible in warfare (and what is not) existed long before the formulation of the first multilateral conventions in the nineteenth century. Whether inspired by religious, economic, racist or moral considerations, belligerents have always waged war according to certain practices and norms.[7] In the history of warfare in the Western world, the treatment of POWs followed usually five prevalent practices (by no means mutually exclusive):

1 **Killing of prisoners of war**. This encompassed the whole gamut between immediate execution upon capture, via gradual starvation in inhumane internment places to placing certain prisoners (or certain categories of POWs) on trial to account for crimes committed prior to their capture.

2 **Utilization of prisoners as labor**. As with the case of killing, this practice ranged from permanent enslavement, through uncompensated work for the duration of hostilities, to paid labor under comparable conditions to those of the local population.

3 **Internment of prisoners in enclosed and guarded areas**. These areas could be relatively large or extremely confined as with the case of prisoners interned in ship hulks (a British custom during the eighteenth and early nineteenth centuries) or in prison cells.

4 **Release on parole under certain stipulated conditions**. A parole was a contract agreed to by the prisoner and the captors that allowed the prisoner a relatively large degree of freedom in return for assenting not to escape. During the Napoleonic Wars, for example, the custom of parole was the accepted norm with regards to captured enemy officers, and the amount of freedom they enjoyed was quite striking. In a few cases paroled prisoners would even be allowed to return home under the condition that they would not re-join their army (or face execution if recaptured).

5 **Outright release**. The release of prisoners could be the result of the cessation of hostilities, the outcome of a negotiated prisoner exchange (sometimes referred to as 'pro-rata cartels') or the consequence of a ransom paid by families. The custom of ransom was especially prevalent in Europe during the late middle ages and the early modern period when fixed monetary scales were agreed for ransoming prisoners from huge sums to ransom generals to trifling amounts for the release of common soldiers.[8]

Between the middle decades of the nineteenth century and World War I, considerable efforts were made in Europe and the US to transform the cultural practices of warfare into a binding set of principles and regulations. These efforts found expression in a large number of declarations, conventions and legal codes, culminating in the Hague Conventions formulated at the peace conferences of 1899 and 1907 (a third peace conference was scheduled for 1915 but did not take place because of the war). According to military historian, Michael Howard, the impetus to codify a *jus in bello* (laws of conduct in warfare of which the treatment of POWs is a part) came from two significant developments in the nineteenth century. First, the emergence of the bourgeoisie and its culture as mainstays of Western European and American societies. Although bourgeois culture was not particularly averse to war itself, it was nonetheless ill at ease with the brutalities of warfare, which had become more noticeable through the introduction of new communication technologies (primarily photography and telegraph). Thus, it was not a coincidence that mid-nineteenth century conflicts such as the Crimean War, Solferino and the American Civil War all spawned attempts to formally curb the degree of human sufferings in warfare. Furthermore, the fact that nineteenth century European armies increasingly relied on universal conscription (rather than on marginal social elements) meant that a larger chunk of society had a personal attachment to the enlisted citizenry which now constituted the bulk of the army.[9]

The second crucial development during the nineteenth century was the introduction of weapons of great destruction which exponentially increased the deadliness of war both on and off the battlefield.[10] Asphyxiating gases, dumdum bullets and even the discharge of explosives from the air (initially from balloons) became major concerns for Western diplomats well before World War I. As John Keegan poignantly described in his classic study, *The Face of Battle*, modern warfare grew considerably more lethal and much longer in duration in comparison to eighteenth century engagements. Consequently the potential of destruction reached such a scale that warfare changed 'from an unpleasant [experience] for a minority of the participants to an intolerable experience for the majority'.[11]

The widespread belief during the second part of the nineteenth century that in warfare – just as in other areas of human action – progress could be achieved, found expression in the idea of the multilateral treaty. The multilateral treaty was to be the embodiment of internationally recognized 'laws of war', which in the words of an American delegate to the first Hague Conference 'would result in the humanizing of warfare'.[12] From the first multilateral treaty in 1856 (the Paris Declaration on Maritime Law) to the Second Hague Convention of 1907 (which in fact included no less than thirteen separate conventions), a corpus of international law emerged which codified what is considered permissible in modern warfare and what is deemed impermissible. The provisions dealing with war captivity formed part of the 1907 Hague Convention (IV) Respecting the Laws and Customs of War on Land (Section 1, 'On Belligerents', Chapter II, Articles 4–20, Chapter III, article 21).[13]

Regarding the treatment of prisoners of war, the Hague Convention touched specifically only three of the five traditional practices, namely internment, utilization as labor and parole. The document did not deal directly with the age-old custom of killing prisoners, although article 4 did stipulate that prisoners 'must be treated humanely', which seems on the surface to preclude capital punishment.[14] Nevertheless, the door was left open for executions in article 8 of the section where it was explicitly stated the captor state is permitted to treat acts of insubordination 'by the adoption towards them of such measures of severity as may be considered necessary'.[15] In the same vein, the discussion of outright release was confined to the last article of the section (article 20), which stated simply that 'After the conclusion of peace, the repatriation of prisoners of war shall be carried out as quickly as possible.'[16] The only exceptions to that rule were doctors, medical orderlies and chaplains who were supposed to be returned to their forces without delay.[17]

The bulk, however, of the POW section in the 1907 Hague Convention was devoted to prescribing the law with regards to internment, labor and parole. In the area of internment, article 5, specified that prisoners 'may be interned in a town, fortress, camp or any other place, and bound not to go beyond certain fixed limits, but they can not be confined except as an indispensable measure of safety and only while the circumstances which necessitate the measure continue to exist.'[18] In other words, prisoners of war were to enjoy freedom of movement within the designated area of internment and were to be confined to their lodgings only for reasons of their own personal safety. The exact nature of the place of interment was left open for each captor power to decide, although the wording of article 5 suggested that some sort of military facility was envisioned. Within the designated internment area the prisoners were to receive 'board, lodging and clothing on the same footing as the troops of the government who captured them'.[19] Thus, the Hague Convention created a linkage between prisoners of war and the detaining power's troops that remained the guiding principle in the subsequent Geneva Conventions of 1929 and 1949. The linkage created between the POWs and the soldiers of the captor power had two important implications: first, no minimum standards were defined for lodgings, food and clothing. The formulation 'on the same footing as the troops of the government who had captured them' was rather nebulous, especially because all European armies employed multiple norms for lodging, food and clothing, depending on the function and location of specific troops. Moreover, local troops were in a much better position to supplement their diet and clothing than prisoners. Second, the linkage automatically privileged the higher ranks among the prisoners, chiefly commissioned officers. As Joan Beaumont has shown in her analysis of hierarchy and privilege in the treatment of prisoners of war, the right of POW officers to receive preferential treatment was unquestionably accepted in all the pre-World War I conventions; surprisingly, according to Beaumont, this codified preferential treatment 'became more explicit as the supposedly more egalitarian twentieth century progressed'.[20] Articles 16, 18 and 19 of the Hague Convention respectively guaranteed interned prisoners of war the rights of free postage, freedom of religion, proper burial and proper death notification. However, as already described above, article 18 (proper death notification) was very rarely observed by the Russian military authorities, contributing in turn to the great difficulties in ascertaining the number of POWs in Russia.[21] Moreover, death certificates were on a few occasions falsified by the Russian military, misstating intentionally the prisoner's cause of death (for example, with typhus presented as 'colitis'). This was ostensibly done to hide the existence of typhus epidemics and to prevent the German government from retaliating against Russian POWs.[22]

The Hague Convention permitted the widespread utilization of rank-and-file labor. Article 6 of the POW section allowed the captor army to employ captive enemy soldiers in 'public service, for private persons, or on their own account'.[23] Work done for the state was to be 'paid for at rates in force for work of a similar kind done by soldiers of the national army, or if there are none in force, at a rate according to the work conducted.'[24] Notwithstanding, article 6 did not stipulate that the POWs themselves should benefit directly from their labor. Rather, it recommended that 'the wages of prisoners shall go toward improving their position, and the balance be paid to them on their release, after deducting the cost of their maintenance.'[25] The option of postponing actual payment of wages while simultaneously deducting maintenance created the possibility of exploiting the POW population as unpaid forced labor (liable to be punished with severe measures for any acts of insubordination). Exempted completely from these measures were POW officers who were not required under any circumstance to perform any form of work they did not wish to do. Moreover, article 17 of the POW section stipulated that officers 'shall receive the same rate of pay as officers of corresponding rank in the country where they are detained, the amount ultimately refunded by their own government'.[26] Thus, as with the case of lodging and internment, the Hague Convention envisaged a huge gap between the ranks in terms of work and pay, and did not specify minimum standards for those on the lower rungs of the military social order.

In addition to internment and labor, the Hague Convention also sanctioned the practice of release on parole. Article 10 of the POW section stipulated that 'prisoners of war may be set at liberty on parole if the laws of their country allow, and, in such cases, they are bound, on their personal honor, scrupulously to fulfill, both towards their own government and the government by whom they were made prisoners, the engagements they contracted.'[27] It is interesting to note that release on parole was open to prisoners of all ranks, not just to POW officers. This was an expansion of the early modern custom of parole that pertained primarily to officers. Still, the emphasis placed in article 10 on the notion of personal honor, and the fact that honor was the defining feature of an officer's code of conduct (and what primarily distinguished him from other ranks) suggests that parole was intended mainly for officers. In any case, the fact that apart from officers all other prisoners were liable to perform work greatly reduced the chances of parole being granted to other ranks. Article 11 of the POW section stated that 'a prisoner of war can not be compelled to accept his liberty on parole'.[28] The reason it was necessary to include such a qualification had again much to do with the officers' code of honor, which required officers to attempt to escape while in captivity. As shall be discussed below, Emperor Franz-Joseph steadfastly refused to permit his officers in Russia to give their word of honor and accept parole. According to the Austrian Red Cross nurse, Countess Anna Revertera, only on his deathbed in November 1916 did he acquiesce to the entreaties of the Austrian and Hungarian Red Cross and agreed to what he perceived as the 'dishonorable' practice of parole.[29] Finally, article 12 of the POW section contained the warning 'that prisoners of war liberated on parole and recaptured bearing arms against the Government to whom they had pledged their honor, or against the allies of that Government, forfeit their right to be treated as prisoners of war and can be brought before courts'.[30]

As mentioned in the preceding chapter, the Hague Convention called for the establishment of two important services: first, article 14 of the POW section ordered 'the institution of an inquiry office for prisoners of war on the commencement of hostilities in each of the belligerent States . . . to reply to all inquiries about the prisoners.'[31] This inquiry office was expected to provide the following information regarding each individual prisoner: 'regimental number, name and surname, age, place of origin, rank, unit, wounds, date and place of capture, internment, wounding and death as well as any observation of a special character'.[32] The fundamental problem regarding this list was that nowhere in the Hague Convention was it written that POWs were obliged to give this information to the military authorities of the captor army (who in turn would forward it to the inquiry office). Rather, the only information prisoners of war were specifically ordered to provide was their 'true name and rank'.[33] The consequences of this discrepancy became glaringly evident in the case of Austro-Hungarian POWs in Russia: the Habsburg military authorities could never really ascertain how many k.u.k. soldiers were in Russian captivity and in turn could not provide reliable information to the families of POWs and MIAs. The second important service prescribed in the Hague Convention was the creation of 'a channel for charitable effort' designed to funnel relief from the home state to its captured soldiers. Article 15 of the POW section stipulated that 'Relief societies for prisoners of war, which are properly constituted in accordance with the laws of their country . . . shall receive from the belligerents, for themselves and their duly accredited agents every facility for the efficient performance of their humane task within the bounds imposed by military necessities and administrative regulations.'[34] The juxtaposition of a permissive clause ('shall receive every facility') with a restrictive clause ('within the bounds of military necessities and administrative regulations') meant that it was up to the belligerents themselves to define the exact nature and boundaries of POW relief; whether charitable activity would assume the 'humane' nature envisioned in the first part of article 15 or conversely whether it would assume the restrictive character of the second part.

In the case of unforeseen eventualities or in areas where the negotiators in the Hague could not reach an agreement (for example, whether resisters in occupied territories are entitled to POW status), the Hague Convention recommended two possible routes: first, to appeal to a common moral ground that professedly bound the signatories together. This principle was formulated by the Russian international law expert Fedor Martens in the what has since been widely known as the Martens Clause:

> Until a more complete code of laws of wars is issued, the high contracting
> Parties think it right to declare that in cases not included in the regulations
> adopted by them, populations and belligerents remain under the protection

and empire of the principles of international law, as they result from the usages established between civilized nations, from the laws of humanity, and the requirements of public conscience.[35]

The second alternative in dealing with the Hague Convention's 'blind spots' was to encourage belligerents to conclude separate agreements regarding specific issues. In the case of POWs on the eastern front, representatives from the four major belligerents – Russia, Germany, Austria-Hungary and Turkey – met in Scandinavia regularly throughout the war for negotiating sessions, highlighted by a number of high-level meetings: in Stockholm in November 1915, December 1916 and August 1917, in Copenhagen in October 1917 and in Oslo later that month. The first gathering, which took place between 22 November and 1 December 1915 under the auspices of Prince Carl of Sweden, was by far the most important. Headed by senior representatives from the belligerent countries (Prince Max of Baden from Germany, Counts Spieglfeld and Albert Apponyi from respectively Austria and Hungary and Senator Arbusov from Russia) the delegations included key civil servants in POW affairs administration as well as repatriated POWs who could provide eye-witness accounts of conditions in captivity.[36]

In contrast to the language of the Hague Convention, which was general and vague (as it is often the case with multilateral conventions), the agreement hammered out in Stockholm was a paragon of specificity. The Stockholm Protocol, signed on 1 December 1915 and ratified by eastern front belligerents by May 1916, included a detailed explication of the privileges and obligations of prisoners of war and of the agencies assisting them. Its main paragraphs outlined the workings of relief committees, offered ways of reforming flawed registration methods, defined how a death certificate should look, specified the appropriate way to dispatch packets and money orders to POWs, determined what reading material could be sent to POWs and most importantly perhaps set precise standards for lodging, clothing and hygiene for officers and men.[37]

The signatories agreed, for example, that POWs would be able to write Red Cross postcards at the first assembly station – rather than wait until arrival at the main assembly stations as previously done – so they can inform their families about their new status as POWs. The postcards would be then sent as quickly as possible via Copenhagen to the home country and forwarded to the addressees. Official POW lists composed in the captor state were to use the home country's alphabet when writing a prisoner's first name, last name and place of birth. The signing parties hoped that this would eliminate errors emanating from improper transliteration of Latin alphabet into Cyrillic and vice versa. The Stockholm Protocol recommended that the captor countries utilize the help of bilingual POWs to compose these lists. By combining early notification and more rigorous registration – each list was required to specify also rank, regiment, date and place of capture and permanent address prior to capture of each POW – the belligerents sought to reduce the number of MIAs and multiple registrants. Unfortunately, the system came into use only after the great majority of POWs had already been captured on the eastern front and therefore did not make a great impact.[38]

The Stockholm Protocol called for an increase in the number of censors handling POW mail to alleviate post logjams.[39] If this proved impossible, the protocol specified the number of letters and postcards each POW was permitted to write as well as their maximal length: two letters (each up to four pages) and four postcards a month for regular POWs, two letters (each up the six pages) and four postcards a month for each officer. There were no limits on the number of letters each POW was entitled to receive and few limits on the books he was allowed to receive. Thus, POWs could receive any book via the official relief committees, provided it was published before the end of 1913 and contained no handwritten markings of any kind. Books in languages not used widely outside their core area (such as Hungarian) were required to include a French translation of their title page. POWs could also receive books directly from their friends and family – and not merely from the relief committees – but these had to have their bindings removed (presumably to prevent unlawful materials smuggled into camps).[40]

The Stockholm Protocol included precise definitions of what POWs were entitled to in terms of material well-being: the lodgings of rank-and-file POWs had to conform to a norm of five square meters of space per prisoner (53.8 square feet); each prisoner was expected to receive a blanket and a sack to be filled either with straw or wood shavings; bath and laundry facilities were to be a requirement in each camp 'with a roof and stable walls to be provided in the ratio of one toilet seat for every fifty people'.[41] In comparison, some of the minimum standards now defined for POW officers were: fifteen square meters (161.4 square feet) of space per officer; a standard issue of a mattress, a pillow, a blanket, a chair or a stool, a trunk for clothes and dishes, a bowl, a glass, a hand towel and a bucket; officers were to be assigned rank-and-file POW orderlies at a ratio of at least one orderly for every four officers.[42] As with the Hague Convention, the Stockholm Protocol reflected contemporary class hierarchies and the perceived gulf between a refined gentleman officer and coarse lower-class soldier.

Finally, from the very first month of the war the belligerents on the eastern front concluded various *ad hoc* agreements through the mediation of Sweden, Denmark and the US (until the entry of the latter into the war 1917). These covered a myriad of issues such as the activities of charitable organizations (such as the American YMCA) the distribution of clothing via Tientsin in China or visitations of Red Cross nurses from the home country in POW camps.[43] All in all, the Hague Convention and the specific agreements negotiated during the war sought to safeguard the lives of military internees within the cultural and social norms of the times. This legal framework was not flawless with many loopholes and ambiguities, especially before the Stockholm Protocol came into being in mid-1916. Still, the ultimate test of any such agreement is the willingness of the signatories to adhere to its provisions and its spirit.

The 'Prototype' Thesis

There is much about World War I captivity that evokes images of subsequent totalitarian brutality: undernourished prisoners interned in barbed wire enclosures; cramped cattle trucks converted to carry human loads; camps that supply cheap labor to industrial and agricultural enterprises; frequent outbreaks of characteristic encampment diseases such as typhus, typhoid fever and dysentery; even some of the names of internment locations during World War I are eerily familiar: Mauthausen in upper Austria billeted Italian prisoners of war, Theresienstadt (Terezín) in Bohemia housed captive Russian soldiers (as well as Austro-Hungarian political prisoners such as Franz-Ferdinand's assassin Gavrilo Princip) and the vast area of Siberia was home to scores of large and medium-sized POW camps. Nevertheless, despite such powerful memory triggers, one must still ask whether we are dealing here with more than just superficial resemblance. Should World War I captivity be indeed viewed in any sense as an early example of organized oppression? Can we detect continuities between mass incarceration of POWs during World War I and the murderous incarceration practices of totalitarian regimes, above all

Nazi concentration and extermination camps and the Soviet forced labor camps or gulags.[44]

According to historian Peter Pastor, one POW internment system during World War I should indeed be considered a precursor of the subsequent totalitarian examples, the Russian incarceration system. In the introduction to *Essays on World War I: Origins and Prisoners of War*, a collection of essays on the subject from 1983 that included contributions from such specialists as Ivo Banac, Gerald H. Davis and Arnold Krammer, Pastor maintained that Russian POW camps during the First World War were 'new types' of internment facilities much akin to the communist gulags and Nazi concentration camps.[45] 'Contrary to Solzhenitsyn's claim', he argued, 'this new type seems to have come into being, not under the communists, but under the tsarists. Their first victims were the prisoners of war.'[46]

If Pastor is correct, then there are two possible and important implications regarding the efficacy of the Hague Conventions: first, the POW section in the Hague Conventions played a negligible role in influencing the treatment of POWs in Russia, and consequently we are dealing here with yet another example of multilateral conventions failing to prevent atrocities and failing in making warfare more humane. The unimpressive performance of conventions is indeed a significant aspect of twentieth-century history, appearing even more troubling in light of late-twentieth century brutalities. The second possibility is that the POW section of the Hague Convention did indeed play a meaningful role in prescribing treatment, but in itself the Hague Convention was a flawed document that enabled this oppressive 'new type' of internment system to emerge. Alternatively, if Pastor's understanding of the Russian system is inaccurate – and it is possible to demonstrate that the Hague Convention framework did offer protection to captured soldiers – then one must ask why this aspect of World War I has been hidden in the grand narrative of the Great War. To weigh the advantages and disadvantages of these alternatives one must first examine the prototype argument in greater detail.

In Pastor's mind there were four striking elements in the Russian POW internment system that justify categorizing it as a 'prototype' of Soviet gulags and Nazi concentration camps. First, there was a deliberate qualitative hierarchy between the various camps in the system, from 'the "first circle" reserved for Slav captives expected to be won over to the Russian cause. These camps were found in European Russia', to 'the "lower depths" – the worst camps – found near the Arctic Circle, in Siberia and in Central Asia. They were inhabited primarily by captured Germans, Austrians and Hungarians.'[47] In other words, it was the national identity of a prisoner that determined the quality of treatment he was to receive from the Russian state, a discriminatory policy that drew its main inspiration from the political ideology of Pan Slavism.

Second, regardless of this intentional differentiation between the various camps in the system, 'they were all', according to Pastor, 'dismal and often inhumane communities'. Even POW camps in European Russia, whose main purpose was ostensibly to facilitate recruitment of prisoners from certain ethnic groups to the Russian army, threatened the survival of their inmates and fell very short of the mark set in the Hague Convention. Thus, drawing on Solzhenitsyn's memorable image of the gulag system as a barbarous chain of islands, Pastor labeled the Russian POW system as a *voennoplennyi arkhipelag* (prisoner-of-war archipelago), which played a key role in the 'acclimatization of the European mind to the existence of concentration camps'.[48] Implicit in Pastor's argument is the idea that Russian POW camps during World War I were *sui generis*; that they were exponentially worse than POW camps in other belligerents and that the practices carried out by the Russian military authorities had no parallels in other warring countries. In the same vein, Reinhard Nachtigal, in his analysis of the typhus epidemic in the Russian camp of Totskoe, argues that Russian POW camps showed the highest mortality rates of any belligerent, and that the undeniably dreadful conditions in Totskoe could be considered 'an example of the treatment of POWs' in Russia during the war.[49] He goes so far as to quote the senior Austro-Hungarian official, Ernst von Streeruwitz, who characterized Totskoe as a *Totenlager*; a designation which nowadays has unmistakable connotations to Nazi camps although Streeruwitz had used it to signify mass mortality.[50]

The third element that distinguished the Russian system was, according to Pastor, the utilization of prisoners of war for large-scale building projects in hostile environments. In Pastor's opinion 'their situation had a great deal in common with that of the *zeks* of Stalin's camps. Like the victims of the 1930s, hundreds of thousands of prisoners of war died on similar projects and in comparable camps as a result of accidents, malnutrition and disease.'[51] The largest and most criticized of these building projects was the construction of the Murman Railway, stretching 1,400 kilometers (875 miles) and connecting Petrozavodsk on Lake Onega with the Arctic Ocean near

Murmansk. The construction of the line had begun well before World War I and been given top priority by the Russian military once the war had started. Between July 1915 and October 1916 an estimated number of 70,000 POWs reinforced the Russian working force that had been already working in this extremely inhospitable region (long cold winters punctuated by humid mosquito-infested summers). News of the tough working conditions filtered back to Germany and Austria-Hungary, leading to considerable wartime publicity and to reprisals between Russia and Germany. The German historian Reinhard Nachtigal, who examined the Murman Railway controversy, argued that the Russian Supreme Command preferred to use ethnic German and Magyar POWs in Murman because of the rough working conditions in the arctic circle region.[52] Following escalating reprisals and with the help of Swedish mediation the use of POW labor on the Murman Railway was halted in October 1916, two months before the line was completed. According to Swedish Red Cross nurse Elsa Brändström, 25,000 prisoners of war died while working on the Murman Railway, and of the remaining 45,000 roughly 70 per cent suffered from various ailments such as scurvy, tuberculosis and rheumatism.

The fourth conspicuous aspect of the Russian internment system, according to Pastor, was the attempt 'to subvert the enemy citizenry's loyalty through propaganda'.[53] Although Russia was not the only belligerent attempting to accomplish this (Austria-Hungary and Italy similarly targeted perceived 'disaffected' elements among the POW population, and France and Britain backed various émigré groups), it was nonetheless the only place where remaining loyal to one's home state could literally be a life-and-death decision. In Pastor's mind, the appalling living conditions in Russian camps meant that 'many of those who did join [the anti-Habsburg forces] made their decision solely in the hope that life in the volunteer barracks would be superior to that in the prisoner-of-war camps.'[54] After the fall of the Provisional Government in November 1917, the Bolsheviks adopted the practice of agitating in POW camps, relying on 'hunger and the need for self-defense' as recruiting tools.[55] Thus, the dilemmas of collaboration in Russian POW camps were of a different magnitude from anywhere else in World War I, providing a foretaste of World War II dilemmas.

In addition to the four structural elements of the Russian POW internment system, Pastor pointed to a visit Stalin made in late 1916 to the Siberian town of Krasnoyarsk, and speculated whether 'Stalin's view of labor camps was influenced by his sight of the Krasnoyarsk camp, which housed 15,000 prisoners of war.'[56] In other words, Russian POW camps might have been prototypes not only in the sense of early examples of ideological maltreatment, but also in a much more direct sense: they served as an actual blueprint upon which the gulags were modeled.

It is important to note that the inaccessibility of Soviet archives until the 1990s hindered empirical research into the history of gulags and their economic, political, psychological and punitive roles within Soviet society. Since the collapse of the USSR, Russian historians have begun revising Solzhenitsyn's original portrayal of the gulag system – which had been based on the accounts of 227 witnesses – by utilizing archival material.[57] It is now quite clear that the gulag system was first developed in the mid 1920s by the secret police (OGPU) under Feliks Dzerzhinski with the aim of rapidly industrializing the Soviet Union by relying on what was considered 'expendable labor'. The gulag complex reached its zenith in terms of industrial production in the early 1950s with a turnover throughout the years of an estimated eighteen million inmates (with an additional fifteen million experiencing non-camp forms of forced labor). Recent additions to the literature about the gulag corroborate Solzhenitsyn's basic condemnation of the system as dehumanizing, exploitative and often outright murderous. Thus, the question regarding putative links between this notorious system of mass incarceration and the one that had existed in Russia during World War I (only a few years before the establishment of the 'gulag archipelago'), retains its validity and importance.

Notes

1. Peter Pastor, 'Introduction' in Samuel Williamson and Peter Pastor (eds) *Essays on World War I: Origins and Prisoners of War*, pp. 113–17.

2. See for example Thomas Nipperdey, *Deutsche Geschichte 1866–1918*, Munich: C. H. Beck, 1992, vol. 2, p. 758; John Keegan, *The First World War*, New York: Knopf, 1999, Introduction; Omer Bartov, *Murder in our Midst: The Holocaust, Industrial Killing and Representation*, New York: Oxford University Press, 1996; Norman Naimark, *Fires of Hatred: Ethnic Cleansing*

in Twentieth Century Europe, Cambridge MA: Harvard University Press, 2001, Introduction.

3. B. H. Liddell Hart, *The Revolution in Warfare*, London: Faber & Faber, 1946, pp. 60-1.

4. According to Bartov 'Industrial Killing' constitutes 'a mechanized, rational, impersonal and sustained mass destruction of human beings organized and administered by states, legitimized and set into motion by scientists and jurists, sanctioned and popularized by academics and intellectuals'. Omer Bartov, *Murder in our Midst: The Holocaust, Industrial Killing and Representation*, New York, 1996.

5. Vejas Gabriel Liulevicius, *War Land on the Eastern Front: Culture, National Identity and German Occupation in World War I*, Cambridge: Cambridge University Press, 2000, p. 279.

6. This contrasts with World War II where two key belligerents – the Soviet Union and Japan – were not signatories of the 1929 Geneva Convention.

7. The nature of the enemy often determined which customs and constraints would be followed. European armies were considerably less restrained when fighting 'infidels' or 'savages' than when they fought fellow Christians. Michael Howard, 'Constraints on Warfare', in Michael Howard, George Andreopolous and Mark Shulman (eds) *The Laws of War: Constraints on Warfare in the Western World*, New Haven: Yale University Press, 1994, Chapter 1.

8. Joan Beaumont, 'Rank, Privilege and Prisoners of War', *War and Society*, 1 (May 1983), p. 68.

9. Michael Howard, 'Constraints on Warfare', in Michael Howard, George J. Andreopoulos and Mark R. Shulman (eds) *The Laws of War: Constraints on Warfare in the Western World*, New Haven: Yale University Press, 1994, pp. 5-6.

10. Howard.

11. Keegan, *The Face of Battle*, p. 324.

12. This statement was made by Frederick W. Holls, the secretary and counsel of the American delegation at the 1899 Peace Conference. See his *The Peace Conference at the Hague and its bearings on International Law and Policy*, New York: Macmillan, 1900, ix-x. Quoted from Adam Roberts, 'Land Warfare: from Hague to Nuremberg' in Michael Howard, George Andreopolous and Mark Shulman (eds) *The Laws of War: Constraints on Warfare in the Western World*, New Haven: Yale University Press, 1994, p. 121.

13. Convention (IV) Respecting the Laws and Customs of War on Land, The Hague, 18 October 1907. Annex to the Convention: Regulations Respecting the Laws and Customs of War on Land, Chapter II Prisoners of War, Article 9. The relevant articles about prisoners of war appear in articles 4-20 of the annex. The regulations will henceforth be quoted as: 'The Hague Regulations: Article #'. One can easily access the document in Jonathan F.

Vance (ed.) *Encyclopedia of Prisoners of War and Internment*, Santa Barbara CA: ABC Clio, 2000), pp. 362–4.
14. The Hague Regulations: Article 4.
15. The Hague Regulations: Article 8.
16. The Hague Regulations: Article 20.
17. This was the result of Chapter 3, Article 21 which stipulated that wounded and sick are to be treated according to the 1906 Geneva Convention. The 'protected personnel' of the wounded and the sick were not to be made prisoners but returned to their forces immediately. On this see Jonathan Vance, 'The Geneva Conventions of 1864 and 1906', in *Encyclopedia of Prisoners of War and Internment*, pp. 109–10, p. 364.
18. The Hague Regulations: Article 5.
19. The Hague Regulations: Article 7.
20. Joan Beaumont, 'Rank, Privilege and Prisoners of War', *War and Society*, 1 (May 1983), p. 69.
21. For their part the Austro-Hungarian military authorities were far from innocent. During the first year of the war, they buried dead Russian soldiers in mass graves without proper identification. See Manfried Rauchensteiner, *Der Tod des Doppeladlers: Österreich-Ungarn und der Erste Weltkrieg*, Böhlau: Graz, Vienna, Cologne, 1993, pp. 152–4.
22. Reinhard Nachtigal, 'Seuchen unter militärischer Aufsicht in Rußland: Das Lager Tockoe als Beispiel für die Behandlung der Kriegsgefangenen 1915/1916', *Jahrbücher für Geschichte Osteuropas*, 48 (2000), pp. 377–9.
23. The Hague Regulations: Article 6.
24. Ibid.
25. Ibid.
26. The Hague Regulations: Article 17.
27. The Hague Regulations: Article 10.
28. The Hague Regulations: Article 11.
29. It is interesting to note that following the Korean War, President Eisenhower, ordered a new 'Code of Conduct for Members of the Armed Forces of the United States', which among other things stipulated that 'I will not accept parole nor any special favors from the enemy.' (Note also the interesting usage of the first person singular.) See Doyle, pp. 57–8.
30. The Hague Regulations: Article 12.
31. The Hague Regulations: Article 14.
32. Ibid.
33. The Hague Regulations: Article 7.
34. The Hague Regulations: Article 15.
35. Fedor Martens (1845–1909) was a professor of international law at St Petersburg University and one of the leading contemporary authorities on the subject. He represented Russia in the 1899 and 1907 Peace Conferences and was awarded the Nobel Peace Prize in 1902. James Brown Scott, *The Hague Conventions and Declarations of 1899 and 1907*, 2nd edition, New

York: Oxford University Press, 1915, pp. 101–2; Adam Roberts characterizes the Martens Clause as 'an inspiring fudge' that concealed 'the incurable incompatible interests of states'. Adam Roberts, p. 122.

36. Ernst Streeruwitz, 'Die Stockholmer Konferenz 1915', *In Feindeshand*, vol. 2, pp. 331–5; Elsa Brändström, *Among the Prisoners of war in Russia and Siberia*, pp. 186-188; Heinrich von Raabl-Werner, 'Österreich-Ungarns offizielle Kriegsgefangenen Fürsorge', *In Feindeshand*, vol. 2, pp. 324–31.

37. Ernst Streeruwitz, 'Die Stockholmer Konferenz 1915', *In Feindeshand*, vol. 2, pp. 331–5; Elsa Brändström, *Among the Prisoners of war in Russia and Siberia*, pp. 186–8.

38. On the process of registration, see Chapter 1.

39. On censorship practices, see Chapter 4.

40. Ernst Streeruwitz, 'Die Stockholmer Konferenz 1915', *In Feindeshand*, vol. 2, pp. 331–5.

41. Elsa Brändström, *Among the Prisoners of war in Russia and Siberia*, pp. 186–8.

42. Ernst Streeruwitz, 'Die Stockholmer Konferenz 1915', *In Feindeshand*, vol. 2, pp. 331–5; Elsa Brändström, *Among the Prisoners of War in Russia and Siberia*, pp. 186–8.

43. On this see in detail below, Chapters 4 and 5.

44. The word 'gulag' or 'GULag' is an acronym for *Glavnaia Upravlenia Lagerei* or main camp administration. The literature on Nazi concentration camps is enormous, much greater than that on Soviet gulags. Two excellent introductions to Nazi crimes, mass incarceration practices and the various scholarly interpretations about them are Raul Hilberg, *The Destruction of European Jews*, three volumes, New York: Holmes & Meier,1985, and Michael Marrus, *The Holocaust in History*, New York: Meridian, 1987; on the gulags see a review article by Anne Applebaum, 'Inside the Gulag', *New York Review of Books*, 15 June 2000.

45. Peter Pastor, 'Introduction' in Samuel Williamson and Peter Pastor (eds) *Essays on World War I: Origins and Prisoners of War*, New York, 1983, pp. 113–17.

46. Pastor, p. 115.

47. Pastor, p. 114.

48. Pastor, p. 117, transliterations appear as they did in Pastor's text.

49. Reinhard Nachtigal, 'Seuchen unter militärischer Aufsicht in Rußland: Das Lager Tockoe als Beispiel für die Behandlung der Kriegsgefangenen 1915/1916', *Jahrbücher für Geschichte Osteuropas*, (2000), p. 363.

50. Ibid., p. 383.

51. Pastor, p. 114.

52. Reinhard Nachtigal, 'Murman Railway', in *Encyclopedia of Prisoners of War and Internment*, pp. 194–5.

53. Pastor.

54. Pastor, p. 116.

55. Pastor argues that the miserable conditions in Russian camps demoralized the prisoners, made them apolitical and consequently hindered their recruitment into the anti-Habsburg legions. On the question of whether Austro-Hungarian POWs became apolitical in captivity see Chapter 6. It appears to me, though, that if one argues that miserable conditions were the primary reason why POWs joined the anti-Habsburg forces then one cannot also argue that miserable conditions demoralized the prisoners and hindered the recruitment efforts. See Pastor, pp. 113–17.

56. Pastor, pp. 113–17.

57. Anne Applebaum, 'Inside the Gulag', *New York Review of Books*, 15 June 2000; Galina Mikhailovna Ivanova, *Labor Camp Socialism: The Gulag in the Soviet Totalitarian System*, M. E. Sharpe, 2000; Simeon Vilensky (ed.) *Till My Tale is Told: Women's Memoirs of the Gulag*, Bloomington: Indiana University Press, 1999; N. G. Okhotin and A. B. Roginskii (eds) *Sistema Ispravitel'no-Trudovikh Lagerei v SSSR, 1923–1960: Spravochnik*, Moscow: Zven'ia, 1998.

3

The Treatment of POWs in Russia

> The Royal Prussian War Ministry wishes to inform families [of German POW officers in Russia] that previous newsletters contained the misconception that the situation among POWs was not exceptionally bad. This may cause bitterness among the prisoners. Newsletters [written by families of POWs] cannot and should not present a definitive picture of life in captivity because they are based on excerpts of letters from this or that writer. Many writers paint a rosy picture because of censorship or because they do not want to burden the addressee. If POWs will continue to receive letters from home underestimating their difficulties, we will have to terminate these newsletters.[1]

Attempts to assess the treatment of prisoners began immediately after the initiation of hostilities in 1914, preoccupying contemporaries well after the last group of prisoners returned home in the summer of 1921. Involved in these attempts was a wide array of individuals and institutions: numerous administrative organs within the belligerent countries, neutral delegates commissioned by the warring parties, Red Cross societies and other charitable organizations and of course those most affected by captivity, the prisoners and their families.[2] In each case, the assessment relied on a different vantage point and in turn was colored by a different set of biases and self-interests. Consequently, we have today divergent accounts regarding the adequacy of the treatment given to prisoners of war in Russia.

Still, contemporaneous assessments did have a discernable common denominator: they almost invariably based their judgment on one of two available yardsticks; on the articles formulated in the POW section of the Hague Convention, or, alternatively, on the ideal of 'humane treatment' (which in the Hague Convention found expression in Martens's formulation about the 'laws of humanity').[3] Both approaches ultimately involved a discussion of such staples of ethical judgement as intent or mitigating/aggravating circumstances, and provided heaps of factual information to support various assessments. The purpose of this chapter is to examine these assessments (and accompanying evidence) produced by such diverse groups as the Austro-Hungarian Censorship, Russian military district commands, the American Embassy in Petrograd, the Swedish and Danish Red Cross societies, newsletters of POW families and the prisoners themselves, and to determine to what extent they convey irreconcilably different evaluations of the treatment of Austro-Hungarian prisoners in Russia. My intention here is not to conceal disagreements nor hide contradictory assessments, but to make judicious choices between competing positions and interpretations.

To facilitate a focused discussion and to place the issue within its broader historiographical context, I will concentrate primarily on Peter Pastor's main points – the intentional hierarchy between various camps in the Russian internment system, the overall abysmal quality of life in the camps, the utilization of POW labor and the efforts to subvert the loyalties of the prisoners.

Prisoner of War Camps and other Places of Internment

'During our transport in the winter of 1914/1915 from the snowy Carpathian Mountains to Siberia', wrote POW Alexander Dworsky:

> we did not pay attention to the freezing-cold weather and were excited as children thinking about the 'camp' . . . We associated the 'camp' with 'settle down', 'lie' and 'rest', in short, with a place where a person can live well . . . When we passed through train stations along the way, we were curious to find out from prisoners, who had already been there, what their 'camp' was like. All of them answered in amazement that they had never been to a camp.[4]

Dworsky's disappointment at not finding what he considered as the ideal-typical POW camp was shared during the first two years of the war by many Austro-Hungarian POWs. What we consider today as a representative POW camp (a regulated environment enclosed by barbed wire, high fences and watch towers) came into being only gradually throughout the first two years of the war. Furthermore, even after about 300 such ideal typical camps had been created in Russia, a prisoner of war was likely to have lived for extended periods of time in an environment other than a POW camp.

There were two primary reasons for this: first, at the beginning of the war Russia simply did not have enough facilities for the massive influx of captive enemy soldiers. As a result, makeshift solutions such as housing POWs in empty factories, theaters, barns and private houses were often used, with prisoners being transferred constantly from one temporary internment place to another before finally reaching what historian Gerald H. Davis called 'a POW camp of the classic mold'.[5] A survey conducted by Austro-Hungarian censorship in August 1915 found that during the first year of the war, Austro-Hungarian POWs in Russia had been interned in no fewer than '891 different internment places'. Of them only 317 were viewed as 'important concentration places' and only sixty-eight were under-lined as major or medium-sized POW camps.[6]

The great shortage of adequate housing during the first two years of the war might be illustrated by a list compiled by the Austro-Hungarian War Ministry regarding the structures used for POWs in Russia (see Table 3.1). An American delegate, inspecting the condition of POWs in the city of Kharkov found in October 1915 that out of 4,957 POWs 3,946 were housed in the local 'Moscow Circus':

> The principal military prison in Kharkov was formerly a permanent circus of the familiar 'ring' type with a pit, two galleries, and a stage. Nothing has been done to adapt this building to its present uses, except to erect in the pit, or arena, and even on the stage, a series of sleeping platforms in three or four tiers, each tier about 1.50 meters above the one below . . . While under ordinary circumstances this place might comfortably accommodate some 2,500 men, the number now confined there results in great over-crowding and discomfort. The men however appear to be under few restrictions, and I met them smoking, playing cards etc. in the stairs, galleries and indeed in all parts of the building. Whether because of this freedom and 'liberal' treatment, or because they have been here but a short time, and still have a fair amount of pocket money earned in the fields, there were few complaints except with regard to the lack of cleanliness, parasites etc. and the inability of the prisoners to obtain soap, hot water and clean linen.[7]

The second reason why one should be cautious in employing the term 'camp', is the fact that from the fall of 1915 Russia began using POW labor on a wide scale. Consequently, the rank-and-file POWs, who under the conditions of the Hague Convention were required to work for their upkeep, were now scattered around the different regions of Russia performing mostly agricultural, construction and mining work. During the summer months, when the agricultural season in Russia was at its peak, the rank-and-file camps would almost completely empty (except for NCOs and invalids who could obtain

Table 3.1 Buildings Used to House POWs: Summer and Fall 1915

Camp	Geographic Location		Building Type	
	Gubernia	Area of Russia	Officers	Rank-and-file
Almasnaia	Yekaterinoslav	Europe	–	Cinema, private house
Astrakhan	Astrakhan	Europe	Old house	Barracks, factory
Barnaul	Tomsk	Central Siberia	Bakery, brick house	Log barracks, warehouse
Cheliabinsk	Orenburg	Western Siberia	Private houses	Mill
Chita	Transbaikalia	Eastern Siberia	Barracks	Private houses
Dauria	Transbaikalia	Eastern Siberia	Barracks	Barracks
Irbit	Perm	North-Eastern European Russia	Hotel	Theater, museum, bazaar
Kazan	Kazan	Europe	Private houses	Barracks
Kharkov	Kharkov	Europe		Circus, brickwork
Kostroma	Kostroma	Europe	Distillery	Riding school
Krasnoyarsk	Yeniseisk	Central Siberia	Brick buildings	Brick and earth barracks
Nikolsk Ussurisk	Primorskaia	Eastern Siberia	Brick barracks	Brick and wood barracks
Nizhne Udinsk	Irkusk	Eastern Siberia	Barracks	Brick buildings
Novo Nikolaievsk	Tomsk	Central Siberia	Private houses	Earth barracks, brick barracks
Omsk	Akmolinsk	Western Siberia	Prison, private houses	Log and earth barracks, distillery, circus
Orenburg	Orenburg	Europe		Brick buildings in the Caravan court
Perm	Perm	Europe		Factory, school
Radolnoe	Primorskaia	Eastern Siberia	Brick barracks	Brick barracks
Rostov-Yaroslavl'	Yaroslavl'	Europe	Private houses	Factory
Saratov	Saratov	Europe	School	Tobacco factory
Shkotovo	Primorskaia	Eastern	Brick barracks	Brick barracks

Table 3.1 Buildings Used to House POWs: Summer and Fall 1915 *(continued)*

Camp	Geographic Location		Building Type	
	Gubernia	*Area of Russia*	*Officers*	*Rank-and-file*
Simbirsk	Simbirsk	Europe	Private houses	Barracks
Spasskoe	Primorskaia	Eastern Siberia	Brick barracks	Brick barracks
Troitzki	Syr Daria	Central Asia	Brick barracks	Clay barracks
Troizkossavsk	Transbaikalia	Eastern Siberia	Brick building	Brick barracks
Tiumen	Tobolsk	Western Siberia	Private houses	Wood barracks
Yekaterinburg	Perm	Western Siberia	Theater	Theater

* Source: Ernst Ritter von Streeruwitz, *Kriegsgefangene im Weltkrieg 1914–1918*, unpublished manuscript at the Heeresegeschichtliches Museum in Vienna, vol.2 pp. 64–6.

exemptions) and the prisoners were sent in small or medium-sized groups to estates and peasants' farms. Thus, although the designation 'POW camp' is a convenient shorthand for 'a place of internment' and although almost all Austro-Hungarian POWs spent long periods in camps, one should always keep in mind that being captive in Russia during World War I did not exclusively mean being a captive in a barbed wire enclosure. The future rector of the Jagiellonian University in Krakow, for example, POW officer Roman Dyboski, had been interned for lengthy periods in the prisoner of war camp of Krasnaia Rechka (near the city of Khabarovsk in the Russian Far East) and in the mammoth camp in Krasnoyarsk, but had also long intervals as an archivist/teacher at the University of Kazan, an interned guest at the house of a retired Russian field marshal and for a duration of eight months a prisoner 'in the custody of Prince Nicholas Gagarin enjoying a wonderful view of the Moscow River'.[8] A less exalted individual, the German NCO Johann von der Wülbecke, had been interned for two years in two major POW camps in eastern Siberia, Stretensk and Berezovka, but lived also for over a year in the little town of Kherusti (ninety miles east of Moscow) where he and eight other POWs perfunctorily performed various odd jobs and quickly became the talk of the town.[9]

Furthermore, even when prisoners found themselves 'surrounded by palisades or wire fences twelve feet high with watch towers at intervals whence the sentries could overlook everything' it became obviously clear that POW camps varied greatly.[10] In size, rank-and-file camps ranged from the small and medium-sized camps of European Russia, which usually accommodated between 2,000–10,000 POWs, to the much larger camps of Siberia such as Berezovka, Krasnoyarsk and Nikolsk Ussurisk, which at times housed 25,000–35,000 prisoners. Officer camps, which were completely separate from the rank-and-file camps were in comparison a much smaller affair: in the first two years of the war they ranged from a population of several dozen prisoners to a maximum of 1,100 POWs (the camp of Krasnaia Rechka), while from 1916 a trend of concentration occurred and a few larger officer camps emerged, most noticeably Krasnoyarsk (4,500 officer POWs) and Dauria (3,000 officer POWs). In the same vein, in terms of location, POW camps were scattered across the vast areas and different climates of the Russian state. As early as December 1914, there were internment centers in far-flung places: from Minsk and Kishinev in western and south-western European Russia to Nikolsk-Ussurisk and Rasdolnoe in the vicinity of Vladivostok.[11] The geographic dispersal of POW camps was truly amazing: camps were to be found in the black earth areas of southern European Russia, in the forested taiga, in the semi-arid and arid regions of Turkestan (today the various republics of Central Asia), in the Caucasian and Ural mountains and across various sub-regions of Siberia. This geographic diffusion created unique problems in each and every camp: the rice fields adjacent to the POW camp of Kokand (south Turkestan, today Eastern Uzbekistan) had swarms of malaria-carrying mosquitoes that tormented and endangered prisoners; Nargin island in the Caspian Sea, which housed mostly Ottoman prisoners, was notorious for its aridness and snake-infested terrain and Stretensk in eastern Siberia had severe water supply problems which emanated from its location on a cliff overlooking the river Shilka. During wintertime when the Shilka froze it was exceedingly difficult to supply the camp with the needed water. Consequently, prisoners created an informal hierarchy of camps which was inextricably linked to each camp's unique problems. Even relatively small areas, as for example the Primorskaia district in the Russian far east, had a distinct prisoner-created valuation of its six POW camps.

Nevertheless, the key question here is whether, despite the obvious diversity and unique local problems, there was a deliberate attempt on the part of the Russian military authorities to make life more difficult for prisoners in camps in certain regions while making it more tolerable in other areas. In other words, do we see any evidence of an intentionally created hierarchy between the 'first circle' camps of European Russia (intended primarily for Slavs and 'friendly' nationalities) and the 'lower-depth' camps of Siberia and Central Asia (designed for Magyars, ethnic Germans and Jews)?

As mentioned in Chapter 1, the Russian *Stavka* ordered as early as November 1914 that Slav and Alsatian POWs be given the best available lodgings, food and clothing and be granted more freedoms whenever possible. This policy stemmed both from the ideology of pan-Slavism – which emphasized the affinities and common destiny of the various Slav nationalities – and from a wish to subvert the loyalties of POWs belonging to 'disaffected' nationalities. As part of this design, Slav and Alsatian POWs (and after May 1915 also Italian prisoners of war) were separated in the assembly stations in Kiev and Moscow and sent to camps in the European section of Russia. The desire to favor Slavs and other 'friendly' nationalities was by no means confined only to the Russian *Stavka*. The Tsar's headquarters was also firmly committed to this policy as evidenced by a report written in November 1915 by one of the adjutants of Nicholas II, Colonel Mordvinov.[12] The report was brought about by a formal complaint of the Serbian Embassy in Petrograd claiming that Slav POWs had not been given preferential treatment at the assembly camp of Kiev (Darnitsa), and that German POWs were entrusted with positions of authority within the huge assembly camp (which in turn allowed them to discriminate against Slavs and even beat them on a few occasions). Regarding the specific complaints of the Serbian Embassy, Mordvinov concluded that these were 'either baseless or exaggerated'.[13] There were only six Germans working within the administration at Darnitsa and only four employed in the kitchen; 'At my request', he reported, 'all these Germans will be replaced by Slavs.'[14] He could not find even one incident where Slav POWs were beaten by non-Slavs, and both the commandant of the camp, Lieutenant General Khodorovich, and the head physician, Professor Griboedov, assured him that Slavs were indeed given preferences in terms of food and lodgings. The only significant problem that Mordvinov found was the use of German and Austrian trumpet calls for reveille; he instructed the Commandant to switch to Russian signals.[15]

However, beyond the specifics of the Darnitsa complaint, Mordvinov acknowledged that there were many problems with implementing the policy of favoring Slavs. Although, the intent to favor them was there from the beginning of the war, 'they [Slav POWs] exhibited bad behavior, disobeyed authorities and escaped in much greater numbers [than Germans]. Therefore, they needed to be restricted. Also, it was not possible to send them only to European Russia because of the lack of space and the fact that there were many refugees and wounded [Russian] soldiers. Thus, they were sent also to Turkestan and Omsk [military district].'[16] Giving Slav POWs better food proved also quite difficult because, according to Mordvinov, 'food rations are ultimately decided not on the basis of nationality but rather on the basis of work preformed'.[17]

There is considerable evidence to suggest that the policy of preferring Slavs did not translate into superior internment facilities. Reports of inspection teams consistently made the point that camps in Siberia were by no means inferior to those in European Russia. Siberia contained some of the best run POW camps in Russia during World War I such as Dauria (Transbaikalia military district), Berezovka (Transbaikalia) and Spasskoe (Primorskaia) as well as some of the most censured such as Stretensk (Transbaikalia) and the Fortress (*voennyi gorodok*) in Novo-Nikolaevsk (today Novosibirsk). Conversely, the camp of Totskoe on the Samara river in European Russia was probably the worst overall POW camp in Russia (if not in World War I) with a typhus epidemic killing as many as 17,000 out of 25,000 prisoners in the winter of 1915/1916.[18] If based on the inspection reports one were to compile a tentative list of the worst camps in Russia during the war, one would be hard pressed to find a distinct geographical pattern: two camps in European Russia (Totskoe and Orenburg), one in the Ural region (Yekaterinburg), one in Turkestan (Troitzki near Tashkent) and three in Siberia (Stretensk, Novo-Nikolaevsk and Omsk). What seemed to have determined the quality of life in each camp (beyond its unique location) was not prescribed policy but rather more prosaic factors such as the rate of size to infrastructure, the competence of the commandant (*nachalnik*) and his assistant (*praporshchik*) and the degree of cohesion and mutual support among the prisoners. Dr Max Sgalitzer, an Austrian POW physician who had been repatriated in March 1916, told officials in the Austro-Hungarian *Kriegsministerium* 'that there is great diversity in the conditions in different camps and much of it is decided locally'.[19] The Danish Red Cross delegate, F.Cramer, inspected South Eastern European Russia and Turkestan in the fall of 1915 and concluded that 'although the main directives regarding the treatment of POWs come from the central authorities in Petrograd . . . there are great differences between different military districts and camps within these districts'.[20]

This decentralization might be explained in part by the small number of people handling POW affairs within the bureaucracy of Russian Military Districts (the level of command which was supposed to monitor individual camps). The Turkestan Military District Command, for example, informed the General Staff in September 1916 that it had 'only two officers and four clerks' to handle the affairs of 200,470 POWs in the district.[21] In periods of extra work one officer and seven clerks were added to this staff, but only on a temporary basis. According to the memorandum the duties of the staff at the district command were numerous and included among other things:[22]

- Issuing administrative orders.
- Registering various categories of POWs.
- Composing complex and detailed reports to the General Staff.

- Applying rules regarding the maintenance of POWs.
- Supervising locations, housing, finances, food, work assignments.
- Handling all requests for locating POWs.
- Reviewing salaries paid to POWs by employers.

Consequently, the Turkestan Military District Command requested additional personnel to be assigned to handle POW affairs, and its staff was increased in October 1916 to include three officers (the top ranking being a general) and fifteen clerks.[23] The inability of military district commands to effectively supervise individual camps (especially in Siberia where military districts were of enormous size) gave local commandants considerable leeway to run things as they saw fit. Only when things became embarrassingly out of hand did military districts intervene in the everyday running of camps; typhus epidemics or formal complaints from nearby towns usually led to interventions as well as bizarre incidents such as in the camp of Tobolsk where Austro-Hungarian officers received weapons and the commandant's permission to duel in affairs of honor (the event apparently had drawn a large number of civilian spectators from the city).[24]

It is very clear then that although the Russian leadership (both military and political) intended to favor Slav, Italian and Alsatian POWs, they did not make it a high priority and did not allocate sufficient personnel to implement it. Moreover, other priorities, such as utilizing POW labor, regularly took precedent over awarding Slavs preferential treatment and offset the original intention. A report written by Austro-Hungarian censorship in August 1916 concluded that many Czech POWs in Russia were profoundly disappointed by the discrepancy between the ideology of Slavic brotherhood and the actual reality in the camps.

> It has become an enormous sobering experience: although a few selected POWs have managed so far to achieve in Russia a position of comfort, the great majority of prisoners of the Czech nationality groan under oppressive inhumane treatment, just like their companions in distress [*Schicksalsgenossen*] from other nationalities of the monarchy.[25]

Prisoner of war František Kopal writing from Poltava back home to Moravia expressed similar sentiments in a somewhat different style: 'we had the opportunity to get to know our Slavic brothers . . . The rod is still master in Russia and the greatest talent is to know how to count up to forty.'[26]

Thus, there is very little evidence to suggest that a hierarchy of POW camps, based on the ethnic identities of the prisoners, had been instituted in Russia during World War I. A different hierarchy, however, based on the criterion of rank, was indeed established and had considerable effect on the quality of life within the camps.

Living Conditions in POW Camps

In assessing living conditions in POW camps during World War I one needs to remember two important things: first, the Hague Convention envisioned two clear plateaus of treatment, one for officers and one for rank-and file prisoners. Officers were to receive salaries from their captors and were not obliged to perform any kind of work, while rank-and-file prisoners did not enjoy any kind of concrete protection beyond a vague promise of linking their conditions to those of soldiers in the army of the captor state. Second, most captivity literature (memoirs, diaries and novels) published after World War I was authored by POW officers. Thus, the image of life in captivity was skewed toward what Joan Beaumont called 'the experience of the privileged élite': escape plans, 'prison universities' and maintaining one's [manly] honor in the face of the enemy.[27]

It is possible to get a sense of the disparity between these two worlds by juxtaposing two letters, one written by a POW officer and one by a POW rank-and-file. The first letter found its way into a newsletter composed by families of German POW officers interned in the camp of Omsk. Written in the fall of 1916, the letter specified what officers were able to eat with a monthly contribution of twenty rubles from each officer (out of a fifty ruble salary):

> Mornings, coffee with milk and pastries baked on the premises; for lunch, soup, meat – cooked in various ways – with potatoes and gravy, from time to time also cabbage or carrots and desserts – in this there is great variety from doughnuts [*Spritzkrapfen*], through artistically decorated cakes to everything the region has to offer; Evenings, rice pudding, potatoes and eggs and dessert.[28]

The overall positive assessments contained in the newsletters written by families caused some consternation in Berlin leading to a warning that 'these newsletters would be terminated' if they would continue to paint such 'a rosy picture of captivity'.[29] In contrast, the second letter written in October 1917 by a rank-and-file prisoner,

Franz Bejcek, from the POW Camp of Bui (fifty miles northeast of Kostroma, upper Volga region):

> The evening wind whistles through every joint of this miserable barrack. You cannot warm yourself anywhere here. It is never quiet, and, on top of it, one has to deal with plenty of roaches and flees. To it add also these impertinent house animals, the rats, which devour during the night every little precious piece of bread and whatever else they can find. They even try to bite you.[30]

Prisoner-of-war officers in Russia, regardless of where they had been interned, enjoyed living conditions that were by far superior to any other group among the POW population. One can even make the argument that during certain periods of the war (especially the winter of 1916–17) their standard of living was considerably higher than that of their home states' civilian population. What enabled officers to benefit from such a position was the decision of all major belligerents to adhere to the provisions of the Hague Convention. Although this adherence was by no means complete and

Figure 3.1: Rank-and-file POWs eating 'Russian style' from a collective bowl.

Source: War Archives, Vienna.

the respective foreign ministries often filed complaints with neutral countries (usually about issues of status such as the right to wear military insignia within POW camps), there was agreement about three important issues: the payment of monthly salaries – in Russia, fifty rubles for subaltern officers (including cadets and captains), seventy-five rubles for staff officers and 125 rubles for generals – the complete exemption from any form of work and the maintenance of an officer's personal and professional dignity (use of batmen, preclusion of any form of physical punishment and allocation of superior facilities).

The payment of a monthly salary enabled officers to ameliorate the general living conditions in the camps substantially. Until the quick devaluation of the ruble in 1917, this monthly infusion of cash enabled POW officers to purchase food, clothing, furniture, heating materials, recreational supplies, bandages and medications from outside sources. There is no evidence to suggest that this practice was at any time discouraged by Russian camp officials. Rather, it seems that in most cases it was actually encouraged because it enabled camp authorities either to siphon off some of the funds earmarked for officers or to become themselves purveyors. The availability of outside markets to interned officers enabled them to pursue many extra-curricular activities that negated some of the boredom of camp existence. The camp of Berezovka in the Transbaikal region became well-known among the POW officers in Russia for its trade academy whose courses received accreditation after the war. *S'Vogerl*, the camp newspaper of the far eastern camp of Rasdolnoe, reported that:

> [T]he Russian Commandant [in Berezovka] allocated a whole barrack for it [the trade academy]. For physical education there is a tennis court (membership fee twenty rubles), a soccer field which is also used for exercises, and for amusement there is also a skittles [*Kegel*] lane. Music and theater are also energetically pursued. They received many newspapers among which are English, French and Swiss ones. The foreign language ones are translated, read out loud and then posted in corridors. The library is extraordinarily rich, because there are many officers from Przemysl who brought with them a major part of the fortress's library.[31]

Prisoner-of-war officer, Hans Weiland, who wrote a history of the camp of the Krasnoyarsk camp, estimated that the library there contained over 200,000 volumes 'representing the work of all the cultural nations'.[32]

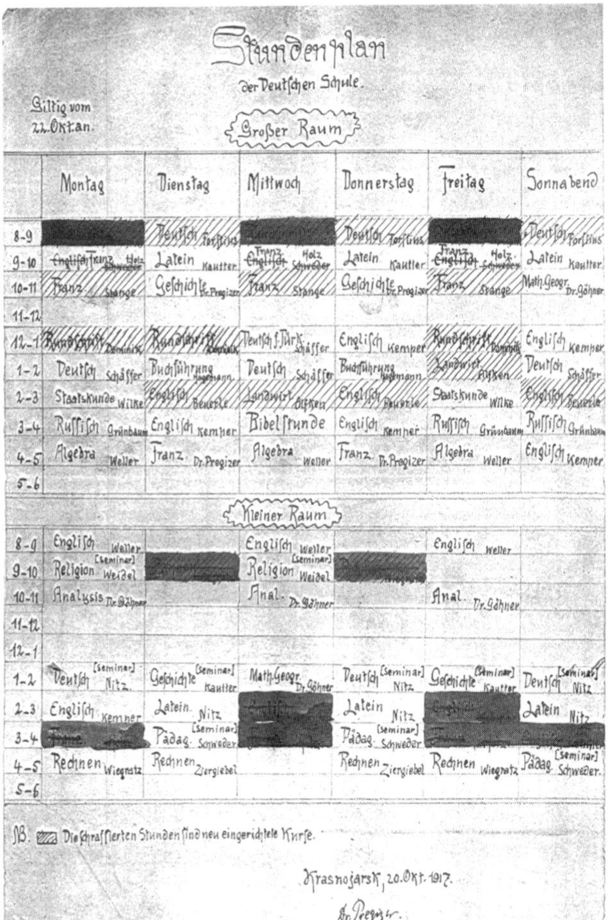

Figure 3.2: Class schedule from the officer camp of Krasnoyarsk.

Source: Military Archives Freiburg im Breisgau, Germany.

During the first two years of the war officers' lodgings had an air of normalcy about them. Qualitatively they were not very different from the lodgings career officers had been used to before 1914 and not much worse than what a young middle-class man could afford in fin-de-siècle Austria-Hungary. Consisting usually of vacated Russian officers' barracks (most of which were one or two storied brick buildings) or private houses in town, officers lodgings offered many of the things deemed essential for civilized existence such as a bed, mattress, desk, chairs and a trunk/closet (albeit all purchased by the officers themselves). During that period staff officers had the luxury of receiving private rooms, while every three to four junior officers shared a room. Each of these rooms had a full-time batman to perform the necessary cleaning duties, which according to the military norms of the time were done without pay.[33]

In camps such as Omsk, Khabarovsk and Krasnaia Rechka, where POW officers lived in large barrack halls instead of separate rooms, a sense of privacy was created by hanging curtains and dividing the rooms into sub-sections. These semi-private spaces (*'Boxen'* in camp slang) enabled officers to preserve a sense of individuality either by withdrawing from the company of other officers, or by using crafts and decorations as means of self expression. 'Our hall is pretty colorful', wrote one officer from Khabarovsk, 'everywhere there are these small quarters which are made by hanging curtains for every 3–4 gentlemen: one can choose white for his wall, the other flowers, the third light blue and together they create the most wonderful color effects.'[34]

The accelerating devaluation of the ruble in the years 1916–17 and the fact that the Russian military increasingly opted for concentrating POW officers in large officers' camps (rather than scattering them around the country), meant that officers had to deal with increasingly crowded lodgings and a diminished capacity to make improvements. Competition over available space intensified and the problems relating to who had precedent over whom became increasingly difficult to solve: Did, for example, higher ranking recent arrivals 'really' outrank veteran POW officers (who had not been promoted because of their internment)? Should disability and older age count for something in allocating lodgings or, as POW Lieutenant Dr Jenö Schönfeld put it, 'is it in order that twenty-five year old career officers get much better accommodations than forty year old *Landsturm* or reserve officers?'[35] Some of the camps tried to address the swelling number of grievances by instituting a ritual of an 'incomplete duel', which would follow all the customs and procedures of a regular duel except for the actual *Rencontre*: a POW officer who had felt his honor compromised or slighted would challenge the alleged offender to a duel. Seconds would then be chosen and a formal protocol would be drawn up by witnesses. The protocol was then stored for safekeeping with the understanding that all affairs of honor would be settled after repatriation. In the camp of Krasanoyarsk alone, as Hans Weiland noted:

> duel protocols accumulated in piles and mountains. The commander of the prisoners, Colonel Franz von Renvers, demanded in the Spring of 1918 from the Danish Red Cross official, Möller-Horst, additional train cars to save the protocols and transport them home. The Dane smiled and refused this stupidity saying that he needed the cars for people and bread. In tight circumstances man becomes small and petty. A place by the window can be half a kingdom.[36]

The downward mobility of the POW officers became more pronounced with the Bolshevik revolution in November 1917. In addition to being declared 'class enemies' by the new regime, POW officers stopped receiving their monthly salaries and were required to subsist on a quickly deteriorating Russian economy. Many officer camps developed workshops, which traded with the surrounding region and provided for basic everyday necessities. Still, this did little to offset the increasing misery among the officers who by the spring

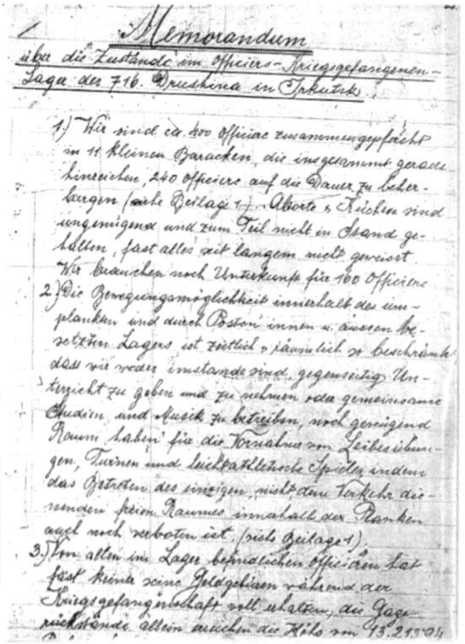

Memorandum

über die Zustände im Offiziers-Kriegsgefangenen-Lager der 716. Druschina in Irkutsk.

1.) Wir sind ca. 400 Officiere zusammengepfercht in 11 kleinen Baracken, die insgesammt gerade hinreichen, 240 Officiere auf die Dauer zu beherbergen (siehe Beilage 1). Aborte u. Küchen sind ungenügend und zum Teil nicht in Stand gehalten, fast alles seit langem nicht [illegible]. Wir brauchen noch Unterkunft für 160 Officiere.

2.) Die Bewegungsmöglichkeit innerhalb des umplankten und durch Posten innen u. aussen besetzten Lagers ist zeitlich u. räumlich so beschränkt dass wir weder imstande sind, gegenseitig Unterricht zu geben und zu nehmen oder gemeinsame Studien und Musik zu betreiben, noch genügend Raum haben für die Vornahme von Leibesübungen, Turnen und leichtathletische Spiele, indem das Betreten des einzigen, nicht dem Verkehr dienenden freien Raumes innerhalb der Planken auch noch verboten ist (siehe Beilage 1).

3.) Von allen im Lager befindlichen Officieren hat fast keiner seine Geldgebühren während der Kriegsgefangenschaft voll erhalten, die Gagerückstände allein erreichen die Höhe von 13.215.04 [illegible]

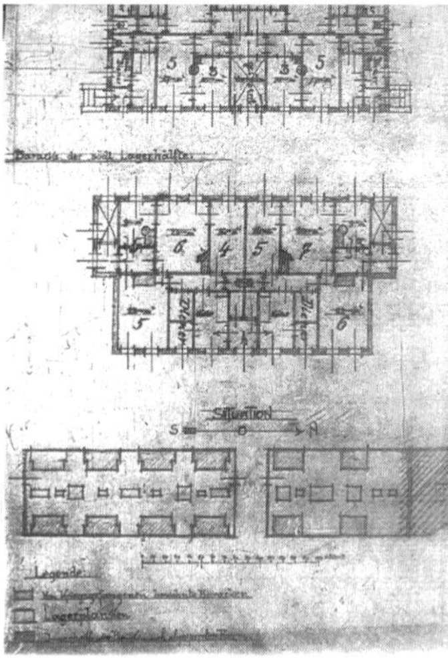

Figure 3.3: Memorandum written by officers in Irkutsk complaining of overcrowding with accompanying diagrams.

Source: Russian State Military-Historical Archive (RGVIA)

of 1918 were not better off than their fellow prisoners. This down-ward trend was somewhat compensated by a significant increase in the officers' sphere of self-management. The presence of the Russian military became less pronounced after the first Russian revolution in March 1917 and completely disappeared in the wake of the Bolshevik revolution. The 4,000 officers in the camp of Krasnoyarsk, for example, held elections for their own 'camp parliament' and a 'coalition government' was formed based on the support of the Reich Germans, the Austro-Germans and the Turkish POW officers (where-as Hungarian POW officers formed the main opposition party). According to Hans Weiland:

> the ministers in charge of the individual areas – finance, welfare com-mittee, sanitation (ambulance and hospitals), food supply, dining's halls, lavki [i.e. small shops], bakeries, housing committee, bank, workshops (tailor, cobbler, carpenter), factories (soap, tannery, leather etc.), baths, laundry, disinfection, wood procurement, schools, orchestra and theater – received their appointment from the general assembly and had to submit monthly reports to trustees of their constituency (barracks).[37]

This increasing ability to manage one's affairs (albeit in a much more chaotic and dangerous environment) helped to combat the lethargy, so characteristic of officer camps prior to 1917, and injected a sense of purpose into everyday life.

In many respects the living conditions of the rank-and-file pris-oners were a mirror image of those of the officers. Whereas the years 1914–16 constituted a relatively favorable period for POW officers, they were the most trying years for the men. The massive influx of captured soldiers from Austria-Hungary coupled with the complete lack of preparedness to house and clothe them led to overcrowding and diseases in many of the camps. This was exacerbated by the propensity of the Russian military to dump new transports of prisoners in camps without first augmenting existing infrastructure. On 19 March 1915 (Old Style), the governor of Siberia, Sukhomlinov, sent an urgent request to the General Staff saying that camps in Omsk, Tomsk and Novo-Nikolaevsk needed to be expanded. 'POWs are constantly coming and there is not sufficient housing. We ask for finance, time is not waiting.'[38] A month later the Primorskaia Military District Command in Khabarovsk informed the General Staff by telegram that 'there is danger of epidemics breaking out because of the lack of housing'.[39] According to Russian General Staff figures, during the first eleven months of the war 8,366,637 rubles and 65 kopecks were spent on POW accommodations (used for converting existing structures or building new ones) which sufficed for about half the number of prisoners who were already in Russia.[40] The result was oppressive overcrowding in the camps: the camp of Orenburg, for example, doubled the number of its occupants between September and December of 1915 resulting in a sharp deterioration of living conditions. The American inspector Frederick A. Sterling wrote:

> About thirty men are packed into rooms not over fifteen by twenty-five feet, using a rough plank platform, raised a couple of feet from a rough flooring over a cellar, for sitting, eating and sleeping . . . They have in many cases no stoves and in order to keep warm wood is burned like a camp fire on a cleared space on the floor, the smoke from which has no exit except the door, kept half open to prevent suffocation . . . Five feet from the door it was impossible to distinguish anything on account of the darkness and smoke. I was compelled to retreat. The men choking with inflamed eyes, were continually going outside to breathe the fresh air.[41]

Similarly, just before Christmas 1915, 1,800 POWs were added to the camp of Antipikha near the Transbaikalian town of Chita. Since the regular quarters had been already filled to three-times the prescribed capacity, the newcomers had to be housed in canon shacks (*Kanonenschuppen*). 'Their condition', wrote POW officer Ladislaus Baczy to a Hungarian parliament member, 'is simply indescribable. They are covered with filth, water constantly drips from above and the whole crowd is infected with typhus.'[42]

The overcrowding in many of the camps, the abysmal sanitary conditions and the dearth of clean clothing contributed to outbreaks of infectious diseases among the rank-and-file prisoners. Epidemic typhus carried by body lice, was an especially severe menace in many POW camps during the first two years of the war. Characterized at first by high fever and pain in the muscles and joints, the louse-borne typhus generates a dark-red rash that breaks out on the *derrière* and shoulders, and spreads out to the rest of the body. During the second week of the disease, the infected persons become delirious, often loosing control over their bowel movements, and after two to three weeks they either die from the effects of the disease or undergo a remission and recover.[43] In the most severe outbreaks of typhus among the POWs, the mortality rate reached 50–70 per cent of a camp's population, overwhelming the usually meager number of doctors and medics.[44] During the typhus epidemic in the Transbaikalian camp of Stretensk, all the Russian camp personnel left the camp, cordoned it off and left the prisoners to fend for themselves. This course of action was criticized harshly by the American inspector Dr William Warfield, who sent an urgent telegram to the Department of State calling for pressure to be exercised 'on the highest Imperial authorities . . . without formality or delay' (Warfield was asked to leave Russia on account of his scathing comments).[45] The Swedish Red Cross nurse, Elsa Bränd-ström, who visited Stretensk at the height of the epidemic was appalled by what she saw: 'A young man lay in the corner. No dumb animal in his father's farm had ever perished in such filth. "Give my love to my mother; but never tell her in what misery I died" were his last words.'[46] Hereward Price, the English expatriate who had been captured while fighting with the German army, had the misfortune of being in Stretensk during the epidemic:

> at the height of the plague there were three patients to two beds, and you might wake up one night to find a dead man on either side of you, and so you would lie through the long hours till morning came. The corpses were taken to a little wooden house and there kept for weeks . . . the ground was frozen too hard for a spade to turn, so all night we could see the glare of the fires on the hills burning a hole into the frozen ground to make graves for the dead.[47]

The situation of the rank-and-file prisoners improved during the years 1916 and 1917. Between the summer of 1916 and the descent of Russia into anarchy and Civil War in the spring of 1918, no major epidemics were reported in any of the POW camps, and the mortality rates of prisoners significantly decreased. There were four main reasons for this improvement: first, the launching of the Austro-Hungarian and German relief efforts in the fall of 1915 gradually eased shortages in clothing, food and medication, and provided the men with some financial means to make improvements (see Chapter 5). Second, the beginning of widespread utilization of POW labor meant that prisoners were now scattered in smaller groups in work places, which in turn reduced the overcrowding and the chances of large scale epidemics. It meant also that the rank-and-file now had some money at their personal disposal (albeit small sums) which enabled them to supplement their diet and purchase additional clothing. Third, the construction of necessary infrastructure – latrines, water supply, baths and barracks – began at last to catch

Figure 3.4: POW officers delousing their beds in the camp of Rasdolnoe.
Color illustration in the camp journal.

Source: Military Archives Freiburg im Breisgau, Germany.

up with the demand. The scathing reports of neutral observers and the fear of reprisals against Russian POWs in Austria-Hungary and Germany, provided some impetus for this expedited pace of construction. Finally, the gradual disintegration of the Russian imperial army, especially during the revolutionary year of 1917, meant that fewer soldiers were now being captured. The last big catch of prisoners occurred during the Brusilov offensive of June and July 1916 and the population of POWs in Russia stabilized at the two-million level.

Still, despite the improvement of the years 1916 and 1917, the living conditions of the rank-and-file prisoners in Russia were among the worst in World War I. The available figures regarding mortality rates – computed in 1929 by Dr Leopold Kern on the basis of *Kriegsministerium* data – place the overall mortality rates of prisoners of war in Russia at 17.6 percent or 411,000 out of 2,330,000 Austro-Hungarian, German and Turkish POWs. This puts Russia along with

Serbia (25 per cent), Romania (23 per cent), Turkey (13 per cent) and Bulgaria (12.5 per cent) as the places where prisoners had the worse chances of survival. On the other end of the scale, POWs had much better chances of survival in central and western Europe and the US: the mortality rate of POWs held by the US was a very low 2.0 per cent, in Germany 3.5 per cent of the POW population died in captivity, while the figures for Britain, France, Austria-Hungary and Italy were respectively 3.9, 5.3, 6.5 and 7.0 per cent. According to Kern's figures, 751,000 prisoners of war died in captivity during World War I, a figure which constituted 8.7 per cent of the total number of men captured during the war.

The figures for Russia were indeed high in comparison to those of the technologically more advanced belligerents further to the west, but overall they reflected the norm in eastern Europe and the Balkans. The rank-and-file prisoners suffered considerable hardships in World War I POW camps, especially in Russia and the Balkans, and a portion of the blame should be directed towards the Hague Convention which did little to ensure them adequate living cond- itions. Nevertheless, the Hague Convention, did manage to create reasonable living conditions in officer camps which mirrored the high status of officers in contemporaneous European societies. However, even the countries with the worst mortality rates in World War I treated POWs much better than the eastern front belligerents of World War II: 3,300,000 Soviet prisoners died in German POW camps during World War II, which constituted 58.0 per cent of the number of prisoners captured by Nazi Germany. Similarly, 1,100,000 out of 3,200,000 German POWs (or 35 per cent) died in Soviet captivity a figure that is slightly misleading because it includes also the German soldiers who had been captured at the end of the war. Erich Maschke estimated that perhaps 90 per cent of German soldiers captured before 1944 died in Soviet camps. Clearly, the eastern front POW camps of World War II were qualitatively different from their World War I predecessors.

Prisoners of War as Labor

The conscription of fifteen million men in Russia during the first three years of the war created severe manpower shortages that resulted in bottlenecks in many important economic sectors. In this respect, Russia was no different from other belligerents and the way it sought to alleviate the shortages was also very common during

POWs and the Great War

World War I, namely, to utilize increasingly the labor of women, children and captured enemy soldiers in war-essential industries. However, during the first year of the war, the growing need for manpower was counterbalanced by suspicion vis-à-vis certain national groups among the POW population and uneasiness regarding their contact with the Russian civilian population. Thus, the Russian government issued in October 1914 and in February 1915 regulations that restricted the use of German and Magyar POWs especially in sectors where they might have contact with the civilian population, first and foremost agriculture.

According to POW Regulations (*polozhenie o voennoplennykh*) published during the first year of the war, prisoners working for the state were to receive no pay whatsoever, while those working for private employers or the administration of agricultural districts (*zemskaia uprava*) were to receive the same pay as a Russian laborer performing the same work. However, there were many different deductions permitted that reduced the actual wages by at least two-thirds. According to the senior Austro-Hungarian official Ernst von Streeruwitz, if the gross wage of a POW sank below fifty-five kopecks a day, the permitted deductions would erase his net pay completely.[48]

The preference given to the employment of Slavic POWs was officially rescinded in May 1916 following a barrage of requests for labor coming from private employers. As a result, many German and Magyar POWs, who had previously been interned in Siberia and Turkestan, were sent to work in European Russia. But even before that date there was a noticeable increase in the number of POWs employed in various Russian sectors. Between the fall of 1915 and May 1916, for example, the number of prisoners employed in agriculture increased from 295,000 to 460,000, and the number of POWs working in road construction doubled from 70,000 to 140,000. Overall, when the employment of prisoners of war reached its full capacity – 1.64 million according to Russian figures – the distribution between agriculture (big estates and small holdings) and industry (including construction and mining) stabilized roughly on a ratio of 2:1 although there was a constant wrangling between interest groups regarding POW labor allocation.[49]

Among the prisoners employed in agriculture, the best lot befell those working with peasants on small farms. Constituting about one-third of the POW agricultural labor force, these prisoners worked in small groups under the supervision of the peasant employer, at times without any military guards. 'They were treated like the

Russian labourers', wrote Elsa Brändström, 'and only the low mental level of many of their peasant companions made it difficult . . . this disadvantage was set off by the good nature which they were, as a rule, treated. They lived together with the peasant and his whole family often in the same room, in winter along with fowls, calves and lambs.'[50] Edwin Erich Dwinger, who wrote *The Army behind Barbed Wire (Die Armee hinter Stacheldraht)*, the most popular account of life in Russian captivity, described the five months spent in 1917 working with Siberian peasants on the shores of Lake Baikal as his best period in captivity:

> Rest at evening in Goloustonoje. We sat in front of the house on the bench . . . and below us gleamed the blue, gently stirring sea. The good Hilde-brandt [their Russian-Jewish guard] chatted of everything imaginable, while the astonished proprietress, and often a couple of neighbors, listened attentively. How kind all these were to us.[51]

The immediacy and the intimacy of working with the peasants – especially peasant women – found expression in an oft-repeated anecdote circulating among the prisoners: according to the anecdote a prisoner who had worked a couple of years for a peasant woman returns white-faced to his fellow prisoners in the camp, asking them to hide him. The prisoner explains to his mates that the husband, expected to return any moment from the front, would be quite shocked to find a new baby in his household and the prisoner's life would be in danger. His friends do their best to hide him but to no avail, the peasant tracks him down and addresses him – 'how shall I thank you for all you did for me and my farm? The cows are full of milk, the pigs have little ones, and four calves have been born. And do you know, brother, the boy is a prize baby.'[52] The anecdote aimed undoubtedly to underscore ostensible moral differences between Russians and central Europeans, as well as to highlight the 'good-heartedness' and 'earthiness' of the archetypal Russian peasant. At its heart, this anecdote belonged to a certain colonial discourse about the goodness and simplicity of the natives. Still, it reflected the very real phenomenon of meaningful relationships that developed between prisoners and Russian women. Austro-Hungarian censorship collected the names of several thousand POWs who either married Russian women or intended to do so. As will be discussed in greater detail in Chapter 4, Austro-Hungarian officials were greatly worried by these attachments and regarded them as an indication of disloyalty on the part of the prisoners. Nevertheless, the letters themselves almost always contained a moving human story that had little to do with patriotism, but forcefully underscored the personal ramifications of warfare. Thus, for example, Klaudia Andreieva wrote from Omsk to Josef Srb of Dolný Slivno near Mladá Boleslav (Jungbunzlau) in northern Bohemia:

22nd of September 1916

Praised be Jesus Christ!
    I regret to inform you the following sad news. Your son Josef has converted to the Greek-Orthodox church because he wanted to marry me, a Russian. We could not get married in church until the conclusion of peace and we decided to wait. In the meantime I had his child. God made it that we would be afflicted by a grave illness, and your son, Josef, died from it leaving me a child and no means whatsoever. We ask you in Christ's and the Holy Mother's name, to forgive your son and not to deny support for his child. The child is not to blame for our offence. Please write me in Russian. I love the child and will never leave him . . . The child received the name Vladimir in his baptism.[53]

However, the majority of prisoners allocated to agriculture in the years 1914–17 did not find themselves on the small holdings of peasant employers but rather on the latifundia of nobles. Although conditions on big estates varied considerably from one to another, and some places had indeed the distinct flavor of forced labor (constant supervision of armed guards, physical punishments and extremely meager wages), the overall assessments of latifundia work are usually positive. Austro-Hungarian censorship concluded in the fall of 1915 that those 'working in the fields are usually satisfied and complain as a result much less. The problem of their lodgings loses its significance for POWs employed in this manner.'[54] Still, agricultural work was an excruciatingly difficult job for those not accustomed to it (particularly during the busy summer months) and as a rule very little consideration was given by the Russians to the occupational background of a prisoner.[55] An anonymous irritable Czech POW wrote his sister in 1915:

We are here in a remote corner of a south Russian gubernia, completely cut off from the rest of the world. We must drudge here restlessly for a Russian estate owner, from sunrise to sunset . . . It goes without saying that the best work is not left for us. I worry about my health but what can we do when we are treated here like slaves. One can endure a lot if the food is good. But one works here from three in the morning and gets a little bit of millet soup around nine o'clock, turnip soup around noon, millet soup again around four . . . when one returns some black noodles. It is good that we at least receive a sufficient amount of bread.[56]

The working conditions in construction and industry were generally worse than those in agriculture. Except for POWs employed as artisans in their civilian professions, who usually received the highest wages among the prisoners, industrial laborers regularly worked long hours in inauspicious conditions without the advantage of proximity to food sources (as agricultural workers). Up to the first Russian revolution at the end of February 1917 conditions were especially deplorable in mining and construction. Elsa Brändström wrote that it was

hardly possible to describe the existence of these men without seeming to exaggerate, for the conditions under which they were forced to live almost surpassed the bounds of mental and physical endurance . . . It is difficult to imagine a more dreary and wretched existence than of these working prisoners of war.[57]

The availability of able-bodied men in an economy depleted of its male work force, naturally channeled prisoners to the most physically taxing jobs. Thus at mid-1917 prisoners of war constituted 60 per cent of iron ore miners, 30 per cent of foundry workers and 28 per cent of peat extractors in Russia.[58] Moreover, the fact that employers could pay POWs significantly less than comparable industrial workers increased their desirability to the point of hiring prisoners of war in areas of Russia where unemployment was high.[59] Consequently, prisoners of war amounted to 27 per cent of the industrial force of the Moscow-Tula, Donets, Ural and Western Siberian districts.[60] The Polish-speaking prisoner, Boleslaus Westwalowicz, reported from Simbirsk that 'the work here is hard, one has to work from sunrise to dusk, stand on one's feet and hammer; my hands are completely ruined and injured by wire cuts. My situation is awful. Without the aid of the wife of my employer I would have already fallen off my feet.'[61]

The worst conditions of any working environment prevailed along the Murman railway line which connected the Petrograd region with the ice-free port of Murmansk on the Arctic Ocean. Traversing Karelia and the Kola Peninsula, the Murman Railway became at the beginning of the war a top priority of the Russian army when the routes across the Baltic and Black Seas were cut off by the Central

Powers. To expedite the construction of the railway, the Russian government sent between July 1915 and October 1916 an estimated 70,000 prisoners of war to reinforce the existing workforce of Russian, Chinese, Finnish and convict laborers. Although funds had been allocated by the Russian government for housing, maintenance and clothing, much of the money, according to Elsa Brändström, was embezzled by guards and engineers.[62] Thus, the laboring prisoners had no proper accommodations and often slept in branch-huts or even on the bare ground. POW Leo Krämer, who had been sent to work on the Murman Railway in March 1916, described his first impressions of the place:

> The kitchen consisted of a kettle placed in a hole in the ground sur-
> rounded by walls; our predecessors [also POWs] dug latrines in the meter-
> high snow, close to the house; to get water we needed to walk half a Verst
> [circa 600 yards] to a small lake and every day dig a new hole in the ice
> sheet . . . In the following morning, two sleds came with blankets and
> straw sacks and took back two prisoners to a supply station five Verst
> away where we received food for three days; the meat we cut up with
> saws, the bread with picks.[63]

The great distances along the line (over 950 miles) and the limited accessibility meant that fresh food could only rarely reach the prisoners. As a result, scurvy was a common affliction and medical facilities were in most cases hundreds of miles away. During the summer months some of the snow would thaw creating swamps and a horrendous mosquito problem. The combination of hard labor in extremely difficult conditions led to many deaths among the POWs: Elsa Brändström estimated that 25,000 POWs died on the Murman railway while 32,000 others suffered from scurvy, tuberculosis, rheumatism and diarrhea. The employment of prisoners of war along the Murman line was finally halted in October 1916, following reprisals by Germany against Russian POW officers and counter reprisals by Russia against German POW officers. The line itself was completed two months later in December 1916.

The first Russian revolution in 1917 brought with it a few import-ant changes for working POWs. First, as part of the overall collapse of discipline within the Russian army, guards supervising working POWs became much more lax. The Moscow Military District Com-mand reported that between March and July 1917, the number of POWs escaping from work places in the Moscow area increased more than sevenfold vis-à-vis a similar period in 1916: from 308 to 2,264.[64]

This does not mean that the escapees made an attempt to return back home, but rather that they wandered within Russia in the hope of finding better conditions. The Turkestan Military District Command interrogated POW Josef Glaubauf on June 17 1917 (old style) who had been captured in the town of Kopal by the local ataman. Apparently, POW Glaubauf was sent to a factory in Pavlodar with a party of 500 prisoners and 500 working Russian soldiers. The soldiers proceeded to arrest the management of the factory, and the prisoners concluded that no one would pay them for their work. Consequently, Glaubauf and a few of his friends decided to return to the POW camp in Omsk, having no problem whatsoever avoiding the six guards on the premises. Unfortunately, Glaubauf lost his friends and his way, and was discovered by a few Kirgizians who gave him food and clothing and instructed him to proceed to the town of Kopal where he was promptly arrested by the ataman.[65]

The Russian revolution also brought with it increasing interaction with Russian workers, which translated into both competition and cooperation. As far as competition is concerned, working POWs were often perceived by their fellow workers as a foreign element driving salaries down and vying for the same jobs. A flyer circulating in Samarkand in the summer of 1917 informed Russian workers: 'Comrades! It is the decision of the Military Revolutionary Committee, jointly with the Union of Metal Workers, Mechanics and other professions, to fire all prisoners of war from all places of work, following the decision of the Union of Metal Workers, Mechanics and other professions.'[66] The increasing power of local soviets placed POW workers in a precarious position: on the one hand they were still under the direct control of the Russian army and the Provisional Government, which attempted to take advantage of them as much as they could (and at one point limited the wages of POWs to 20–50 kopecks a day); on the other hand prisoners realized that the balance of power shifted within Russia and that it was in their best interest to cooperate with the workers' movement. Thus, there are various reports of POWs joining strikes and demanding both higher wages and better working conditions. Ernst von Streeruwitz, the head of the Political Section in Abteilung 10.Kgf of the Austro-Hungarian *Kriegsministerium*, described his section receiving during the summer of 1917 numerous reports about Austro-Hungarian POWs in Russia demanding pay raises.[67] In one instance, in June 1917, the 'Peace Chamber' in the mines of Sudshenka near Tomsk sent a telegram to the owner of the mines 'insisting that the pay of POWs and Russians be matched, and that the pay of both should be raised simultaneously to 7–8 ruble for an eight hour shift'.[68] Prisoners of war, who had been paid until then two rubles per shift, expressed their willingness as part of the deal to 'sacrifice 7–15 percent of their earnings for families of soldiers, for a workers' library and for the needs of local workers' organizations'.[69] Because such demands were occurring frequently, the Austro-Hungarian *Kriegsministerium* instructed the Danish Legation in Petrograd to convey to Austro-Hungarian prisoners 'in no uncertain terms, that it is much more difficult to protect them when they are wheeling and dealing'.[70]

The unstable situation of working POWs was further exacerbated by rising inflation in Russia. The price index rose between the end of 1916 and the end of 1917 from 221 to 512 (1913 = 100), reducing in turn the value of POW wages.[71] Thus, during the revolutionary year, the rank-and-file prisoners experienced the same pauperization trend that affected POW officers and the rest of the Russian population; a trend that would only become stronger with the Bolshevik revolution and the Russian Civil War.

Although the treatment of working POWs in Russia was far from uniform, it does seem quite wretched from a Western liberal perspective. Overall, about 180,000 POWs were affected by the atrocious conditions prevailing in large-scale construction projects and a few additional industrial enterprises, and the great majority of the remaining rank-and-file prisoners worked long hours for wages well below prevailing standards. Still, except for cases like the Murman railway, this use of rank-and-file prisoners was by no means an anomaly during World War I. Germany and Austria-Hungary utilized captive enemy soldiers in a similar way, and very rarely allowed them the same degree of interaction with the local population that POWs in Russia enjoyed . In his book *War Land on the Eastern Front*, Vejas Gabriel Liulevicius examined the policies of the German occupation forces in the Baltic area during World War I (an area which came to be known as *Ober Ost*). The working conditions of Russian POWs and local forced labor in the *Ober Ost* seem to have resembled those in the big projects across the border:

> POWs and even refugees displaced from the front were organized into work gangs . . . In the Lithuanian area, numbers in the work gangs reached 60,000, shuttled around the country, from one work project to another. Conditions and exertions were terrible, yet each worker was allowed only 250 grams of bread and a liter of soup each day. As a result of poor nourishment, many reportedly died of exhaustion.[72]

Despite atrocious conditions in some work sites during World War I, they do not seem to be the rule during that conflict. Deplorable conditions appear to have represented big projects organized by the respective militaries, although much more empirical research is required on this subject. The majority of working POWs performed their labor in predominantly civilian settings (both in agricultural and industry) although they were guarded, of course, by soldiers and required to adhere to military discipline. Nevertheless, this was much better than working in the big projects and Elsa Brändström was probably right in suggesting that most kinds of work were preferable to the 'gnawing unrest and the despairing feeling of emptiness' that characterized the camps. In the final analysis, Russia, like other belligerents made ample use of what the Hague Convention had permitted, and violated it repeatedly when military or economic necessity demanded it.

Propaganda and Recruitment Among the Prisoners

The attempts of consecutive Russian governments to subvert the loyalty of Austro-Hungarian POWs are probably the best known chapter of World War I captivity. The subsequent exploits of the predominantly POW composed Czechoslovak Legion in the years 1917–20, especially its 'anabasis' through Siberia, acquired legendary proportions in the annals of the Russian revolution and the ensuing civil war. Some of the Czechoslovak Legion's most controversial actions generated polemical literature that probed the aims and the historical significance of this fighting force. The ability of an army of about 40,000 prisoners of war to become so spectacularly powerful in the spring and summer of 1918, eclipsed the fact that during the first three years of the war the various military formations recruited among the prisoners, including the Czechoslovak Legion, were small and demoralized.

The idea to exploit national discontents among the subjects of the enemy was by no means a Russian monopoly during World War I. Germany, Austria-Hungary, Italy, France and Britain all engaged in one way or another in attempts to destabilize their enemies by supporting various and often contradictory claims of disaffected national groups. In the Russian case, its patronage of anti-Habsburg groups drew an impetus from the ideology of pan-Slavism, which regarded Russia as the leader and protector of smaller Slavic nations, and from a desire to weaken its enemy.[73] According to Orlando Figes, years of perceived humiliation by the 'Teutonic powers' (especially the formal annexation of Bosnia-Herzegovina by Austria-Hungary in 1908), persuaded the Tsar and most of the Russian bourgeoisie, state administration and officers corps to support pan-Slavist tenets by 1914.[74] Nevertheless, this desire to aid and dominate the smaller 'Slavic brethren' was circumscribed by other factors: by the deeply engrained suspicion regarding the Western orientation of some of these Slavic nationalities (and their politicians), the awareness that multi-national Russia was itself susceptible to the same destabilization tactics; the fact that Russia's own immediate interests (for example in the economic sphere) collided in many cases with the explicit wishes of other Slavs and, finally, a sense that certain policies and tactics undermined cherished notions of legality and legitimacy. Thus, until the collapse of the Tsarist regime in February 1917, Russia approached the idea of enlisting POWs gingerly and half heartedly.

This ambivalence can be exemplified very well in the case of the Russian-sponsored Czech fighting force.[75] Proposed during the first days of the war by leaders of the small Czech colony in Russia, the volunteer Czech Company (*Česká družina*) came quickly into being in late August 1914 following audiences these Czech leaders had with three of the most senior members of the Russian *Stavka* (Generals Sukhomlinov, Yanushkevich and Belaev) and with the Tsar himself.[76] Established formally in Kiev – the center of the Czech community in Russia – on August 28, 1914, the *Družina* was designed as a reservoir of future administrators who would manage what was hoped the soon-to-be conquered Czech lands. Although formally a unit of the Russian army, the *družina* was represented in all political matters by the Association of Czechoslovak Societies in Russia (*Svaz československých spolků na Rusi*; or Svaz) who received for that purpose a letter of authorization by the Russian Ministry of the Interior.[77] The initial role of the *družina* as a facilitator of Russian territorial expansion was further highlighted during a second audience with the Tsar in September 1914. In an emotional speech by one of the leaders of the Svaz, the industrialist Otakar Červený, the future 'free and independent crown of Saint Wences-laus' was described as linked with the 'glorious Romanov Crown', eliciting, reportedly, great satisfaction from the Tsar and promises of help.[78]

Still, despite the solemn phrases and high expectations, the *družina* had, at this point, little military value. At its inception the company attracted only 777 volunteers, all of whom were citizens of the Russian state (and thus liable in any case for military service). When the early hopes for a breakthrough of the Russian 'steamroller' into Bohemia, Moravia and Austrian Silesia were dashed, the *družina* evolved into a small intelligence-gathering unit positioned opposite Czech units in the Austro-Hungarian army. The capture of many Czech and Slovak prisoners of war during the first year of the war created the theoretical possibility of expanding the small Czech Company into a full-fledged army. The Svaz leadership sent various memos on the subject to the Russian authorities and even acquired the partial support of the Tsar's brother, Grand Duke Nikolai, who was the nominal Commander in Chief of the Russian army.[79] However, at this stage, the Svaz leaders encountered strong opposition from the Russian premier, Prince Goremykin, and his Foreign Minister, Sergei Sazonov, who were alarmed by what they perceived as meddlesome interference in Russian foreign policy. In a memorandum written by Sazonov in April 1915 he stated that the Svaz request for its own army was contrary to the Hague Convention and consequently should not be granted. Moreover, in Sazonov's mind the whole notion of Czech independence was ridiculous and therefore the Russian government should not lend it support.[80]

The result of the disagreement within the Russian government was an unenthusiastic embrace of the project to create a Czechoslovak fighting force. For their part, the Russian military authorities concentrated Czech and Slovak POWs within the confines of European Russia, ordered that Slavs would be given preferential treatment within a reasonable framework and allowed Svaz delegates access to POW camps. However, they did not actively disseminate propaganda or pressure POWs to enlist in the *Družina*. In fact, there were a few steps taken by the Russians that actually discouraged mass enlistment: the stipulation that POWs assume Russian citizenship prior to their enlistment, harsh reprimands of Svaz members who threatened *Kaisertreue* Czech POWs and unequivocal priority given to utilizing POWs as labor. Thus, it was left to the Svaz itself to traverse the huge distances within Russia, talk to Czech and Slovak POWs and distribute Czech and Slovak nationalist literature (first and foremost the newspaper *Čechoslovák*). The relatively small number of POWs who volunteered to the unit prior to the spring of 1917 suggests that these efforts enjoyed only a mild success: between the beginning of the war and February 1915 the *družina* had 1,433 volunteers, of which 278 were POWs; between March 1915 and March 1916 only sixty-five out of 869 volunteers were prisoners, and between March 1916 and May 1917 the Svaz managed to recruit 6,930 POWs, which constituted a huge increase compared to the previous two years but still only a small fraction of the estimated quarter of a million Czech and Slovak POWs in Russia.[81]

Similarly, the recruitment of Austro-Hungarian POWs from South Slav nationalities into the Serbian army and of Italian POWs into the Italian army met with only moderate success.[82] The Russian government oscillated between full-fledged support of South Slav and Italian units – even attempting at one point to forcibly recruit South Slav POWs – to complete curtailment of the volunteer movement in the fall of 1916 under Prime Minister Stürmer.[83] The designated 'propaganda camps' for anti-Habsburg volunteers, established in Tiumen (Slavs in general), Tsaritsyn (Czechs), Odessa (South Slavs) and Kirsanov (Italians), seem to have been only negligibly better than regular POW camps. A Slovene volunteer in Odessa described how badly disappointed he was upon discovering the state of affairs there: 'They assigned me to a rope factory, which was cold and filthy. We were full of lice, without straw mattresses or blankets, and in clothes that were no match for the frost of 1916.'[84] Moreover, the frightful fighting conditions on the Italian front and the disastrous campaign of the South Slav Corps in Dobruja in August and September 1916 further hurt the willingness of POWs to volunteer. After its debacle against Bulgaria, the demoralized South Slav Corps split into internal fractions and a mutiny broke out at the end of October 1916. According to Ivo Banac 44 percent of the POW South Slav volunteers either deserted or withdrew from the corps following this mutiny.[85]

The February revolution ushered in a new phase in the history of the anti-Habsburg military formations. The ambivalence that characterized the attitude of the tsarist imperial regime was replaced by explicit support on the part of the Russian provisional government. Pavel Miliukov, the Russian Foreign Minister during the first two months of the revolution, issued the first statement on the part of any major entente politician which called for 'a liberation of the oppressed peoples of Austria-Hungary and the establishment of a solidly organized Yugoslavia'. The Chairman of the Paris-based Czechoslovak National Committee, Thomas Garrigue Masaryk, a *persona non grata* during the tsarist regime, was now allowed to come from Paris in May 1917 and launch a massive recruiting drive among Czech POWs. The hesitancy of Prime Minister Kerensky to send POWs from labor duties to the national units was allayed by the performance of the Czech brigade in the battle of Zborov (3 July

1917) . In a context of an increasingly disintegrating Russian army, the Czech brigade was one of the few forces that proved successful during the ill-fated 'Kerensky offensive'. Kerensky, who visited the unit immediately after the battle, promised full support in building a Czechoslovak army (henceforth known as the Czech/Czechoslovak Legion). Consequently, the Czech National Committee dispatched 300 agitators to the provinces to locate Czech and Slovak prisoners and enlist them in the legion.[86] Between May 1917 and May 1918 three recruiting drives were launched, which proved extraordinarily successful in comparison to the pre-revolution drives: Between May and September 1917, 83,328 Czech and Slovak POWs were located of whom 21,760 volunteered; in the period September–December 1917, 124,000 Czech and Slovak POWs were discovered and 9,780 volunteered; in the first two months of 1918, 137,193 Czech and Slovak POWs were found but only 1,500 chose now to volunteer.[87] Clearly, the months immediately after the battle of Zborov constituted the period when the Czech Legion appeared the most attractive to POWs. Still even during this period the great majority of Czech and Slovak POWs rejected the overtures of the recruiters. When, for example, a recruiting officer attempted in August 1917 to enlist volunteers in the working detachment of *Kamenskii Zavod*, he found, according to one letter, only 'three fools who were willing to support the continuation of the war', this despite four days of activity among the many prisoners there.[88] All told, in the years 1914–18 about 40,000 Czech and Slovak POWs volunteered to fight against Austria-Hungary, or 16 per cent of the estimated 250,000 Czech and Slovak prisoners of war in Russia.

There is a touch of irony in the fact that the Czechoslovak Legion achieved its most noted victory in May 1918 at a point when its attractiveness to prisoners was waning. The Bolshevik revolution and even more importantly the advance of the German army into Ukraine and the Baltic area in the winter of 1917/18, created an extremely precarious situation for the Czechoslovak Legion whose soldiers faced execution if captured by the Central Powers. The Czech National Council decided therefore to transport the legion to France where it could still contribute to the military effort of the Entente and gain support for an independent postwar Czechoslovakia. In February 1918 the French Government recognized the Czechoslovak Legion as part of the French army and approved its transfer to the western front via Vladivostok. On its way to the far east in May 1918 (and despite Masaryk's promises to the Bolshevik leadership that the

Czech forces did not wish to intervene in the internal affairs of Russia) the legion clashed with the Red Army units in the Ural town of Cheliabinsk. The People's Commissar of War, Leon Trotsky, consequently ordered the complete disarmament of the legion, and instructed Red Army units to curb what he perceived as basically a reactionary force. However, the ill-organized Red Army was no match at this point of its existence for the more-disciplined Czech soldiers who proceeded to seize control of the entire Trans-Siberian railroad.

During the spring and summer of 1918 the Czechoslovak Legion constituted the most significant military force within Russia, providing military protection to various anti-Bolshevik forces that mushroomed in eastern European Russia and in Siberia. Although not formally a part of the White or allied interventionist forces, the Czechoslovak Legion did nonetheless play an important role in the early part of the civil war by exposing the weaknesses of the Red forces. The presence of 40,000 armed Czech and Slovak POWs in Russia became an important bargaining chip for Czech émigré politicians negotiating the postwar settlement. The involvement of the legion in the Russian Civil War became negligible during 1919, and the successes of the Red Army forced the legion's leadership to re-evaluate its position. Thus, in February 1920, an armistice agreement was signed between the Czechoslovak Legion and the Soviet forces, and as a result the head of the White government in Siberia, Admiral Kolchak, was handed over to the Bolsheviks to be executed. The Czechoslovak Legion finally sailed from Vladivostok in September 1920 and became the core of the Czechoslovak army.

Attempts to recruit POWs into pro-Bolshevik units began in the weeks following the October revolution. Both *Pravda*, the organ of the Bolshevik Party, and *Izvestia*, the voice of the Soviets, appealed to prisoners 'to support the socialist revolution... and come to the defense of the peace and brotherhood of all nations'.[89] Those groups of POWs not targeted by previous Russian regimes (especially Magyar, German and Jewish POWs) were the first ones approached by the nascent Bolshevik regime. German and Hungarian newspapers were distributed in massive numbers among the prisoners, and a congress of the 'international Social-Democratic POWs' was summoned to Samara at the end of January 1918. The congress had an air of a staged event with delegates solemnly requesting permission to join the Red Guards and defend the socialist homeland. At the beginning of February 1918 this request received formal approval by the Soviet government, and German and Hungarian Red

Guard units were consequently formed with the future leader of the Hungarian Soviet Republic, Bela Kun, appointed as chief organizer among Magyar POWs. There are no exact figures regarding how many POWs actually joined the Red Guards in the months following the congress. Estimates vary between a handful of POW volunteers to 90,000 (a wildly optimistic assessment by the head of the All-Russian POW bureau, Ivan Ulianov). Before June 1918, the number of internationalists probably did not exceed a few thousands, of whom the great majority were Magyar. Soviet-era historiography tended to stress the ideological commitment of these volunteers to the Bolshevik cause, while studies emanating in the west usually underlined pragmatic reasons for enlistment such as want of food or fear of the notoriously anti-Magyar and anti-German Czech Legion.[90] With the outbreak of full-scale civil war in Russia, the new regime began exerting substantial psychological and physical pressure to induce prisoners to join the Red Army. As a result, the number of Internationalists fighting with the Bolsheviks increased significantly, although, as Peter Pastor has shown, the length of their service was at times limited to no more than a few days or weeks.[91] Assessments of the total number of POWs who served at one point or another with the Red forces range from 50,000 to 190,000; thus, it is very difficult to assess the size and relative importance of the POW contingent in the Red Army. Arnold Krammer, who argued for the higher figure, maintained that 'the Internationalists helped tip the military balance in the Bolsheviks' favor . . . and may well have changed the course of history'.[92] On the other hand, Soviet historians, who generally praised the volunteers for their ideological commitment, did not regard their contribution as decisive neither during the first months of the Civil War or after the summer of 1918 when the Red Army grew in size and sophistication.[93]

In his study of South Slav POWs in Russia, Ivo Banac portrayed Austro-Hungarian POWs as 'the prize in the contest between the two rival modern ideologies; small-nation *Staatenbildung* and Leninist socialism'.[94] This depiction of the prisoners as a ripe fruit ready to be plucked by the hungry ideological forces of modernity does some injustice to the complexity of the story. During the first two-and-a-half years of the war, the desire of the imperial Russian regime to subvert the loyalties of these prisoners gave way in many cases to a much stronger desire to exploit them as labor. Thus, paradoxically, the Russian government both allowed propaganda to reach camps and simultaneously shielded most prisoners from it. After the

February revolution prisoners became more exposed to ideological overtures, but their ability to debate various alternatives also increased. In other words, they were far from passive human material ready to be influenced and molded. As will be described in detail below (Chapters 4, 5), prisoners of war interacted, reasoned and weighed their options, and attempted to steer a course which made sense in the context of the period.

The Treatment of POWs and the Perception of World War I

During recent years a relatively large number of comprehensive overviews have been published about World War I. Niall Ferguson, Martin Gilbert, John Keegan, Hew Strachan and Jay Winter have aspired in their books to present a broad history of the war, whereas Manfried Rauchensteiner, Holger Herwig and Roger Chickering attempted to write a thorough history of the Austro-Hungarian and/or German war effort. There is something quite exceptional about this barrage of works about World War I: a boom in studies about a specific historical event is usually a good indication that an important anniversary is near, or, conversely, that important new material has been discovered. In the case of the World War I this is plainly not the case. Nevertheless, the popularity of some of these books, especially John Keegan's *The First World War*, which reached number three on the New York Times best sellers list, and Jay Winter's BBC/PBS series *The Great War and the Shaping of the Twentieth Century*, attest to the public resonance of World War I themes.

One way to look at the recent crop of works on World War I is in the wider context of books covering the twentieth century. The chronological conclusion of the century produced many popular as well as scholarly books, attempting to delineate – in the words of Gary Wills– the 'real twentieth century'.[95] The idea that World War I marked in many ways the 'true' beginning of the twentieth century and had a crucial influence on the subsequent eight decades, found expression in Ivan Berend's concise phrase 'the short twentieth century'.[96] Although there are various interpretations in regard to the most important aspects of this short century, there is a widespread agreement about the fact that this century had an astonishingly brutal side, exposed emblematically by the carnage on the western front. Thus, World War I is seen as a quantum leap in terms of disregard for human life, state-sanctioned killing and the hollowness of international law. 'After that cataclysm', wrote Adam Roberts, 'only very few especially blinkered inhabitants of Europe could talk with real confidence of the distinction between "civilized" and "barbarian" – a distinction which had been taken for granted in much of the previous discussion, including the Hague peace conferences.'[97] The literary historian, Paul Fussell, called World War I 'a hideous embarrassment' to the idea of progress and maintained that a certain pre-modern innocence was irrevocably lost in the years 1914–18.

Yet, in analyzing the treatment of POWs in Russia during the First World War, I attempted to demonstrate that there was at least one crucial aspect of the war where international legislation did play an altogether positive role. In contrast to Peter Pastor, who portrayed POW camps in tsarist Russia as 'prototypes' of communist gulags and Nazi concentration camps, I tried to show that the treatment of prisoners had more to do with nineteenth-century social thinking than with Auschwitz and the Gulag Archipelago. While Pastor is undoubtedly right in maintaining that the treatment of prisoners of war in Russia was far from being satisfactory – and was often downright deplorable – there are compelling reasons for rejecting his 'prototypes' thesis:

First, the 'camp' was an ill-defined entity through most of the war. It certainly did not exist during the first two years of the war when an unexpected mass of captive enemy soldiers reached Russia. Rank-and-file POWs were interned in a host of different buildings and makeshift settings, and spent a great deal of time outside their internment places. Moreover, although many of these internment facilities were cramped and unsanitary, they were not, in many cases, fundamentally different from the kind of housing used by Russian troops.[98] Prisoner-of-war officers, on the other hand, enjoyed the sort of internment deemed by the contemporary European elite worthy of their class. This included pay, furniture, servants, superior food (much better than the food consumed by the civilian populations of Russia and the Central Powers) and ample free time to study and to pursue hobbies. Thus, rather than giving a taste of things to come, Russian POW camps mirrored the hierarchical thinking of the nineteenth century with its huge gap between officers and men.

Second, although the living conditions of the rank-and-file prisoners were woeful, they did not even remotely resemble those of inmates of totalitarian camps. Mortality rates in Russian POW camps during World War I were just a fraction of those of POWs in the Soviet

Union during World War II or Soviet POWs in Nazi Germany. Russian World War I rates were not much different than those of other East European or Balkan belligerents and in some cases even lower. Moreover, living conditions of POWs in Russia improved in the years 1916–17 and major outbreaks of typhus epidemics were eliminated from the summer of 1916. Russian authorities, like their counterparts in Germany and Austria-Hungary, permitted thorough and repeated inspections of camp facilities by both neutral Red Cross observers and delegates from the home countries (something absolutely inconceivable under the totalitarian camp structure). Finally, the Stockholm Protocol, signed by the three eastern front belligerents in the winter of 1915/16, attests to the belief in the efficacy of multilateral international agreements and the wish to preserve some measure of human dignity during warfare. The Stockholm protocol and the subsequent agreement reached during 1917 served as the basis for the POW sections in the 1929 Geneva Convention.

Third, the exploitation of POW labor was by no means a Russian monopoly during World War I. Germany and Austria-Hungary utilized captive enemy soldiers to replace their own recruited manpower and took advantage of the wide latitude of the Hague Convention. Conditions of working POWs varied immensely: from the primitive but generally agreeable settings of the Russian peasant farm to the unconditionally brutal environment of the Murman railway. Altogether, about 180,000 POWs worked in settings that resemble forced labor conditions under Stalin. This is by no means an insignificant number, and it justifiably caused alarm in Austria-Hungary and Germany during the war. Still, the great majority of prisoners worked under conditions that were not different from those of Russian workers albeit for a lower pay. Working outside enabled them to interact with the Russian population (especially in agriculture), earn money, ameliorate their diet and clothing situation and most importantly live outside of the cramped and hazardous lodgings of camps.

Finally, the Russian tsarist government was very ambivalent about subverting the loyalties of Austro-Hungarian POWs and enlisting them in anti-Habsburg military formations. More often than not, the Russian government laid obstacles in the paths of recruiters from the various ethnic legions, and did not allocate significant funds or personnel for these projects. The minute number of people handling POW affairs at the military districts and at the camps indicates that we are not dealing here with a coercive totalitarian apparatus and an inordinate pressure exerted on the prisoners. Moreover, from the beginning of the war there were vocal critics of the legions; Russian Foreign Minister, Sergei Sazonov, expressed apprehensiveness about the political character of the ethnic legions, and was outspoken in his recommendations to curb them. It seems, therefore, rather exaggerated to argue that the tsarist government made 'attempts to enlist the majority of the prisoners'.[99] It was rather under the Provisional Government and the Bolsheviks that more concentrated efforts were made to recruit the prisoners. However, even these enjoyed considerably less success than the favorable assessments of post-World War I nationalist and Soviet historiography.

World War One has been often portrayed as the event where Europe embarked on the road to barbarism. Millions of senseless deaths, coupled with the war's legacy of political instability, made 'the First World War the worst cautionary example of war horror'.[100] It created a grand narrative which would significantly influence the perception of later wars such as the Vietnam War or Israel's involvement in Lebanon. Yet, history is not a study of absolutes and not everything that had been perceived before the war as right and humane was ignored and discarded during the conflict. The treatment of POWs proved that even though the Hague Convention was not a perfect document, it did ensure that over 90 per cent of those captured during the conflict would return home.[101]

Notes

1. 'Bericht Nr.7 über das Offizierslager OMSK (nur für den Privatgebrauch der Angehörigen)', 1917 Bundesarchiv (BA), Militärarchiv Freiburg (MA), N 448/3.

2. Until 1917 the US represented the interests of Austria-Hungary and Germany in Russia, while Spain represented Russia vis-à-vis the central powers. In addition to various Red Cross Societies the American YMCA was also heavily involved in the distribution of relief during the first three years of the war. There was a German relief committee in the Chinese city of Tientsin which funneled funds and clothing to the prisoners. Various ethnic committees within the Russian empire provided support for 'their' co-nationals. Especially active were the Polish Association for the Aid of War Victims and various Jewish communities scattered over Russia. See more details in Chapter 5.

3. See Chapter 2.

4. Alexander Dworsky, 'Im Lager', in Hans Weiland and Leopold Kern (eds) *In Feindeshand*, two vols, Vienna, 1931, p. 106.

5. Gerald H. Davis, 'The Life of Prisoners of War in Russia 1914-1921', in Samueal Williams and Peter Pastor (eds) *Essays on World War I: Origins and Prisoners of War*, p. 167.

6. AOK (1915)/ GZNB/Kart:3729/Akt:1509; AOK (1915)/ GZNB/Kart: 3737/Akt:2887. Thirty-six of the camps listed in the survey were underlined as major camps. It is not clear, however, what were the criteria for designating the different camps. If one follows Elsa Brändström's typology than a small POW camp consisted roughly of 2,000-6,000 POWs, a medium camp of 6,000-10,000 and a large one had more than 10,000. Elsa Brändström, *Among the Prisoners of War in Russia and Siberia*, pp. 68-96.

7. 'Kharkov and Kursk', U.S National Archives 763.72214 suffix 1084.

8. Roman Dyboski, *Seven Years in Russia and Siberia (1914-1921)*, translated from the Polish by Marion Moore Coleman (Cheshire CT: Cherry Hill Books, 1970) pp. 35-6.

9. Johann von der Wülbecke, 'Meine Erlebnisse in russischer Kriegsgefangenschaft', BA/MA (Freiburg im Breisgau), Msg. 200/932.

10. The quotation is from Elsa Brändström, *Among the Prisoners of War in Russia and Siberia*.

11. Untitled report dated December 31,1914. Paragraph 4: 'An Internierungsorten, Lagern und Gefangenenetappenstationen in Russland wurden bisher bekannt . . .' AOK (1915)/GZNB/Kart:3728/Akt 1385.

12. 'Vcepoddanneishii doklad fligel' - Adiudanta Vashego Impertorskogo Velichestva Polkovnika Mordvinova (The Report of Your Royal Majesty's Adjutant, Colonel Mordvinov), November 1915 RGVIA fond 970/ op.3/ d.1973/pages 95, 95(ob), 96.

13. Ibid.

14. Ibid.

15. Ibid.

16. Ibid.

17. Ibid.

18. It is not clear exactly how many died during this typhus epidemic partly because medical documents were falsified. Estimates range from 12,000-17,000. The epidemic in Totskoe is described in detail by Reinhard Nachtigal, 'Seuchen unter militärischer Aufsicht in Rußland: Das Lager Tockoe als Beispiel für die Behandlung der Kriegsgefangenen 1915/1916', *Jahrbücher für Geschichte Osteuropas*, 48 (2000), pp. 363-87.

19. Max Sgalitzer. 'medizinische und persönliche Erlebnisse in russischer Kriegsgefangenschaft', Kriegarchiv/Kriegsministerium (KM)/Akt 1916 14.A 63-13.

20. RGVIA f.12651/op.11/d.114.

21. RGVIA f.1396/op.2/d.1943/ll.20, 20(ob), 40, 40-41.

22. RGVIA f.1396/op.2/d.1943/ll.15-16.

23. RGVIA f.1396/op.2/d.1943/ll.5–6, 8–11.

24. Avigdor Hameiri, *Be'gehenom shel Mata: Reshimot Katzin Ivri Be'shevi Russia* (Hell on Earth: The Memoirs of a Jewish Officer in Russian Captivity) published in Hebrew (Tel Aviv: Mizpah Publishing, 1932), Chapter 35. Affairs of honor in captivity were usually postponed after a detailed protocol (signed by witnesses) had been taken down. Both parties agreed that the protocol would be taken back to Austria-Hungary after the war and the affair would be settled as customary by a duel.

25. KA/AOK (1916/1917)/GZNB/Kart.3747/Akt. 4395.

26. Ibid.

27. Joan Beaumont, 'Rank, Privilege and Prisoners of War', *War and Society*, 1 (May 1983), p. 67.

28. 'Bericht 2 über das offizierslager Omsk: nur für den Privatgebrauch der Angehörigen', April 1917, BA/MA (Freiburg im Breisgau)/ N 448 3/ p. 7 (number according to MA stamping); in the camp of Khabarovsk, officers contributed 28 Rubles for food, which was prepared by 'Mr. Tewatge, the most important hotelier in town who delivers four times a week delicious fish from the Amur river, two meals a day, tea, coffee, sugar. For those who suffer stomach pains, cocoa, apples and Nestle's condensed milk are ordered.' 'Bericht 7 über das Offiziersgefangenenlager Khabarovsk: nur für den Privatgebrauch der Angehörigen', 17 March 1917. BA/Ma Msg.200/20.

29. See Chapter 3, note 1. 'Bericht Nr.7 über das Offizierslager OMSK (nur für den Privatgebrauch der Angehörigen)', Bundesarchiv (BA), Militärarchiv Freiburg (MA), N 448/3.

30. Buj (Kostroma) Franz Bejcek nach Wien, 14 October 1917 (letter written originally in German). KA/AOK (1917/1918)/GZNB/Kart:3756/Akt 4980/ p. 6- 'Mannschaft'/letter # 45.

31. 'Nachrichten eines Zugvogels', *S'Vogerl* Nr.1 Rasdolnoe, pp. 40–3, BA/ MA MSg. 220/399.

32. Hans Weiland, 'Kriegsgefangenenlager Krasnojarsk', in Hans Weiland and Leopold Kern (eds) *In Feindeshand*, vol. 1, p. 176.

33. Some of the food and clothing supplied to the officers did, however, trickle down to the batmen and they were generally much better off than the regular rank-and-file (who as a rule greatly disliked the batmen).

34. Ilse Raettig, 'Bericht 9 über das Offiziersgefangenenlager Chabarowsk (nur für den Privatgebrauch der Angehörigen)', Bundesarchiv (Germany)/ Militärarchiv (Freiburg im Breisgau)/ Msg.200/20.

35. 'Lt. Dr. Jenö Schönfeld nach Ungarn, Sept. 11 1917' AOK. (1917)/ GZNB/Kart:3755/Akt:4909 letter # 12 (written originally German).

36. Hans Weiland, 'Kriegsgefangenenlager Krasnoyarsk', in *In Feindeshand* vol. 1, p. 178.

37. Hans Weiland, 'Kriegsgefangenenlager Krasnoyarsk', *In Feindeshand*, p. 183.

38. RGVIA f.2000/op.9/d.25/l.274.

39. RGVIA f.2000/op.9/d.25/ll.34-37, 40.

40. RGVIA f.2000/op.9/d.25/l.72.

41. The National Archives of the United States/Department of State/ file 763.72114/1148, p. 4; also published in: US Legation Russia, *Reports of the Delegates of the Embassy of the United States of America in St Petersburg on the Situation of the German prisoners of War and Civil Persons in Russia*, Zurich: Art. Institut Orell Füssli, 1917, enclosure 6 pp. 30-1.

42. 'Ladislaus Baczy an Emerich Diossy, Reichstagabgeordneter in Szentmihalyiur' Behandlung der österr. Kgf. in Antipicha b. Tshita (Russland): Ungarische Zensurgruppe, AOK (1916)/GZNB/Kart. 3740/Akt 3511.

43. Today epidemic typhus is treated effectively with antibiotics.

44. The ratio of doctors to POWs in Russia was 1:1500.

45. Special representative of the Department of State William Warfield, to the Department of State, 17 January 1916, United States National Archives, Department of State, 763.72114 suffix 1277. To expedite matters Warfield sent his telegrams from Harbin in China to the Department of State, who then relayed them to the American Embassy in Petrograd. Thus, the telegram that had reached Petrograd was the following: 'Warfield telegraphs Department from Harbin. Quote. Violent typhus epidemic broken out in Stretensk. Siberia. Camp, nine thousand men, over fifty per cent sick and over fifty deaths daily. Newly established camp. New arrivals. Insufficient equipment. Unsanitary. Only hospital building accidentally burned after outbreak. Only two doctors. One Austrian one German; primitive hospital supplies given by Swedish Red Cross only equipment available. Demoralized camp deserted by authorities. Temporarily in charge six German officers hitherto unrecognized.' United States National Archives, Department of State, 763.72114 suffix 1169.

46. Brändström, p. 99.

47. Price, Boche and Bolshevik, p. 140.

48. Ernst Ritter von Streeruwitz, *Kriegsgefangene im Weltkrieg 1914–1918*, unpublished manuscript at the Heeresegeschichtliches Museum in Vienna, vol .2, Section B, Chapter 13.

49. Verena Moritz, 'Die österreichische Kriegsgefangenen in der russischen Wirtschaft (1914 bis Oktober 1917)', *Zeitgeschichte*.25 (November-December 1998), pp. 380-9; Gerald H. Davis, 'The Life of Prisoners of War in Russia 1914-1921', in Samuel Williamson and Peter Pastor (eds) *Essays on World War I: Origins and Prisoners of War*, New York: Columbia University Press, 1983, pp. 162-96.

50. Brändström, p. 130.

51. Edwin Erich Dwinger, *The Army behind Barbed Wire: A Siberian Diary*, translated by Ian Morrow, London: George Allen & Unwinn, 1930, p. 179.

52. See for example Dwinger, p. 181; Brändström, pp. 131-2. Another version of this story presents a Russian peasant woman worried by the imminent birth of a child fathered by a Magyar POW. When asked by the doctor if she is worried by her husband's reaction she replied that this does

not matter so much. What really matters is the fact that the child will speak Hungarian and she doesn't understand a word of it.

53. Russische B. Gruppe, Gruppenleiter Hermann Safir, 'Spezialbericht: Eheschliessung und Tod eines österr.kgf. in Russland', AOK (1916)/GZNB/ Karton 3745/ Akt 4117/4.

54. 'Lage unserer Kgf. In feindlichen Auslande', AOK (1915)/ GZNB/ Karton 3735/ Akt 2565, p. 4.

55. Ibid., pp. 14-15.

56. AOK (1915/1916)/GZNB/Karton 3738/Akt. 3230/p. 10.

57. Brändström, pp. 133-4.

58. G. H. Davis, 'the Life of prisoners of War in Russia 1914-1921', p. 175.

59. Moritz, pp. 384-5 and note 58.

60. Davis, 'the Life of prisoners of War in Russia 1914-1921', p. 177.

61. 'Patrikiejewo Gouv. Simbirsk, Kgf. Boleslaus Westwalowicz an Anna Rymarz in Hard Fussach bei Bregenz, September 30th 1915', AOK (1915)/ GZNB/Karton 3735/ Akt 2565/ letter 169.

62. Brändström, p. 137.

63. Leo Krämer, an der Murmanbahn: Im Frühjahr 1916, in *In Feindeshand* vol 1, pp. 231-2.

64. RGVIA f.1606/op.2/d.1063/l.102.

65. RGVIA f.1396/op.2/d.1992/l.184.

66. RGVIA f.1396/op.2/d.1987/l.146.

67. Ernst Streeruwitz, 'Der Umsturz in Rußland und die Kriegsgefangenen', in *In Feindeshand*, pp. 268-9. Streeruwitz's contribution is based on a manuscript he had written prior to 1931. The exact date, however, is not given.

68. Ibid., p. 269.

69. Ibid., pp. 268-9.

70. Streeruwitz, in a nutshell, argued that because Austria-Hungary in principle did not negotiate with Russian POWs and because the Habsburg Monarchy was in no position to give Russian prisoners similar pay hikes or increased rations, a discrepancy was being created between the treatment of POWs in Russia and in Austria-Hungary. This discrepancy, Streeruwitz continued, elicited protests from the Russian provisional government and the Russian army (he cites one example) and a backlash against Austro-Hungarian POWs in Russia was a very real possibility. 'The good and loyal prisoner', he concluded, ' did not think in his hour of need and distress about equal treatment or social problems; half decent treatment and sufficient food is all he should have aspired to.' The example Streeruwitz cites is dated also June 1917. According to Streeruwitz General Grigoriev the commander of the military district in Tomsk published the following warning: 'The camps where Russian fighters find themselves in Germany, Austria-Hungary and Turkey are becoming from day to day increasingly wretched places. So many from these unlucky have suffered deaths resulting from insufficient nourishment and the diseases associated with it . . . if their [i.e. Russian POWs] condition will not be improved immediately, the Russian regime would be

forced to use the same standards in the treatment of POWs in Russia.' Ibid., pp. 268-9.

71. Moritz, p. 385.

72. Vejas Gabriel Liulevicius, *War Land on the Eastern Front: Culture, National Identity and German Occupation in World War I*, Cambridge: Cambridge University Press, 2000, p. 73. *Ober Ost* is a short form of *Oberbefehlshaber Ost* – Supreme Commander in the East the title of the German highest military commander.

73. See Orlando Figes, *A People's Tragedy: a History of the Russian Revolution*, New York, 1996, pp. 241-52; Dominic Lieven, *Russia and the Origins of the First World War*, Oxford: St Martin's Press, 1983; Paul Vyšný, *Neo-Slavism and the Czechs 1898-1914*, Cambridge: Cambridge University Press, 1977.

74. Ibid.

75. Regarding the Czech Legion and the South Slav Legion see respectively: Vlastimil Vávra, 'Formování České družiny', *Historie a Vojenství*, 1 (1990) pp. 107-18; John Bradley, *The Czechoslovak Legion in Russia 1914-1920*, (Boulder CO: Columbia University Press, 1991); Josef Kalvoda, 'Czech and Slovak Prisoners of War in Russia during the War and Revolution', in *Essays on World War I: Origins and Prisoners of War*, pp. 215-38; Karel Pichlík, *Zahranicní odboj bez legend*, Prague: Nasé Vojsko, 1968; Margarete Klante, *Die Geschichte der Tschechischen Legion in Rußland*, Berlin: Ost-Europa Verlag, 1929; *Za svobodu: obrázková Kronika Ceskloslovenského hnutí na Rusi 1914-1920*, four vols, Prague, 1924; Josef Kudela, *Přehled vývoje čsl. revolucního hnutí na Rusi*, Prague, 1923; František Steidler, *Ceskoslovenské hnutí na Rusi*, Prague, 1922. See also Alon Rachamimov, 'The Czech Legion', in Jonathan F. Vance (ed.) *Encyclopedia of Prisoners of War and Internment*, Santa Barbara CA: ABC Clio, 2000, pp. 68-9. Ivo Banac, 'South Slav Prisoners of War in Revolutionary Russia', in *Essays on World War I: Origins and Prisoners of War*, pp. 119-48.

76. The number of Czechs residing in Russia before 1915 was estimated by Pichlík at 60,000-100,000, most of them arriving after the 1850s. Pichlík, p. 47. Kudela thinks 100,000 is a very high estimate and makes an argument for the lower estimate (Kudela, p. 6). Contrary to the prevailing opinion in the literature, Bradley makes the argument that it may have been a pet project of the Russian High Command all along and not of the Czechs in Russia. According to Bradley, the leaders of the Czechs' societies endorsed the idea only after it was suggested to them by the military and because they wanted to protected those Czech settlers who had not naturalized in Russia. See Bradley, pp. 14-17.

77. From September 1914 to January 1915 the Svaz had a different name: *Rada Cechů v Rusku* (The Council of Czechs in Russia), Kudela, p. 12.

78. Bradley, p. 17.

79. In December 1914 Grand Duke Nikolai authorized the conscription of any Czech POW who volunteered immediately after his capture and passed the scrutiny of the Svaz.

80. Bradley, p. 21.
81. Kalvoda, p. 223.
82. The Italian Consul in Omsk Gazzirelli visited 528 Italian POWs in the camp of Omsk at the end of November 1915. According to a report prepared by a Russian representative to the meeting, the consul promised the prisoners the world for volunteering: 'exemption from fighting Austria-Hungary, permission to work in their profession, salaries from the Italian government and ample food. At one point Austro-Hungarian officers of Italian nationality stood up and announced that they were proud to be Austrians and are not prepared to fight for Italy.' RGVIA f.2000/d.11/op.6/ l.43–44.
83. Stürmer was apparently thinking of a separate peace with the Central Powers and wanted to eliminate the most obvious thorn in the eye. Stürmer's German name, his loyalty to the Tsarina (who was of German origin) and the large number of German family names in his government led to rumors and accusation about Russia being governed by a 'German clique'. See Banac, pp. 123–7 and Figes, pp. 274–88.
84. Quoted from Banac, p. 126. Originally from Anton Kovačić, 'pota dobrovoljca-kmeta', in Turk et al. (eds) *Dobrovoljci kladivarji jugoslavije*, Lubliana, 1936, p. 575.
85. Banac, p. 127.
86. Kalvoda, p. 224.
87. Ibid., pp. 224–5. The numbers of POWs visited by the recruiters are by no means mutually exclusive; some prisoners were visited more than once.
88. 'Bericht über die Lage unserer Kriegsgefangenen in Rußland; Mannschaft, Nationales, Brief 146:Viktor Mayer nach Ungarn 14.VIII.17, p. 18', Österreichisches Staatsarchiv: KA/AOK (1917)/GZNB/ Karton 3755, Akt. 4909.
89. Quoted in Arnold Krammer, 'Soviet Propaganda among German and Austro-Hungarian Prisoners of War In Russia', in *Essays on World War I: Origins and Prisoners of War*, pp. 244–5. On this subject see also: Inge Pardon and Waleri Schrawiljov (eds) *Lager, Front oder Heimat. Deutsche Kriegsgefangene in Sovietrußland 1917–1920*, two vols, Berlin: G. K. Saur, 1994; Ivan Völgyes, 'Hungarian Prisoners of War in Russia', *Cahiers du monde russe et Soviétique*, 14 (1973); M. Birman (ed.) *Internatsionalisty v boyakh za vlast' Sovetov*, Moscow, 1965.
90. See Robert Ezerov, 'Die sowjetische Historiographie und die deutschen und österreichischen Kriegsgefangenen-Internationalisten', *Zeitgeschichte*, 25 (1998) pp. 343–7; Peter Pastor, 'Hungarian POWs in Russia during the Revolution and Civil War', in *Essays on World War I: Origins and Prisoners of War*, pp. 154–9; Völgyes, section 5; Krammer, pp. 244–7.
91. Pastor, 'Hungarian POWs in Russia during the Revolution and Civil War', p. 159. The rate of desertion among the Internationalists seems to have been very high; on desertion in the Red Army, see Mark von Hagen, *Soldiers in the Proletarian Revolution: The Red Army and the Soviet Socialist State, 1917–1930*, Ithaca: Cornell University Press, 1990, pp. 67–80.

92. Krammer, pp. 257-8.

93. See in Pastor, 'Hungarian POWs in Russia during the Revolution and Civil War' p. 159; also Mark von Hagen , Chapters 1-2; Ezerov, pp. 343-5.

94. Banac, p. 120.

95. Garry Wills, 'A Reader's Guide to the Century', *The New York Review of Books*, 15 July (1999), p. 24.

96. Berend in turn rephrased Fernand Braudel's 'the long sixteenth century'.

97. Adam Roberts, 'Land Warfare: from Hague to Nuremberg' in *The Laws of War: Constraints on Warfare in the Western World*, p. 126.

98. After the German Red Cross nurse, Alexandrine von Üxküll, complained about conditions in the camp of Achinsk (western Siberia) she was taken to inspect a nearby Russian army camp and admitted that Russian soldiers shared the same miserable conditions. See Üxküll.

99. Pastor, Introduction, p. 115.

100. Samuel Hynes, *The Soldiers' Tale: Bearing Witness to Modern War*, New York: Penguin Books, 1997, p. 55.

101. The estimated total mortality figures are the following : 751,000 dead out of 8,510,000 POWs or (8.7 per cent mortality rate) see in *In Feindeshand: Die Gefangenschaft im Weltkriege in Einzeldarstellungen*, statistical appendix.

4

In Search of the 'Good and Loyal Prisoner': Austro-Hungarian Censorship and the POWs

> The good and loyal prisoner did not think in his hour of need and distress about equal treatment or social problems; half decent treatment and sufficient food is all he should have aspired to.[1]
>
> Ernst Streeruwitz
> Kriegsministerium, Abteilung 10.Kgf

Patriotism in a Multi-National State

The expanding nature of warfare during the nineteenth century created throughout Europe a sense that the size of a country's military was crucial to maintaining (or enhancing) its international standing.[2] Consequently, broadly conscripted reserve-based armies were gradually added to smaller professional cores, bringing with them a new kind of soldier into the center stage of the military endeavor: the citizen soldier. Serving now only a limited number of years in active duty (three in Austria-Hungary) these citizen soldiers were expected to mobilize quickly upon the threat of war and fight willingly for their country.[3] The fact that in their civilian lives these men were not under constant supervision of the army meant that it was impossible to motivate them exclusively by negative means (such as punishment and discipline).[4] Rather, these civilian soldiers needed to bring with them a sense of serving and fighting for a common cause, or have the military become the *Schule der Nation*.[5]

The difficulties in convincing soldiers that the state as a whole was their *patria* are well documented in connection with self-described nation states such as France, Italy and Imperial Germany, where linguistic, cultural and emotional attachments were often predominately local at least until the last decades of the nineteenth century.[6] The task was even more daunting in a dynastic multi-national state such as the Habsburg monarchy where the state was the patrimony of its ruling house (and not its peoples), and where, in the words of Oscar Jaszi, a 'growing chasm between dynastic and national patriotism could not be bridged by the anxious efforts of the official administration'.[7] In other words, in contrast to the nation states of western Europe, the Habsburg monarchy lacked a self-evident collective 'us' into which a host of separate identities could be hierarchically intertwined. The seemingly rational western European progression of identities (individual→village/town→region→nation→state) that aimed to mobilize every person on behalf of the state, did not seem to flow smoothly in multi-national Austria-Hungary even in theory (e.g. individual→region→nation→another European state or individual→nation→imaginary future state **and/or** current Habsburg state etc.).

Yet, the willingness of the Austro-Hungarian troops to mobilize on behalf of their state in the summer of 1914, and the apparent widespread support for the initial war effort attest to the existence of imperial loyalties among the population (if not to their depth).[8] Pictures of celebrating crowds in the major cities of Austria-Hungary are not markedly different from the pictures we have of jubilant patriotic masses in France, Russia and Germany. The reports of the Austro-Hungarian Army High Command (*Armeeoberkommando* or AOK) show that, contrary to pessimistic prewar assessments, general mobilization proceeded smoothly, and almost no resistance was encountered even in 'problematic' military districts in the Czech speaking areas.[9]

If 'patriotism', then, in Carlton Hayes's basic definition, is the 'love of country or native land', and if the willingness to sacrifice one's life for one's country is an indication of this love, then Austro-Hungarian citizens appear in the summer of 1914 to have been just as patriotic as their counterparts in other parts of Europe.[10] Still, as an anticipated short war became a long and costly one, as military setbacks piled up and as a significant part of the Austro-Hungarian imperial army found itself in Russian, Serbian, and Italian captivity, the Army High Command began viewing a considerable section of this recruited citizenry as 'unpatriotic' and 'disloyal'.

My main goal in this and the next two chapters is to examine the various opinions and forms of behavior that received the tag of 'patriotic' (and those which were conversely designated 'suspicious', 'disloyal' and 'unpatriotic'). I would like to argue here that beyond veneration of the Emperor/King, personal sufferings and hatred of the enemy, the Habsburg military and political leadership struggled to define the meaning of 'patriotism' and 'loyalty'. Instead, it preferred to lump a wide array of actions and opinions as 'suspect' and 'disloyal'. In doing so it utilized a double standard regarding perceived 'loyal' nationalities and perceived 'disaffected' nationalities, and failed to recognize a real sense of state support that found expression among its recruited citizenry. This chapter focuses specifically on the Austro-Hungarian POW censorship during World War I, the organ responsible for assessing the loyalty of the Habsburg prisoners of war in enemy countries. I will present here the organization and the personnel of the POW censorship, its methods to assess the loyalty of the prisoners in Russia and the reasons why it concluded in the winter of 1917–18 that returning POWs might destabilize the monarchy.

The Austro-Hungarian POW Censorship

During the long years of captivity letters and postcards were the principal means of communication between POWs and their families and friends back home. It was this correspondence that enabled POWs to keep in touch and share some of their experiences in captivity: to notify their families that they had fallen captive, to complain, to give instructions, vent their frustrations, express homesickness, request money or gossip about an acquaintance who for example had been cheating on his wife.[11]

The large number of Austro-Hungarian POWs in enemy hands and the similarly imposing numbers of captive enemy soldiers in the Habsburg monarchy meant that the volume of this correspondence was enormous.[12]

The daily average of incoming and outgoing POW mail reached a robust 8,000 articles in September 1914, rising to 75,000 in the beginning of 1915, 266,000 in the beginning of 1916 and finally 455,000 in November 1916, a level that stayed constant until the Bolshevik revolution a year later.[13] Each single letter would typically take at least a month before reaching its addressee, dallying at times as much as six months en route. Miss Sascha Kronburg of Vienna sent between 23 February 1915 and 7 October 1915, 147 articles of mail to her fiancé, Lt Alfred Mayer interned in the far-eastern camp of Rasdolnoe. Having some connections abroad she sent some of this mail via England, Romania and the US (the latter two were neutral

Figure 4.1: Prisoners writing their first letter from captivity.

Source: *Za Svobodu*

at the time), using simultaneously also the official Red Cross route via Sweden. As perhaps only someone in love might do, she compiled detailed statistics of the average duration each route required: Sweden an average of 105 days, the US fifty-five to sixty-five days, England fourty-five days and Romania thirty days. Beyond the sheer quantity of letters sent, it is astonishing to note that in the midst of a war on an unprecedented scale almost all the articles of mail sent from Vienna to the Russian Far East arrived at their destination.[14]

The reason for the relative delay in the official Red Cross route was the wartime practices of censorship; primarily the Austro-Hungarian POW censorship. In contrast to the Russian military authorities who read samples of mail, the Austro-Hungarian POW censorship was instructed to read all incoming and outgoing mail and grew into a sizable and surprisingly efficient institution, considering the task at hand. The practices of censorship in wartime Austria-Hungary were shaped (as many other political practices in the dual monarchy) by a combination of legal, quasi-legal and illegal measures, as well as by a host of political considerations.[15] The legal basis for censorship went back to the *Ausgleich* and to a series of laws passed in the years 1867–9 in both halves, which allowed for the suspension of certain civil liberties during wartime. Most important, in this context, was the expected suspension of the rights to secrecy of correspondence, to freedom of the press and to free assembly. This suspension was foreseen as a temporary measure with the ultimate control resting with the parliaments of both halves.

The institutional contours of the censorship were sketched in 1912 in a series of secret meetings between officials in the Austro-Hungarian War Ministry, the joint Ministerial Council (*Ministerrat*) and members of the General Staff. Josef Redlich, the Austrian constitutional historian and liberal statesman viewed the meetings and ensuing top secret *Dienstbuch J-25a* as 'completely unlawful', and estimated that they were designed to give the army broad powers under the guise of preventing critical information from reaching the enemy. Thus, *Dienstbuch J-25a* called for the establishment of a War Supervisory Office (*Kriegsüberwachungsamt* or KÜA) within the Austro-Hungarian War Ministry with jurisdiction – it was hoped – in both halves of the monarchy. The KÜA had 'the assignment to implement military and other measures appropriately and quickly in order to prevent espionage, sabotage and the circulation of unauthorized information'. As the Austrian historian Gustav Spann has pointed out, the KÜA was in name and purpose a completely new entity within the legal framework of the *Ausgleich*, although its sponsor attempted to conceal it within the recognized joint *Kriegsministerium*.

The quasi-legal status of the KÜA became apparent during the first weeks of the war, when the Hungarian government of Count Tisza successfully blocked its full operation in Hungary, defining precisely what it could and could not do on Hungarian territory. Specifically, all political and press matters were separated from the supervision of the KÜA in Vienna and handled separately from Budapest. As a result, Hungarian newspapers reported much more freely and broadly on the war than their counterparts in the Austrian half. Moreover, since the Hungarian Parliament continued to meet throughout the war while Austrian *Reichsrat* was adjourned until May 1917, the activities of the KÜA in Hungary were monitored by the legislature in Budapest whereas in Vienna the KÜA became an unencumbered military-bureaucratic tool. In specific terms the KÜA had five main groups:

Group I. The Political Group (*Politische Gruppe*).
Group II. The Censorship Group (*Zensurgruppe*).
Group III. The Import-Export Group (*Ein-und Ausfuhrgruppe*).
Group IV. Machine Intelligence Group (*Maschinenevidenzgruppe*).
Group V. Special Missions (*Besondere Arbeiten*).

Group II – the censorship – was further divided into three sections:

1 Press censorship (supervised by officials from the Foreign Ministry, the Interior Ministry, the Ministry of Justice, the Ministry of Finance and the army) containing two main sub-sections – the political press censorship (dealing with political subjects), and Military Press Censorship (dealing with military issues).
2 Letter censorship (*Briefzensur*) (supervised by officials from the Ministry of Justice, the Ministry of Finance, the Commerce Ministry and Army officers) having four sub-sections:
   (a) Foreign correspondence.
   (b) Inland correspondence.
   (c) Field post (*Feldpost*).
   (d) POW correspondence.
   This latter sub-section was not an 'official' part of the imperial bureaucracy (it had been refused the 'k.u.k' epithet), but rather of the Central Information Bureau of the Red Cross (*gemeinsames Zentralnachweisbureau* or GZNB).
3 Telegram correspondence (including all wireless communication).

Considered by far the best organized sub-section within the Austro-Hungarian letter censorship was the POW censorship (GZNB). Its structure and methods of operation served in the fall of 1916 as the model for a complete reform of the whole letter censorship section. What made the POW censorship unique from the very beginning of the war was its centralized structure. In contrast to sub-section (a) (foreign correspondence), which operated from twenty-two different locations until the fall of 1916 (three from then on),[16] sub-section (b) (inland correspondence), which focused on perceived 'problem areas' and read only samples, and sub-section (c) (field post), which delegated authority to junior officers in the units themselves, the GZNB processed all incoming and outgoing POW mail from Vienna. This enabled the POW censorship to function simultaneously as an intelligence-gathering unit and as a gatekeeper.

The thoroughness and versatility of the GZNB censorship not only won it accolades within the Austro-Hungarian censorship apparatus, but also led it to serve as a model for the 1916 reform of the *Zensurdienst* in Germany (to the considerable delight and pride of General Max Ronge, head of the Intelligence Bureau – *Evidenzbureau* – in the AOK).[17]

Under the direction of a career officer – Major Theodor Primavesi – the GZNB grew very quickly in size, employing in the beginning of 1916 more than 1,150 censors who read mail in more than thirty-five different languages, divided into fifteen language groups (see Table 4.1).[18] The KÜA's personnel guidelines instructed all the censorship to use

> as a rule persons **unfit for front-line service** (*felddienstuntaugliche Personen*) . . . In case of emergency, also rank-and-file soldiers fit for front-line service could be recruited, whose civilian occupation and social and civilian position (*soziale Zivilstellung*) would guarantee proper fulfillment of their assignments (professors, governmental officials, bank clerks etc.).

Thus, according to the War Supervisory Office, the desired profile of an Austro-Hungarian censor included linguistic, intellectual and social credentials. Still, political considerations were even more important: censors were required to be absolutely trustworthy from a political point of view with a special group within the GZNB – the *Hyperzensur* – in charge of assessing the reliability of each individual censor. In addition, each language group commander had to assess regularly the political tendencies of his censors, and report 'Slavo-philes', 'Austrophobes', 'irredentists', or any other case of 'question-able' opinions. Judging by the constant complaints of the GZNB command, the army rarely allocated enough personnel qualified to meet the many qualifications and the heavy work load.[19] Thus, the GZNB turned to civilians, who worked for a small honorarium or as volunteers, and who would constitute almost half of the people employed in the GZNB (and more than half of those actually reading the letters in the language groups; see Table 4.1).

Every mail article sent by or sent to Austro-Hungarian prisoners of wars (or to POWs held in Austria-Hungary) would first be handled by the *Sortiergruppe* (Sorting Group). The *Sortiergruppe* would sort out the correspondence into languages creating bundles of 1,000 articles of mail. The *Sortiergruppe* was also responsible for conducting

Table 4.1 The personnel of the GZNB censorship – 21 January 1916

Department*	Officers	Rank-and-file	Civilians	Total
Command	4	4	6	14
Information	1	5	0	6
Blotting out and interception	0	19	0	19
Comptroller (hyperzensur)	1	5	1	7
Post	2	92	0	94
Other depts	7	73	3	83
Balkan group	0	2	7	9
Czech	11	78	49	138
German	11	90	92	193
English/French	2	5	11	18
Hebrew	0	6	3	9
Italian	11	66	65	142
Croat	2	22	8	31
Polish	16	44	24	84
Romanian	2	11	11	24
Russian	4	25	152	171
Serb	3	20	15	38
Slovak	1	9	8	18
Slovene	1	3	5	9
Ukrainian	6	19	25	50
Hungarian	3	5	6	14
TOTAL	**88**	**593**	**491**	**1172**

* Some language groups were divided into sub-groups (for example six Russian sub-groups, three German, two Czech and so forth) which I condensed into one figure. The surprisingly small number of Hungarian censors, reflected the paucity of POW correspondence in that language. In many cases, Magyar POWs in Russia were specifically prohibited from writing in their mother tongue due to the lack of qualified censors on the Russian side able to read Hungarian fluently.

Source: The personnel distribution of the GZNB Censorship is taken from 'Übersicht über den gesamten bei der Zensurabteilung in Verwendung stenhenden Personalstand', KA/AOK (1915)/GZNB/Kart. 3734/Akt.2438 ad 21 January 1916.

a first search for the correspondence of 'suspicious' people or conversely marking 'suspicious-looking' correspondence written by people not identified yet as 'suspicious'. From the *Sortiergruppe* the mail would be forwarded to the heart of the GZNB operation – the language groups (*Sprachgruppen*). It was there that all the POW mail was read, assessed, analyzed and subsequently forwarded to the appropriate groups (see Chart 4.1).

The language groups handling the most mail were the German, Czech, Russian and Italian groups. The first two dealt primarily with the mail of Austro-Hungarian POWs in enemy countries, while the latter two focused on the correspondence of Russian and Italian

Chart 4.1: The mail sorting process at the GZNB

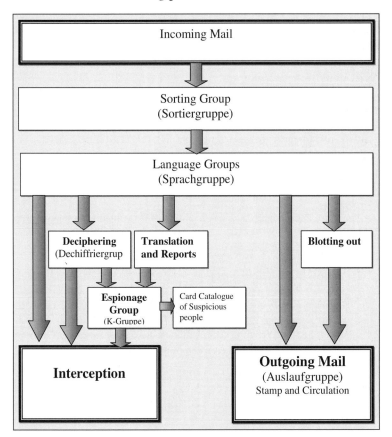

POWs held in the Habsburg Monarchy. The Hungarian-language group was a relatively small cog within the GZNB apparatus, despite the fact that Magyars constituted the second largest national group among the Austro-Hungarian POW population in Russia (see Chapter 1). This was because the Russian military authorities strongly discouraged Magyar POWs from using Hungarian in their letters. The Russian military simply did not have enough qualified censors to read correspondence in Hungarian, and stories circulated among the Hungarian POWs about thousands of sacks of mail lying somewhere in censorship limbo. A Czech-language censor by the name of Voskovec, who was employed by the Russian censorship in Petrograd, sent a message to his fellow censors in Austria-Hungary stating that 'there is currently no censor here for this language [Hungarian]. There was one but he died. One should use a different language or everything stays put.'[20] The matter even reached the Prime Minister of Hungary, Count István Tisza, but to no avail, Magyar POWs in Russia (and their families back home) had to write in one of the recognized languages – usually German or Russian – or find someone who could do it for them.

The great majority of letters – a monthly average of 95–98 per cent – processed by the language groups proceeded smoothly to the *Auslaufgruppe* (outgoing mail) where they received a censorship stamp and were released from GZNB control. The criteria for determining what was permissible or impermissible were defined by the KÜA at the beginning of the war and updated periodically. According to instructions from 1914:

The aim of censorship is the strictest possible control over the correspondence of prisoners of war, civil internees and their family members – and includes the following principal points:

a) The censors must pay attention that correspondence with political or military themes will not be overlooked. This includes, for example, information about troop movement, measures or planned measures in the area controlled by the army, descriptions of the war, mobilization, historical reminiscences that are linked to the current military leadership, information about uprisings, epidemics etc.

b) Letters that contain such elements are to be intercepted [*inhibiert*]. Postcards with pictures of foreign leaders are also to be intercepted. Likewise, letters whose contents break the law or the pertinent regulations are also to be intercepted, particularly the following: §58 high treason, §63 lese-majesté, § 65 disturbing the public order, §308 circulating unsettling rumors . . . Suspicious letters should be handed over to the head of each language section, who will register them in a ledger [*Konsignation*]. The ledger will then be made available to the proper authorities, always accompanied by a German translation.

c) Letters that do not contain the above-mentioned objections but nonetheless contain non-permissible remarks, e.g. about the present situation, about price increases . . . or about things that could be depressing to the reader are to be blotted out [*remediert*].[21]

In other words, when dealing with letters which appeared problematic, censors could choose one of the two options: either intercepting (*inhibieren*) them, or blotting out (*remedieren*) problematic sections. In the first case, the letters would be translated and transferred to the Espionage Group (*Kundschaftsgruppe* or K-Gruppe). The K-Gruppe took particular interest in espionage, sabotage, treason and desertion, and created a card catalogue with the names of all those suspected of such activities.[22]

The K-Gruppe would receive also periodic and special reports from individual language groups based on a synthesis of a large

Figure 4.2: Letter Written by POW officer (and future historian) Hans Kohn to his friend Robert Weltsch (future editor of the Zionist Newspaper Die Welt). The letter was intercepted by the censorship due to its Zionist content. Written on 7 October 1917.

```
" Chabarowsk, am 19. Dezember 1914.

" Lieber Freund !

" W enn I hr R ubel g endet, t elegrafieret
g rst h ieher; E insendung n icht u nbedingt
n ötig ! T elegramm e rhalten; R udolf
d onkt g benfalls; r echt K rgerlich -
r aunzig g ewesen, g oll t raurig -
g rnste N achrichten w egen I hrer
l ieben L udmilla k ürzlich U bellaunig
r etourniert h aben. E s r egt R udolf
g chrecklich guf : F eier - T age u nd
n un d as W sihmachtsfest g s r ührt
d och E inem ! N ächstens w erde i ch
E uch y ielleicht g ine r echt b illige
R eise - E rinnerung, C habarowsker
E rzeugnis, r edlich b esorgen; g s
h üngt g llerdings n ur d aran; g rst
l eichtere T emperatur h ier g rwarten !
L ustige F eier - T age u nd(
N eujahrs - G egen !
```

Figure 4.3: Deciphered postcard from Khabarovsk (The Russian Far East) 19 December 1914. The first letter of every word create the following encrypted message: 'Wir stehen unter der ärgsten Will-kürherrschaft und werden wie Verbrecher behandelt. Helft uns!' (We are subjected to the worst arbitrary rule and are treated like criminals. Help us!)

number of letters. When the *Sortiergruppe* or the language groups encountered letters that attempted to convey information surreptitiously, they would forward them for deciphering in the *Dechiffrier-gruppe*. The codes handled by the censors ranged from the naively simple (for example talking about 'Uncle Willi' when discussing Germany), through the elusive (marking with tiny dots the letters meant to carry the real message) to the sophisticated (writing between lines with invisible ink, which appears when the letter is ironed).

In the case of letters which required blotting out, the problematic sections would just be translated into German and sent to the K-Gruppe (or integrated into reports). The blotted-out letter would then be forwarded to the *Auslaufgruppe*, stamped and released. The blotting-out techniques were a cause of much satisfaction within the GZNB. Utilizing what historian Gustav Spann termed an 'artisanal approach' to this task, the GZNB censors devised a system of blotting-out text by applying the same writing material in which the letter had been originally written. Thus, the censored parts would be submerged in a background of graphite or ink (of various colors and shades) and made illegible. An attempt to remove the censored section would result in the removal of the original text. The GZNB command took pride in the fact that other belligerent countries (especially Russia) seldom showed the same sophistication in blotting-out text and made it possible at times to read the censored sections.

During the first two years of the war the GZNB was occupied mainly with traditional censorship duties (controlling the flow of information). Yet, the fact that censors read all the POW mail meant that they were in an excellent position to gather valuable information and assess its meaning. Besides mining POW correspondence for specific intelligence (for example about the formation of the *Česká družina* in 1914 or regarding epidemics and food shortages in Russia), one can detect an increasing – albeit unhurried – effort to integrate information into broad reports. The first comprehensive report about 'Our Prisoners of War in Russia and Rumania' was written in March 1917. Prior to that date each individual language group published its own periodic reports, or occasionally a specific issue would be examined comparatively by censors from various groups. During the first two years of the war the question of the loyalty (or disloyalty) of Austro-Hungarian POWs in Russia stood at the center of these efforts.

Austro-Hungarian POWs, the Censorship and the Issue of Loyalty

One of the most interesting assignments handled by the GZNB, during the first six months of the war, was 'to provide a certain picture of the political and military reliability' (*ein gewisses Bild der staatlichen und militärischen Zuverlässigkeit*) of Austro-Hungarian POWs in Russia and Serbia.[23] To do so each language group collected a sample of POW letters and counted how many POWs reported being wounded while being captured. Specifically, the POW censorship was interested in pinpointing particular regiments 'that had been compromised through a significant number of unwounded prisoners of war'.[24] The underlying assumption here was that only wounds could automatically justify a soldier's capture and clear him from suspected cowardice or treason. In other words, only through individual suffering could Austro-Hungarian POWs make an uncontestable claim for not failing their duties as 'patriots'. Dr Burghard Breitner, the noted surgeon and future director of the Austrian Red Cross society, entitled his wartime memoirs *Captured Unwounded* to indicate his feeling of having done something dishonorable. It should be emphasized though that this perception was very common in all armies during World War I. Canadian historian Jonathan Vance has shown that the British Army during the Great War was deeply imbued 'with the nineteenth-century military ethos, which held that to be captured could have resulted only from some personal failing on the part of the soldier'.[25] This ethos was inextricably bound with the emphasis among European general staffs on personal and collective bellicosity (the much discussed 'cult of the offensive' capsulated by the French notion of *la guerre à l'outrance*), as well as by the contemporary cultural link between elan and manliness.[26]

Thus, wounds constituted an individual litmus test for loyalty and patriotism. However, for the Austro-Hungarian AOK they were far more important on a collective level. Therefore, the reports produced by the GZNB emphasized 'the percentages of wounded POWs among the various nations represented in the army'.[27] In December 1914 the GZNB listed the percentage of wounded Austro-Hungarian POWs as follows:

Germans	about 85%
Poles	about 85%
Slovaks	about 90%
Slovenes	about 80%
Italians	about 70%
Magyars	about 95%
Ruthenes	about 70%
Serbs	about 30%
Czechs	about 50%*
Romanians	about 95%

* (in the previous month only 30%)

It is important to emphasize that these and similar figures produced by the GZNB during the first six months of the war are almost certainly exaggerated. Not only that the samples upon which these figures were based seem to have been very small (in one case less than 200 letters), but also because one would be hard pressed to explain the discrepancy between the very high number of wounded men and the relatively much lower mortality rate. The estimated **overall** mortality rate for Austro-Hungarian POWs in Russia was 17.6 per cent according to official Austrian statistics and the medical attention received by Austro-Hungarian POWs in Russia was usually insufficient (especially during the chaotic first year). It seems highly unlikely that so many POWs were injured, yet still managed to survive the ordeal. What seems more likely to have happened is that POWs overstated their wounds in letters to appear more patriotic, more manly and perhaps out of fear of retribution from their state. Moreover, it seems that censors within the individual language groups attempted to exculpate 'their' POWs and present them in a favorable light. A case in point are the figures attributed to Czech POWs in Russia.

During the winter of 1914–15 the head of the *böhmische Zensurgruppe A*, Dr Kolinsky, made two attempts to put the Czech wounded figures in context. The first was in mid-December 1914 when he wrote a correction to the above-mentioned report. Dr Kolinsky stated that the percentage of wounded Czech POWs in Russia was actually sixty per cent and not fifty per cent – this latter figure applied to Czech POWs in Serbia – and that most of the unwounded belong to specific *Landsturm* battalions and do not represent Czech soldiers in general. The second and more serious attempt was in March 1915 when Kolinsky assembled a collection of letters from unwounded Czech POWs, explaining the circumstances in which they had been captured. This collection demonstrates, he argued, that 'although these soldiers fell into enemy hands healthy and unwounded, the accompanying circumstances [*Begleitumstände*] suggest they held out heroically until the last moment.'[28] This last attempt by Kolinsky resulted in a letter of reprimand – most likely from the head of the GZNB censorship Major Theodor Primavesi – stating that 'an attempt has been made to present this nation [the Czechs] as virtuous and their notorious Austrophobe statements as the work of individual agitators . . . The fact is that one **never** finds Germans, Croats and Magyars serving the enemy. These soldiers would rather hunger and die than let themselves be coerced into serving our mortal enemies.'[29]

Although the letter of rebuke was three pages in length, it did not address Kolinsky's argument specifically, but rather criticized in

POWs and the Great War

general terms the conduct of Czech soldiers and POWs. This general critique found further expression in Primavesi's report from that month, which stated that 'one feels revulsion that there is a nation that shakes the entire structure of our proverbial dynastic, brave and loyal army; this incidentally has already been demonstrated through many years of intensive subversive activity [*Wühlarbeit*].'[30] The matter however was not resolved with this condemnation, due to a surprising increase in the percentage of unwounded Magyar POWs detected by the censorship during the first months of 1915.[31] Consequently, the GZNB had to choose now between three different courses of action: label Magyar POWs as 'disloyal', reassess its conclusions regarding the loyalty of Czech POWs or repudiate this method as a faulty indication of loyalty. The absence of data on the subject from the spring of 1915 onwards suggests that the GZNB chose the third option – to relinquish the method altogether. Still, Primavesi's report made a valiant effort to explain why 'the large number of unwounded [Magyar] POWs is not connected in any way with the proven soldierly qualities of the Magyars'. Ironically, to do so he relied on Kolinsky's method of collecting letters that explain 'accompanying circumstances' such as hunger, lack of clothing, freezing weather and lack of ammunition. Thus, although wounds and suffering could constitute a *prima facie* indicator of patriotism they could not do so exclusively.

For the GZNB two additional motifs were solid indicators of patriotism among the POWs: veneration of the emperor/king and hatred of the enemy. Both of these figured prominently in a collection of 'patriotic letters' assembled by the GZNB in the years 1915-16.[32] An example of such a 'patriotic letter' came from the Ukrainian-speaking POW, Olexa Poselskyj, who reacted to the news that Ukrainian POWs from the Habsburg monarchy could obtain Russian citizenship by swearing an oath to the Tsar: 'I don't want to do this for any money in the world. I would rather die than swear an oath of loyalty to another Emperor. I serve only the Austrian Emperor Franz Josef I. I don't want to know about any other.'[33] Another example in these files came from the Polish-speaker POW Jakob Skiba who wrote home on August 16 1916 from a work detail near the city of Perm:

In two days we celebrate the birthday of our 'old master'. This is how we call our Emperor. We would like to organize some sort of celebration in his honor, but don't know if it's going to be allowed. Love and

reverence are really owed this monarch whose life goal was the preservation of peace. All the peoples of Austria love their old master, even in
Russia one utters his name with respect. His whole life was full of
suffering for sins he did not commit. We Poles have a special reason to
love and appreciate him. In the Russian area of Poland we are dispossessed,
our property is confiscated, we cannot speak or sing in Polish, only in
Austria do we enjoy full freedom.[34]

The fact that the censorship expected prisoners to love their
monarch and dislike their captors is not at all surprising. The first
motif constituted an unambiguous indication of loyalty to the
Habsburg ruler (and by extension to the multi-national state he was
heading), whereas the second was an emotional re-affirmation of the
wartime commitment.[35] Beyond these two commonly accepted
motifs, there were additional themes that were understood to be
'patriotic' by the various language groups. A comparison between
these themes uncovers a different standard of patriotism for different
nationalities. As a rule there was a marked difference between what
was accepted as 'patriotism' among Magyar and Polish POWs and
what was accepted as 'patriotism' among Czech and Slovak prisoners.[36] Whereas, the former could combine *Kaisertreue* feelings
with expressions of nationalism, the latter were restricted to the
three *prima facie* indications of patriotism: love of monarch, hatred
of enemy and anguish in being POWs. Thus, for example, a Polish
POW officer, Seweryn Kisielewski, could be considered a patriot by
the GZNB although his letter waxed poetically about 'Our future
Poland . . . this eternal sufferer . . . who waits for the final victory to
restore her lost freedom.'[37] Likewise a Magyar POW could take pride
in the deeds of 'ancient Hungarian heroes' and another could
emphasize 'the sunny future of a strong Hungary'.[38]

In contrast, the GZNB did not recognize indications of Czech
national sentiments as congruent with dynastic patriotism. The kind
of letters that were put in the file of Czech 'patriotic letters' were
restricted to apologetic formulations such as the one written by POW
Havlíček to his [former?] fiancée Rosa Jandl in June 1915:

> I am really jealous of all the comrades, who were lucky enough to die
> for the fatherland, but there was no other option to escape from this awful
> situation. I am so miserable that I have lost you, since you would never
> give your hand to a person who allowed himself to be taken captive. I
> regret that I dodged this terrifying bullet storm, and that no bullet had
> found me.[39]

Most illuminating perhaps were the observations made by the head of the Slovak language group regarding the patriotism of Slovak POWs:

> He [the Slovak] knows that he is fighting for a just cause for his master and emperor, and has the conviction in his childish and humble soul that God will not forsake him in this just battle. Further he knows that . . . he must bring the greatest sacrifices; he perceives the matter as a Christian martyr, approaching resolutely our righteous, holy cause like a deeply devout man who believes in the immortality of his soul . . .[40]

Thus, 'patriotism' in the Hungarian and Polish cases was a broader and more malleable concept than in the Czech and Slovak cases. It recognized a fuller range of opinions and identities, and allocated them a legitimate place within multi-national Austria-Hungary. In the Czech and Slovak case 'patriotism' was a rigid and restrictive concept which de-legitimized identities and opinions.[41]

As mentioned above, the GZNB created during the war lists of POWs whose opinions and forms of behavior were deemed particularly objectionable or suspicious. These included POWs who volunteered for anti-Habsburg units or expressed support for the Entente and various irredentist causes.[42] They included also POWs who insulted the emperor in words the censors occasionally found 'too coarse to repeat on paper', POWs exhibiting suspicious economic behavior (for example, a POW divulging that he 'gained possession of ten gold rings' or POWs demanding higher wages from their Russian employers) and POWs expressing content with their status as prisoners. Although the GZNB did not regard all these activities and opinions as equally severe, it did view all of them as undesirable from the perspective of the state requiring accountability after the war.

Among the most fascinating collections of 'suspicious' correspondence is a file containing 411 letters composed by Habsburg POWs, who had formed close personal relationships with women in Russia and announced their matrimonial intentions.[43] Most of these letters were written by Slavic and Jewish POWs while very intermittently one finds letters from Romanian- or Magyar-speaking POWs. The preponderance of the letters from the first two groups was probably the result of linguistic and cultural affinities with sections of the Russian civilian population. The Slovene POW N. Pongratschitsch wrote to his mother in Styria: 'I have found a little wife,

whom I married here in Russia. I will return home so you can see
your Russian stepdaughter. Please tell Hani she shouldn't think about
me anymore, because I have heard a lot about her.'[44]

In the case of Jewish POWs these relationships were very often
due to the close contacts between local Jewish communities in Russia
and their co-religionists from Austria-Hungary. The Hebrew writer,
Avigdor Hameiri, described in detail how Jewish families would
'adopt' certain prisoners of war and invite them for holiday and
Sabbath meals. This interaction resulted at times in betrothal or
marriage as was the case with R. Judkowycz, who informed Rachela
Lea Freund of Przemysl: 'I have become engaged to a very educated
girl from a very good house, I also live with her and am treated very
well by the people.'[45] Adele Schwarzbach suggested to her brother
interned in Simnik near Omsk 'if you have a pretty girl there, bring
her back with you. If, however, you can marry her there, do so and
stay there.'[46]

On a certain level it was clear to the censors that these relationships were not a political or military act. The head of the GZNB
censorship was even asked whether there was a specific Austrian
law that these marriages break.[47] Still, the increasing number of
reported marriages in the years 1916–17 and the presumably much
greater number of non-matrimonial relationships tipped the scale
toward characterizing them as *Vaterlandsflucht* (fleeing the fatherland). Moreover, the mood expressed in many of these letters
reflected a longing to end the war and return to normality. Julius
Marxiser wrote home in October 1917 from a camp near Tomsk:

> I would like to inform you that I married a Japanese woman here. I am
> doing well. I thought to myself, I am here already three years in captivity,
> why shouldn't I make my life more pleasant when I can? At home nobody
> really cares what happens here to the good soldiers, even the state takes
> care of no one. [48]

The February 1917 revolution in Russia brought with it a more
lax regime within POW camps and allowed prisoners greater interaction with the Russian population (see above Chapter 3). This was
accompanied by increasing efforts to recruit POWs to anti-Habsburg
units, and greater contacts between prisoners and various socialist
organizations. Since the GZNB had even before 1917 a broad, vague
definition of 'disloyalty', it regarded these new developments with
considerable apprehension. The increasing willingness of Austro-

Figure 4.4: Two wedding photographs showing POWs with their new Russian wives.

Source: Kriegsarchiv, Vienna.

Hungarian POWs to write with little restraint and express their opinions frankly, 'as though there is no censorship and no avenging justice' (according to mortified words of the Czech language censor Carl Ritter von Eisenstein), worked to confirm pre-existing suspicions vis-à-vis the prisoners.[49] General Max Ronge, the head of the Intelligence Bureau in the AOK, thought that a considerable number of POWs had been infected in Russia by the 'Bolshevik bacillus', and warned that 'what awaits returning POWs [*Heimkehrer*] is not a jubilant welcome but a thorough examination of heart and conscience.'[50] Thus, when Austro-Hungarian POWs began returning from Russia in the winter of 1917–18 a restrictive repatriation system had been set up as a 'prophylactic political device'.[51]

The fear and distrust of the POWs had short and long term consequences.

First, it added unnecessary hardship to the lives of about 600,000 POWs, who had spent between two and four years in Russian camps and who returned home before Austria-Hungary disintegrated in the fall of 1918. The justification proceedings against them yielded, according to official data of the Austro-Hungarian War Ministry, relatively few cases of 'unjustified behavior'.[52]

Second, the series of large-scale mutinies that broke out among Austro-Hungarian reserve units in the spring and the summer of 1918, in which returning POWs played a prominent role, was sparked most probably by the restrictive policies and rough treatment towards the *Heimkehrer*. Thus, if the mutinies did indeed constitute an important milestone in the break-up of the Habsburg monarchy – as most historians writing on the subject agree – they were triggered primarily by the miscalculations and perceived fears of the Austro-Hungarian military authorities.[53] These fears were the outcome of pre-war prejudices against certain nationalities as well as the manner in which the GZNB interpreted the opinions and behavior of prisoners in Russia.

Third, the narrow definition of 'patriotism' and the broad definition of 'disloyalty', adopted by the GZNB, demanded from POWs passivity, self-sacrifice and uncritical parroting of official slogans. This attitude contradicted four decades of efforts to turn, in the words of Eric Hobsbawm, 'subjects into citizens' and to win over their loyalty.[54] By doing so, I shall argue in Chapter 6, the censorship failed to recognize a real attachment to the Habsburg state that found expression in many of the letters. This perhaps fell short of the mark of what the head of the Department of POW Affairs in the Austro-Hungarian War Ministry – Ernst Streeruwitz – described as the proper behavior of 'the good and loyal prisoner', but it did attest to a sense of citizenship and a fundamental willingness to support the state.[55]

Notes

1. Streeruwitz was the head of the political section of Department 10.Kgf (the department in charge of POW affairs in the Austro-Hungarian War Ministry). He was a prominent Christian Social politician during the Austrian First Republic and served as Chancellor in 1928. These lines were published in 1931 but originate in a manuscript he wrote during the war and edited immediately after it. Ernst Streeruwitz, 'Der Umsturz in Rußland und die Kriegsgefangenen', in Hans Weiland and Leopold Kern (eds) *In Feindeshand: Die Gefangenschaft im Weltkriege in Einzeldarstellungen*, vol. 1, pp. 269–70.

2. The North German Confederacy, for example, fielded 1,200,000 soldiers in 1870, twice as many soldiers as Napoleon had led into Russia and fifteen times more than the largest of the eighteenth century's armies. Michael Howard, *War in European History*, Oxford, 1975, p. 99. See Also, John Keegan, *The Face of Battle: A Study of Agincourt, Waterloo and the Somme*; John Keegan, *A History of Warfare*, pp. 359–66.

3. István Deák, *Beyond Nationalism: A Social and Political History of the Habsburg Officer Corps 1848–1918*; Gunther Rothenberg, *The Army of Francis Joseph*, West Lafayette IN: Purdue University Press, Indiana, 1976.

4. On the development of these negative means in modern society and on the role of the military see Michel Foucault, *Discipline and Punish: The Birth of the Prison*, New York: Vintage Books, 1979.

5. Eugen Weber, *Peasants into Frenchmen: The Modernization of Rural France, 1870–1914*, Stanford CA: Stanford University Press, 1976, p. 298.

6. These local identities needed first either to be weakened or hierarchically intertwined with larger and more abstract forms of identification. In imperial Germany, for example, as Alon Confino has recently shown, the notion of *Heimat* bridged the local and collective levels, representing interchangeably a locality, a region or the entire German nation. This hierarchical extension of identities could proceed more smoothly in states such as France and Germany whose self-definition was that of a nation state. Through membership in the nation (and because the state was the patrimony of the nation) every citizen became an heir to the sacred territory of the state, which in turn conferred a powerful sense of belonging and obligation. Consequently, utilizing fatherland rhetoric to motivate a reserve-based army and expecting unconditional loyalty made considerable sense in the context of a nation state. Alon Confino, *The Nation as a Local Metaphor: Württemberg, Imperial Germany and National Memory 1871–1918*, Chapel Hill NC: University of North Carolina, 1997, part 2. See also Celia Applegate, *A Nation of Provincials: The German Idea of Heimat*, Berkeley CA: University of California Press, 1990; Eric Hobsbawm, *Nations and Nationalism since 1780: Programme, Myth Reality*, Cambridge: Cambridge University Press, 1990, chapter 3.

7. Oscar Jaszi, *The Dissolution of the Habsburg Monarchy*, Chicago: University of Chicago Press, 1929; quoted from Phoenix Books edition 1964, p. 436.

8. 'Imperial loyalties' denote in this work 'loyalty to the Habsburg monarchy'. What each individual understood by loyalty to the Habsburg monarchy is a subject that still needs to be examined in depth. This work aims to contribute to this investigation. The usage of 'empire' and 'imperial' in conjunction with Austria-Hungary is not unproblematic, but for lack of a better alternative is used throughout this work. See Karen Barkey and Mark von Hagen (eds), *After Empire: Multiethnic Societies and Nation Building: The Soviet-Union and the Russian, Ottoman and Habsburg Empires*, New York, 1997. Also, increasing attention has been paid recently to the meaning

of these July and August crowds. It is possible to identify two *loci* of debate regarding the question of war enthusiasm: first, the question of how widespread this 'enthusiasm' really was. Does the fact that thousands of people gathered in a public sphere mean that the population at large greeted the war with enthusiasm. J. J. Becker's research regarding France and most recently Niall Ferguson's *The Pity of War* (and his argument regarding 'the myth of war enthusiasm') raised doubts regarding the widely accepted view of the 'enthusiatic crowds'. Second, Ferguson and even more so Peter Fritzsche analyzed the meanings of these public gatherings from the perspective of various participants. Interestingly, both begin their examination with Hitler's participation in such a public demonstration. Fritzsche's work is particularly interesting vis-à-vis German working-class public gatherings. See, Peter Fritzsche, *Germans into Nazis*, Cambridge MA.: Harvard University Press, 1998; Niall Ferguson's *The Pity of War: Explaining World War I*, New York: Basic Books, 1998; Jean-Jacques Becker, *The Great War and the French People*, Leamington Spa: Berg, 1985.

9. Holger Herwig, *The First World War: Germany and Austria-Hungary 1914–1918*, London: Arnold, 1997, pp. 33–7; Manfried Rauchensteiner, *Der Tod des Doppeladlers: Österreich-Ungarn und der Erste Weltkrieg*, Graz, Wien, Köln: Verlag Styria, 1993; Z. A. B. Zeman, *The Break-Up of the Habsburg Empire 1914–1918: A Study in National and Social Revolution*, London: Oxford University Press, 1961, pp. 42–44.

10. In contrast to the extensive theoretical literature on nationalism, written in the past two decades, there is relatively little on patriotism. See, for example: Hubertus Jahn, *Patriotic Culture in Russia during World War I*, Ithaca and London: Cornell University Press, 1995, introduction; Eric Hobsbawm, *Nations and Nationalism since 1780: Programme, Myth Reality*, Cambridge: Cambridge University Press, 1990, Chapter 3; Carlton Hayes, *Essays on Nationalism*, New York: Macmillan, 1937.

11. Österreichisches Staatsarchiv (ÖStA)/Kriegsarchiv (KA)/Armeeoberkommando (AOK) 1916/ Gemeinsames Zentralnachweisbureau des Roten Kreuzes-Auskunftstelle für Kriegsgefangene (GZNB)/ Kart:3745/Akt:4117/ 2. POW Majer Freund to his wife Rachela in Mosciska Galicia, 30 August 1916: 'I am sick of Jacob Eisler. He is living here with a Christian woman and wants to go to America with her. I want you to tell this to his wife Beily.'

12. According to official Austrian figures there were 1,861,000 enemy soldiers in the Habsburg monarchy. Of them the two largest groups were Russian POWs (1,269,000) and Italian POWs (369,600).

13. However, the deteriorating political conditions in Russia reduced the flow of mail to a trickle in the Spring of 1918 and from the summer of 1918 and onwards mail could be sent back home only in convoluted or makeshift ways.

14. 'Statistik über Sicherheit und Schnelligkeit verschiediener Routen für die Gefangenschaft nach Russland', AOK (1915)/GZNB/Kart:3737/Akt. 2965.

15. The only study of Austro-Hungarian World War I censorship is the Ph.D. dissertation written by Gustav Spann, *Zensur in Österreich während des I. Welt Krieges 1914–1918*, Dissertation zur Erlangung des Doktorsgrades an der philosophischen Fakultät der Universität Wien, Vienna, 1972.

16. The three were Budapest, Vienna and Feldkirch in Vorarlberg.

17. Spann, p. 145.

18. AOK (1915) GZNB, kart:3734 akt: 2438ad. The languages processed by the GZNB included the following: German, Russian, Italian, Czech, Polish, Slovak, Slovenian, Ukrainian, Serb, Croat, Romanian, 'Bessarabian' (today Moldavian), Hungarian, French, English, Swedish, Hebrew, Yiddish, Ladino (or Spaniolit the language of Sephardic Jews especially in the Balkans), Spanish, Lithuanian, Estonian, Latvian, Bulgarian, Greek, Albanian, Arabic, Turkish, Persian, Cherkessian, Finnish, and occasional letters in Chinese, Japanese, and various Caucasian and Central Asian languages. See Heinrich von Raabl-Werner, 'Oesterreich-Ungarns offizielle Kriegsgefangenenfürsorge', *In Feindeshand*, vol. 2, p. 325.

19. At times, these complaints had a touch of the absurd: some censors were reported to experience 'insanity fits', others had 'limited thinking abilities', while there were complaints of 'bums' (*Galgenvögel*), and even criminals. See: Spann, pp. 154–5.

20. AOK (1915)/GZNB/Kart.3729/Akt.1405, 1405ad.

21. 'Instruktion für des Gemeinsamen Zentralnachweisebureau für Kriegsgefangene', AOK (1914/1915)/GZNB/Kart.3726/Akt.13.

22. This card catalog no longer exists today, so it is unclear how extensive it was. It is clear, however, that many types of offenses were deemed suspicious and resulted in landing a person on the list of suspect POWs. They contained patently treasonous acts such as volunteering to fight against Austria-Hungary. They could also contain insults directed against the person of the emperor, suspicious economic activity to letters expressing happiness with being a POW.

23. AOK (1914/1915)/GZNB/Kart.3726/Akt.44 page III.

24. Ibid.

25. Quotes from: Jonathan Vance, *Objects of Concern: Canadian Prisoners of War through the Twentienth Century*, Vancouver: UBC Press, 1994, p. 26 On the AOK's predilection to look for collective scapegoats see above Chapter 1. See also Graydon Tunstall, *Planning for War against Russia and Serbia: Austro-Hungarian and German Military Strategies, 1871–1914*, New York: Columbia University Press, 1993, Chapters 7 and 8; Richard Plaschka, 'Zur Vorgeschichte des Überganges von Einheiten des Infantrieregiments Nr. 28 an der russischen Front 1915', *Österreich und Europa: Festschrift für Hugo Hantsch zum 70. Geburtstag*, Graz, 1965, pp. 455–64.

26. See John Keegan, *The First World War*, Chapter 2; J. M. Winter, 'The Generals' War', *The Experience of World War I*, London, 1988, pp. 70–101.

27. GZNB Kart. 3728, Akt 1385. The GZNB assumed that the language of a letter was an indication of the national identification of the writer.

Although in most cases this assumption was probably true, it was not always the case. There were POWs who spoke several languages fluently and who used them intermittently, and there were languages such as Magyar and Yiddish, which POWs preferred in many cases not to use. The former because of a dearth of Magyar-speaking Russian censors, which resulted in logjams and delays, and the latter because it was usually prohibited by the Russian military authorities.

28. 'Böhmische Zensurgruppe A. 7. Spezialbericht: Einige Schilderungen über die Situation bei der Gefangennahme', AOK (1914/1915)/GZNB/Kart.3726/Akt.630.

29. Emphasis in the original.

30. AOK (1915)/GZNB/Kart.3728/Akt.1385, Section E-3.

31. Due to the paucity of letters written in the Hungarian language, it is not clear how many letters were used or whether this conclusion had been reached by another method (family names, place of origin etc.).

32. AOK (1915)/GZNB/Kart.3731/Akt.1746 These letters were most probably collected for propaganda purposes, even though I found no indication of such usage.

33. Ukrainische Zensur-Gruppe, ibid.

34. 'Meldung von 17. Oktober 1916', Polnische Zensur-gruppe, Ibid letter # 1.

35. István Deák, Mark Cornwall, Rudi Jeřábek and others have made the point that not all the enemies of Austria-Hungary produced the same emotional response from k.u.k. soldiers. Italy it is argued was universally and vehemently disliked, Serbia was disliked by most soldiers while the attitude toward Russia was more ambivalent. This is a very interesting thesis that needs to be examined empirically.

36. Interestingly the files of the GZNB do not contain 'patriotic letters' written in German. There are letters in Hungarian, Ukrainian, Polish, Czech and Slovak and a couple of example in Slovene and Serbian. It is not clear whether letters in other languages were not collected or simply not preserved.

37. 'Kostroma, Kgf. Offizier Seweryn Kisielewski an Sofie Kisielewska in Krakau' 22 November 1915, AOK (1915)/GZNB/Kart.3731/Akt.1746, patriotische Briefe, letter #8.

38. Rusai Janos in Astrachan, 25 February 1916, Ungarische Zensurgruppe, Fäh. N. Csike Gábor Tobolsk, 1 September 1916. AOK (1915)/GZNB/Kart. 3731/Akt.1746.

39. AOK (1915)/GZNB/Kart:3731/Akt:1746.

40. 'Patriotische Briefe der slovakischen Kriegsgefangenen', AOK (1915)/ GZNB/Kart:3731/Akt:1746, p. 1.

41. For the Czech language censors it was probably inconceivable that Czech national motifs would be accepted by the AOK as anything but expressions of separatism and disloyalty. It mattered little in this respect that until May 1917 only a tiny minority of the Czech speaking POWs in Russia (7,273 out of an estimated 250,000, or 2.9 per cent) volunteered for the

Czech Legion and committed themselves unequivocally to a separate Czech state. Josef Kalvoda, 'Czech and Slovak Prisoners of War in Russia during the War and Revolution', in S. Williamson and Peter Pastor (eds) *Essays on World War I: Origins and Prisoners of War*, p. 223.

42. Such as the following letter in Italian written on 30 July 1915 by POW Antonio Vedovalli in Omsk to Erminia Vedovalli in Breguzzo South Tyrol: 'These German barbarians have certainly brought misery upon you. But God knows how to punish these dogs. With my friend I am waiting to be transported to my new fatherland, sunny and beloved Italy where I will enlist and perhaps fight against these arrogant Germans and liberate our villages.' AOK (1916) GZNB Kart: 3743, Akt: 3880/1, p. 2.

43. The language distribution of the letters was the following: 199 (47 per cent) in Czech, 73 in Polish (17.5 per cent), fifty-five in German (13.1 per cent) many of them appear to be from Jewish POWs, thirty-one in Ukrainian, fourteen were written in Slovak, twelve in Serbian, ten in Russian, eight in Hungarian, three in Romanian, three in Slovene, one respectively in Croat, Italian and Yiddish.

44. 'Sonderbericht', Slovenische Zensurgruppe.

45. Zensurgruppe Deutsch C., Gruppenleiter Oblt. Beran March 12 1917, AOK (1916)/GZNB/kart.3745/Akt.4117.

46. Ibid.

47. Ibid, Böhmische Zensurgruppe B. 11 July 1916.

48. Ibid.

49. R. v. Eisenstein, 'Die nationalpolitische Bewegung der Tschechen (Oktoberbericht)', Referat XIV/19 6 November 1917, AOK (1917)/GZNB/kart:3755/Akt 4871, p. 1.

50. Quoted from Hannes Leidinger and Verena Moritz, 'Österreich-Ungarn und die Heimkehrer aus russischer Kriegsgefangenschaft im Jahr 1918', *Österreich in Geschichte und Literatur*, 6 (291) (1997), p. 394.

51. Otto Wassermair, *Die Meutereien der Heimkehrer aus russischer Kriegsgefangenschaft bei den Ersatzkörpern der k.u.k. Armee im Jahre 1918*, Unpublished Dissertation (University of Vienna, 1968); see also Chapter 6.

52. Out of the 120,272 POWs who returned home by May 1918, the behavior of only 1,620 could not be 'justified': 514 *Heimkehrer* were labeled 'suspect of disloyal activity' (no conclusive proof was found), whereas 603 returnees deserted from their reserve units before their investigations could be completed (and of course may have deserted for a variety of reasons). See Otto Wassermair, p. 88.

53. Quoted from Hannes Leidinger and Verena Moritz, 'Österreich-Ungarn und die Heimkehrer aus russischer Kriegsgefangenschaft im Jahr 1918', *Österreich in Geschichte und Literatur*, 6 (291) (1997), pp. 385-403; Herwig, pp. 364-73; Rauchensteiner op.cit, ch.24; Richard Plaschka, Arnold Suppan and Horst Haselsteiner, *Innere Front: Militärassistenz, Widerstand und Umsturz in der Donaumonarchie*, Vienna, 1974, vol. 2.

54. Hobsbawm, *Nations and Nationalism*, p. 88.

55. See the words of, the head of Abteilung 10.Kgf. in the Austro-Hungarian Kriegsministerium, Ernst Streeruwitz, on the first page of this chapter.

5

The Emperor's Clothes: The Austro-Hungarian POW Relief Effort

I do not know what impression I made on the prisoners, but I hope that at least they noted my good will.

Countess Nora Kinsky[1]

POW Relief in World War I: The Uniqueness of the Eastern Front

Prisoners of war are by definition 'in the power of the hostile government'.[2] The home state has usually no direct contact with its captive soldiers and can rely only on indirect means if it wishes to assist them. In case of inadequate treatment (or perceived inadequate treatment) a home government has three main courses of action.

It can opt for retaliatory measures against enemy POWs, hoping to convince the adversary's government to ameliorate conditions in its own camps. However, as the Austro-Hungarian superintendent Heinrich von Raabl-Weber had pointed out, retaliatory measures often backfire and create a spiral of counter-retaliation, counter-counter-retaliation and an overall deterioration of conditions. Germany and Russia were embroiled in 1916 in a retaliatory cycle on the issue of working conditions on the Murman railway, which resulted in a decline in living conditions for Russian and German POW officers (and no improvement for the rank-and-file POWs who worked on the line).[3]

In the same vein, a home government can attempt to stir up national and international public opinion by publishing accounts of life in enemy captivity, accompanied whenever possible by visual (ideally photographic) representations. During World War I there were occasional official publications about the fate of the prisoners, but they seem to have been a low priority for all the warring countries.

161

The first collection of POW letters was published in Austria-Hungary no earlier than 1917. Its editor, Sil-Vara (Geza Silberer), bemoaned the low priority given to the plight of the prisoners even after all other aspects of the war had been exhaustively covered. He therefore strove to describe to the reading public the prisoners' 'first ride into misery, the compulsory transport of the disarmed, the torture of powerlessness, the humiliation of those without rights and the vegetation in the ensuing slavery'.[4] Likewise, occasional posters published during the Great War often juxtaposed the suffering of prisoners of war while presenting the enemy in cruel and inhuman light. It appeared, however, that the propaganda aims of the home country – especially the wish to reinforce negative stereotypes of the enemy – took precedence over creating an awareness for the conditions of POWs.[5]

An alternative approach, which as a general rule has more chances to make an immediate impact on the well-being of prisoners, is reaching an agreement with the enemy government on the distribution of relief. This option requires three necessary preconditions to materialize: first, it requires a shift in the perception of the war from something that would be resolved quickly to a longer affair, in which imminent repatriation of prisoners is unlikely; second, it requires that **both** belligerent governments see some moral and political value in reaching such an agreement; third, it requires that neutral governments and benevolent institutions (most often the Red Cross) become involved as intermediaries. In the case of Austria-Hungary, the realization that the end of the war was nowhere in sight occurred in the winter of 1914/1915 after four months of unsuccessful combat against Serbia and Russia.[6] Moreover, the growing dependence on German military and economic support, coupled with Italy's declaration of war on the Habsburg Monarchy (but not yet on Germany) in May 1915, significantly reduced the ability of Austro-Hungarian leaders to opt out of the war if they so wished. The realization that the war was there to stay had been accompanied in the Austro-Hungarian *Kriegsministerium* by the awareness that all was not well with its POWs in Russia. Whereas during the first few months of the war POWs were generally expressing content with their treatment and living conditions in captivity,[7] a noticeable deterioration began taking place in the winter of 1914–15. Typhus and cholera outbreaks were reported in a few camps and the number of letters containing praise decreased rapidly.[8] The Swedish Red Cross nurse, Elsa Brändström, reported that more than half the prisoners brought in the winter of 1914/1915 to the fortress (*gorodok*) in Novo-Nikolaevsk (today Novosibirsk) died of typhus and other infectious diseases. Prisoners in other internment facilities wrote home about extreme overcrowding and complaints about lack of sufficient clothing were becoming commonplace. Soldiers who went to the war in their summer uniforms found themselves suddenly dealing with a Russian winter without appropriate apparel. Willi Keiner, for example, a young German private wrote back home in November 1914:

> The food here is much better than I thought, we receive bacon, soup, beef, eggs, tea, cigarettes . . . but it is getting very cold all around us and everyone tells us through signs that our uniforms are just too thin . . . twenty men went to sleep in a circle, trying hard to keep our wet feet covered with hay. We fell asleep overly tired and when we woke up we found that only our heads were sticking out of the hay. The [Russian] soldiers had covered us, so we would not freeze during the night.[9]

Like the writer Egon Erwin Kisch,[10] most Austro-Hungarian soldiers did not bring with them much spare clothing and what they had was in many cases lost or stolen when they became prisoners. According to Elsa Brändström, in the beginning of 1915 only very few prisoners had overcoats, 60 per cent of them had worn-out shoes and 20 per cent had no shoes whatsoever, requiring them to wrap 'their feet in straw and rags'.[11]

The grievances of Austro-Hungarian and German POWs in Russia and the complaints of Russian POWs in Austria-Hungary and Germany, expedited discussions of a proposal for POW relief which had been sitting on the desks of the respective foreign ministries since September 1914.[12] According to the proposal, material aid from the home country would be distributed among its captive soldiers, and Red Cross delegations would be permitted to inspect POW camps in Russia, Germany and Austria-Hungary. The delegations would be permitted to talk directly to prisoners and be allowed to distribute money, clothing and food according to their judgment.[13]

What makes the relief action on the eastern front unique in twentieth century warfare was the inclusion of Red Cross nurses from the home country in the inspection teams (alongside neutral delegates and representatives of the captor state). The German historian, Reinhard Nachtigal, argued that only the 'old-European, aristocratic solidarity which linked three warring empires' could have enabled such a POW relief effort, and indeed all the nurses sent by the home state were aristocratic women from some of the most prominent families of three monarchies.[14] The decision to send aristocratic women to distribute relief was rooted in nineteenth-century social thinking about the role of upper-class women in charitable endeavors. Yet, as Heinrich von Raabl Werner explained, these aristocratic nurses were expected to do more than just embody a maternal and caring aspect of their patriarchal regimes:

> They [i.e. Austro-Hungarian nurses] were expected to provide concrete suggestions for improvement . . . negotiate directly with the authorities . . . defeat strong prejudices which gained a foothold [among the prisoners] through systematic agitation! In addition to strengthening the spiritual constitution of the prisoners and intensifying their connection to the homeland through visitations and distribution.[15]

As agents of their state these women were expected to fulfil funct-ions far and beyond their official designations as 'nurses'. Many of them left detailed accounts of their struggle to accomplish various aspects of their mission at the same time, of which the most fascin-ating was Nora Kinsky's *Russian Diary* published posthumously in 1976.[16] These accounts supplement the existing bureaucratic and diplomatic files, and the numerous reports of neutral delegates (primarily Swedish, Danish and American observers). Moreover, through the activity of the GZNB censorship it is possible to look also at how Austro-Hungarian POWs received and interpreted their state's relief effort. Thus, the Austro-Hungarian POW relief effort provides a unique opportunity to study the mutual expectations of subject and (multi-national) state. This chapter will focus on the actions and expectations of the Austro-Hungarian state and its agents, while chapter six below will turn to the expectations of the prisoners themselves as reflected in their correspondence.

The Austro-Hungarian POW Material Relief

From the perspective of the Austro-Hungarian *Kriegsministerium* there were two distinct components to the POW relief program. The first focused on material relief and was aimed at relieving the most acute shortages in clothing and medication. The second centered on a series of visitations and was geared toward boosting morale, reporting and correcting ill-treatment and assessing the Habsburg loyalty of the Austro-Hungarian POWs in Russia. While the first component was handled primarily by the Swedish Red Cross Society and to a lesser extent by a number of other intermediaries (for example the American YMCA organization, the Danish Red Cross and the POW Relief Action in Tientsin China), the second component was entrusted primarily to nurses from Austria-Hungary under the umbrella organization of the Danish Red Cross.[17] It is crucial to remember, however, that although Austro-Hungarian *Kriegsminister-ium* officials differentiated between 'material relief' and 'visitations', the prisoners themselves did not always do so. As will be discussed in detail in chapter six, Austro-Hungarian POWs expressed amazement at times that 'their' nurses could come all the way from Austria-Hungary and bring them very little or nothing at all.

In terms of actual material support, the Austro-Hungarian relief effort fell well short of the needs of its prisoners, although, in absolute numbers it was significant. Between October 1915 and March 1918, the Dual Monarchy dispatched via Sweden forty-three trains (each of twenty-eight cars) carrying a total of 375,000 uniforms, 1,195,000 pairs of underwear, 300,000 blankets, 150,000 pairs of boots and 5,000 Red Cross Packets.[18] Thus, theoretically at least (and as in any relief effort on such a magnitude there are differences between plan and praxis), every sixth Habsburg POW was supposed to receive a new uniform, every second prisoner a new pair of underwear, every seventh a new blanket and one out of thirteen POWs was supposed to obtain a new pair of boots. In addition, Austria-Hungary sent between 1915–18 medicinal supplies worth eight million Austrian crowns to Russia and food worth 14,768,365 Austrian crowns. Altogether, the official aid sent directly from the Dual Monarchy to its POWs was worth 85,572,990 Austrian crowns or roughly forty-two crowns per prisoner.[19] Heinrich von Raabl-Werner, emphasized after the war 'that only a person who takes into consideration the terrible clothing shortages at home could truly appreciate the difficulties of organizing such an effort; it is alone justified by the fact that it saved thousands from the Russian death'.[20] Austria-Hungary financed also the costs of American, Danish and Swedish envoys who represented the interests of Austria-Hungary in Russia. All in all, Elsa Brändström stated that 361,306,300 crowns were transferred from the coffers of the Dual Monarchy for POW relief (which after adjustment for inflation and currency rate changes amounted to 120,515,900 Swedish crowns).

Despite the well-documented material shortages in Austria-Hungary during the war and despite the fact that Raabl-Werner was

Figure 5.1: Distribution of aid at the Khabarovsk camp September 1916.

Source: Kriegsarchiv, Vienna.

without doubt correct in saying that thousands of POW lives were saved by this help, the POW relief effort was still relatively parsimonious. According to Holger Herwig, already during the first year and a half of the war (August 1914–December 1915) Austria-Hungary spent an estimated 20-22 billion crowns on financing its military endeavor.[21] The funds assigned thus for POW relief were just a drop in the water in context of wartime expenditures. The inadequacy of the Austro-Hungarian relief effort was highlighted by imperial Germany's relief effort which was relatively much more generous. Germany sent via Sweden 131,000 uniforms, 50,000 blankets and 46,500 boots which ensured that many of its 167,000 POWs in Russia would get some kind of state-sponsored relief. According to Elsa Brändström, Germany provided a total of 53,444,900 Swedish crowns for its POWs in Russia, which was 4.4 times more per capita than the Habsburg monarchy provided. Moreover, German citizens sent more money to their POWs in Russia than k.u.k. citizens (15,207,000 vs. 8,115,000) and purchased more Red Cross parcels in Denmark. Altogether, German citizens bought over 100,000 standard Red Cross parcels for German POWs in Russia compared to a paltry 5,000 parcels purchased by Austro-Hungarian citizens. According to Johann von der Wülbecke, a German NCO in the East Siberian camp of Berezovka, the discrepancy in the number of parcels created 'ugly confrontations' with the Austro-Hungarian POWs who demanded an equal share of the parcels.[22]

The material relief coming from Germany created two standards of care among prisoners of war in Russia: a modest Austro-Hungarian one and a relatively generous German one. It indicated both symbolically and practically that Germany cared more about its wounded soldiers in captivity than the Habsburg monarchy did. The idea that the state ought to care about its wounded and captive soldiers was relatively a new one in European history. John Hutchinson, in his study of the International Red Cross movement, traces this idea to the second half of the nineteenth century and places it in the context of the emergence of national armies, the beginning of mass conscription in most of Europe, the dissemination of graphic portrayals of warfare by new technologies (photography and telegraph) and the increasing influence of bourgeois sensibilities (most importantly those about civility and civilization).[23] Yet, despite the emergence of this idea, the actual agreements that were being hammered out in the decades preceding World War I dealt primarily with the obligations of belligerent states towards other countries' subjects (military or civilian).[24] What the home country owed its own wounded and captive soldiers was left for each state to decide and act upon. Since there was no major war in Europe in the four and half decades prior to World War I and no prolonged war since the conclusion of the Napoleonic wars, soldiers simply did not know what their states would do for them if they were to be captured by the enemy. Thus, when Germany and its citizenry sent more aid to its captive soldiers, it de facto defined a threshold of caring that Austria-Hungary failed to reach.

Relief distribution in Russia was hampered also by serious logistical difficulties. The Swedish Red Cross, which handled most of the on-the-spot relief distribution, was always significantly understaffed. There were never more than forty-eight Swedish Red Cross delegates in Russia at any given time, dealing with all aspects of relief administration for both Austro-Hungarian and German POWs. Altogether, between the years 1915–1920, seventy-seven different Swedish Red Cross officials were involved in apportioning relief, led by Elsa Brändström, the daughter of the Swedish Ambassador in Petrograd.

The Swedish delegates were in charge of obtaining sufficient rolling stock, despite the debilitating railroad problems in Russia (this was accomplished mostly via their connections in the Finnish Ministry of Public Works). They arranged the passing of trains through customs inspections. The Swedes had to deal with systematic harassment along the train route from bureaucrats, railroad employees and guards, who expected to receive a cut of the cargo. They were expected also to acquaint themselves with a baffling and constantly changing array of railroad regulations in Russia in an increasingly chaotic situation (especially from 1917 and onwards). Most importantly, the Swedish Red Cross delegates had 'to supply the places whose need was greatest'.[25] In the first two years of the operation, Swedish delegates would travel from camp to camp with whole trainloads and distribute relief individually to every needy prisoner. The perception among the Swedes was that relief left in bulk in each location would be taken by Russian camp personnel or by POWs with connections, rather than reaching those who required it most. This system slowed down the operation considerably but ensured that relief would get to its intended recipients. Gradually a different system was devised: Swedish delegates would be sent to individual districts within Russia and open office in the largest town. From this office the delegate would contact POW camps, internment facilities and labor details in the region, and learn about shortages and specials needs. With the permission of Russian military authorities, relief committees composed of POW doctors and other prisoners would be established in camps to determine the specific local needs. The Swedish delegates worked now primarily through these intermediaries, supporting them also with funds intended to erect communal projects such as hospitals, baths, kitchens, disinfecting stations and workshops. According to Brändström, the attitude of the local Russian military authorities toward the Swedish delegates was a combination of suspicion and respect. At least until the Civil War there was tolerance for the activity of these 'foreigners', without which the whole operation would have been impossible.[26]

It was the Swedish Red Cross that gained more recognition, from POWs than any other relief agency. Although understaffed it appeared ubiquitous and steadfastly present in Russia through war and Civil War. Elsa Brändström, in particular, achieved almost a cult status among the German-speaking prisoners, which only grew with her interwar charitable activity among POW veterans and their families. Nicknamed the 'Angel of Siberia' by the prisoners, Brändström became, in the words of Hans Weiland, 'a symbol of sisterly love, noble humanity and self-sacrifice and willingness to help'.[27] A poem written in camp of Achinsk and a picture based on it portrayed Brändström as the sun piercing the darkness of captivity:

The Visit

A little word going by,
A greeting, a praise a friendly smile
Such as we've never experienced in awhile . . .
Sun! You can make us feel glee,
When after a dark night it's you we see.

Hallowed is our whole day,
Because we met you in the morning;
The need is eased, the misery fades away
With you we're again, blissfully hoping . . .
Come again! Come when difficulties sway!

Written by POW Viktor Buchgraber, Achinsk
Dedicated to Elsa Brändström [28]

During the early 1920s Brändström was considered a leading candidate for a Nobel Peace prize, the first women to be so considered. Now largely forgotten, Elsa Brändström still awaits the first scholarly treatment of her life and work, and an attempt to disentangle myth from reality.

Alongside the Swedish Red Cross, material relief reached the prisoners in Russia via two additional channels: Elsa von Hanneken's Relief Commitee for Military and Civilian Prisoners, which was located in Tientsin China (today Tianjin), and the American YMCA organization. Elsa von Hanneken's *Hilfsaktion für Kriegs- und Zivilgefangene in Tientsin* was an impromptu benevolent society, which grew in size and importance during the war. Established originally in October 1914 by German and Austro-Hungarian residents of Tientsin, the committee relied on Elsa von Hanneken's extensive connections among the colonial forces in China and obtained the official backing of the American Red Cross society (until February 1917). While relying initially on privately raised funds, the Tientsin committee became in the spring of 1915 a conduit through which Germany and Austria-Hungary channeled relief funds. With these funds the *Hilfsaktion* purchased clothing, food and medications, and

Figure 5.2: 'Is the sun finally coming into our lives? The visit of Elsa Brändström in an infirmary barrack.'

Source: *In Feindeshand*

supported prisoners in eastern Siberia and the Russian pacific maritime region (the Primorskaia district). The 'odd Chinese clothes' became the butt of many jokes among the POWs, but in three and a half years of activity the committee managed to forward an estimated 180,000 of these funny uniforms to needy prisoners (see Figure 5.3). Between 200–400 individual letters of request would arrive daily in Tientsin making, according to Elsa von Henekken, all kinds of requests: 'one wanted green boots, another silk shirts, many money, blankets, lamps, a thousand of small requests which we attempted to fulfil'. [29] All in all, Germany sent money worth 1,716,800 Swedish crowns to Tientsin while Austria-Hungary transferred funds worth 3,527,000 Swedish crowns.

Until the entry of the US into the war in 1917, the American YMCA was one of the most active organizations pursuing relief work among the prisoners of war. It was active in most of the belligerents,

Figure 5.3: Prisoners in Chinese clothing from Tientsin.

Source: Elsa Brändström, Unter Kriegsgefangenen in Rußland und Sibirien, 1914–1920.

receiving the endorsement and at times also the financial support of home governments (it did rely on its own resources for the most part). Combining philanthropic and missionary work, the YMCA focused its effort on spiritual and communal projects for the prisoners like establishing churches, kitchens, workshops, libraries and sports and music facilities. In Russia the activity of the YMCA focused on the large POW camps in East and Central Siberia, where they visited and supported sixty-eight camps. In its region of concentration the American YMCA served as a reliable channel for transferring private money and correspondence to the prisoners of war.[30] It is not clear how much Austro-Hungarian governmental money was actually allocated to the YMCA for its activity, but it seems very little.[31]

The Austro-Hungarian Nurses

The Mission of the Swedish Red Cross – and other charitable organizations – was complex in terms of logistics but simple in terms of its
goals. The Swedish delegates were there first and foremost to
alleviate the physical – and to a certain degree also the mental –
suffering of the POWs. On the other hand, the mission of the Austro-
Hungarian nurses was not as logistically challenging but much more
complex in terms of its goals. The Austro-Hungarian nurses were
expected to inspect camps (usually in a day or less for each camp),
press local Russian military authorities to rectify the most urgent
problems, distribute money and tobacco, assess the Habsburg loyalty
of the POWs and boost morale. If this was not enough, these nurses
were counted on to symbolize monarchical care by virtue of their
upper-class background and their gender. They were thus expected
to be exceptional in their personal abilities and qualities, and to know
how and when to use their patrician background and femininity.

The first round of visitations began in the fall of 1915 and included
three German and three Austro-Hungarian nurses. The three German
delgates – Countess Alexandrine Uexküll, Erika von Passow and
Magdalene von Walsleben – arrived in Russia already in October 1915
almost two months before their colleagues from the Dual Monarchy.
The Austro-Hungarian delegation had to wait until the final ratif-
ication of the visitation agreement by Russia and the Habsburg
monarchy, leaving Vienna for Russia on 10 November 1915. According to the criteria formulated by the *Kriegsministerium* each
delegate had to possess the following qualifications:[32]

1 She had to be a nurse.
2 She had to be able to converse in a few of the monarchy's languages
   in addition to German and French.
3 She had to be impeccably loyal to the Habsburg state, which
   meant being of an aristocratic background or being married to a
   career officer. In 1916 a qualification was added stating that the
   delegate should be unmarried.
4 She was prohibited from having relatives in Russian captivity
   (qualification added in 1916).

Interestingly, if one examines the background of the first Austro-
Hungarian delegates – and for that matter also the subsequent ones
– it is clear that they were **not** chosen because they matched the
official criteria. Countess Anna Revertera who headed the k.u.k.

contingent was selected due to her extensive Russian contacts: her mother was a Russian princess from the Buturlin family and her father served in the Austrian Legation in St Petersburg. Ilona von Rosty (born Countess Forgách) lobbied to be included in the delegation because her son was a POW officer in the camp of Krasnoyarsk. She was thus added as a representative of the Hungarian Red Cross and by extension of the Hungarian half of the monarchy. The only member of the delegation who actually possessed some experience as a nurse was Käthe von Mihalotzy, who had worked in the Vienna Radetzky Military Hospital from the beginning of the war. According to Mihalotzy, she was also told by the head of Austrian Red Cross Society, Baron Spieglfeld, that 'it was highly desirable that one of the three ladies selected for this mission would be an officer's wife'.[33] However, for Mihalotzy to leave for Russia raised a difficult dilemma: with her colonel husband at the front, she had to leave her daughters in Vienna for three months. She decided nonetheless to take upon herself this assignment as 'a great work of compassion'.[34]

Before leaving for Russia the delegation was briefed by Austro-Hungarian Red Cross and *Kriegsministerium* officials. Anna Revertera wrote a few years after the war that 'the information supplied before the departure . . . proved to be inadequate'.[35] In specific terms, the briefing included an introduction to the three Danish officers, who would accompany the nurses during their sojourn in Russia, a review of international law pertaining to the treatment of POWs, a brief synopsis of what was known about conditions in Russian POW camps and finally a visit to a few POW camps in Austria-Hungary to see how Russian prisoners were treated by the Dual Monarchy.[36] While the delegation was making its preparations to leave, reports appeared in newspapers regarding the trip and the three women were swarmed by relatives of POWs who presented them with letters and money to take to their loved ones in Russia. According to Käthe von Mihalotzy 'the many letters that we were expected to take, but which according to our instructions we were forced to decline, would have required a whole wagon just for themselves.'[37] Mihalotzy's poignant portrayal encapsulates the tensions embedded in the mission from its inception: on one side the expectations and anguish of the families of prisoners (and later on of the prisoners themselves), and on the other side the good will, limitations and weighty burden felt by the three hastily-trained delegates.

On 10 November 1915 the delegation took the train from Vienna to Berlin. In Berlin they were updated about the activities of the three

German nurses who were already in Russia and heard a lecture about the dietary needs of the prisoners (which included also a sample lunch of simulated prison food). News of their stay in Berlin circulated again among the families of POWs and once more they were inundated with requests to take letters and money to Russia.[38] From Berlin they traveled to Denmark, where they had an audience with the Danish queen and meetings with the Austro-Hungarian ambassador and his staff and with Danish Red Cross officials. Revertera, Mihalotzy and Rosty continued their journey via Sweden and Russian Finland to Petrograd where they arrived in the last week of November 1915.

In Petrograd the delegation was delayed a week and half due to the emergence of last-minute disagreements between Russia and Austria-Hungary. The two most important points of contention were whether the delegations would have to submit before leaving Petrograd a binding list of all the camps they intended to visit and whether the Austro-Hungarian nurses could themselves determine who would go to which part of Russia.[39] Anna Revertera described 'tempestuous meetings' with Russian officials and intensive behind-the-scenes negotiations needed to iron out these disagreements. The compromise reached in the beginning of December allowed the Austro-Hungarian delegations 'to visit all camps without having to submit pre-approved routes'.[40] As Revertera correctly pointed out, this leeway enabled the delegations to put camp commanders on their toes and could not have been achieved without having powerful people 'in the court, society and military authorities on our side'.[41] However, the Austro-Hungarian delegations were less successful in deciding their own areas of inspection and had to accept the Russian allocation: Ilona von Rosty was assigned to the Moscow and Kazan military districts, and received also the huge Siberian camp of Krasnoyarsk where her son was interned; Käthe von Mihalotzy was assigned the Turkestan military district and the large European camps in the Samara-Orenburg region; and Anna Revertera received the ridiculously large area of western and central Siberia (except the camp of Krasnoyarsk) and was expected to inspect it within eight weeks and return back to Petrograd.

All three nurses placed their main emphasis on reporting unsatisfactory material conditions in internment facilities. Due to extreme hurry they usually relied on the POW medical personnel among the prisoners to give them accurate description and 'to disregard strenuous efforts to throw dust in the eyes of the visitors'.[42] Käthe von Mihalotzy wrote that 'I reminded myself of a female general, but got quickly used to this idea, like so many other things in this not-so-easy assignment.'[43] As the Swedish and American inspectors before them, the delegates censured locations with deficient lodgings, inferior food and unfair wage practices for working POWs. Accompanied by a Danish and Russian officers, the nurses attempted to rectify some of the most grievous problems. In Totskoe, the worst POW camp in Russia, Mihalotzy's delegation bought clothing and blankets to alleviate the terrible shortages, and purchased crates of medical supplies from a local veterinarian.[44] The impression left on the nurses in some camps was devastating. Revertera felt revolted by the underground earth barracks prevalent in central Siberia and dreaded the physical and psychological impact they had on the prisoners. Mihalotzy stated that 'if I would live three lifetimes, I would still not forget the impressions [from Totskoe].'[45] According to the nurses, the Austro-Hungarian POWs always responded positively to their efforts to pull strings to amend shortcomings. Raabl-Werner thought that Revertera was especially adept in utilizing her personal connections including direct access to the governor of Siberia Sukhomlinov and to the Russian Stavka Chief, General Belaev.

However, the other goals of the mission proved to be more difficult for the delegates, particularly the distribution of money and 'charitable gifts' (*Liebesgaben*). The nurses brought with them approximately 4,500,000 Austrian crowns (about 1,800,000 Romanov rubles) for the purpose of on-the-spot allocation.[46] The Austro-Hungarian *Kriegsministerium* preferred that money would not be given to individual POWs but rather allocated for communal projects in each camp. If distributed individually, officer POWs were to receive between 30 rubles and 50 rubles as a loan (to be paid back by their families in Austria-Hungary), while the rank-and-file were to receive between three and five rubles as gifts. Regarding ensigns, cadets, one year volunteers and NCOs each nurse could determine whether to treat them as separate groups deserving special consideration or as officers/rank-and-file. As will be shown below, the problem of how to divide this small pecuniary pie became one of the thorniest and most aggravating issues to the prisoners. To exacerbate the dilemmas of distribution even further, the nurses ran out of money in the middle of their trips. The dreadful conditions in Totskoe made a dent in Käthe von Mihalotzy's budget, and inaccurate information about the POW camp of Troitsky-Tashkent caused her to bring Christmas gifts (tobacco and soap) for 600 instead of 16,000 men.[47]

The nurses interpreted quite differently the problematic issue of the loyalty of the Habsburg prisoners. When she had time and permission Käthe von Mihalotzy attempted to strengthen the emotional link between POWs and their home state through public meetings, sing-alongs and religious ceremonies. Taking advantage of a sentimental atmosphere in the days prior to Christmas, she seems to have cultivated – either consciously or unconsciously – a sense of homesickness among the prisoners. On 5 December she celebrated dinner and 'Nikolo' (St Nicholas' Day) with a group of officers in the camp of Kuznetsk. In Perovsk she sat down with a group of Hungarian officers, who had been captured in Przemyśl, listening to violin music and singing folk song. 'When we left', she reported, 'we were accompanied by boisterous *eljen* calls and the tunes of the Rakoczy March.'[48] On 24 December 1915 the delegation visited all three camps in the city of Tashkent bringing with them a Christmas tree. 'We went from camp to camp; everywhere they waited for us to light up candles. It was touching to see, and from the addresses to hear, the joy it brought these poor people, to see a nurse from the homeland in their middle.' In the officer's camp she heard recitals of a string quartet and the 'so-called Bukhara vocal quartet'.[49] It is unknown how the rest of the Mihalotzy mission would have proceeded: on that same night she came down with symptoms of typhus and was hospitalized in the private lodgings of a Russian general. According to Mihalotzy two well-known Austrian POW physicians and three Russian doctors treated her. She was strong enough to leave Tashkent in the beginning of February and was surprised with a parting concert. In her absence, the Danish officer Captain Fritz Cramer conducted the inspection of other central Asian camps.

In contrast to Mihalotzy, Anna Revertera adopted a more confrontational approach to the issue of Habsburg loyalty. From her first stop in Perm on 10 December 1915 she noted the places where she found signs of disloyal or 'Russophile' attitude, especially among officers. 'A number of officers [in Perm] lived in a big building in the middle of the city. A terrible, passionate and stormy excitement raged in the heart of everyone: on the one hand wounded fatherland love and on the other open treason.'[50] Revertera does not specify why the latter group of officers were considered traitors, but she did collect names which infused her mission with considerable tension.[51] In Irbit on 16 December she encountered open hostility to her visit from officers and rank-and-file alike: 'Despairing I left that place with what was for me still a strange feeling of indescribable shame and disgrace,

Figure 5.4: POWs in the camp of Chita displaying worn clothes to the Red Cross delegation.

Source: Kriegsarchiv, Vienna

coming from the ranks of these derelicts of duty (*Pflichtvergess-enen*).'[52] As the POW censorship had done via percentages of unwounded/wounded prisoners (see Chapter 4), Revertera constructed a hierarchy of loyalty among various Habsburg nationalities. Using the treatment of the Russian authorities as an indicator, she placed the Austro-Germans and Magyars at the top of the ladder and Czechs at the bottom:

[The Russian authorities'] hand weighs heavily on the brave, patriotic Austro-Germans and passionately patriotic Magyars. The Czechs, who as Slavs are easily won over by anti-Austrian propaganda, are consequently also the unmistakable darlings of the Russians. They enjoy all privileges as soon as they go over, the easiest work and the warmest fire are always reserved to them, whereas their loyal [*kaisertreuen*] comrades hunger and freeze. The Poles, owing to their political situation as a connecting link between all belligerents, have their own special position in captivity. They find brothers among Russian soldiers and among the commandants of the same race. The Bosniaks, Croats and other Slavic men fight along-side their Austrian and Hungarian comrades, and share freely in their misery rather than partake in the advantages of deserters. Often they request me with touching simplicity to take from them the name 'Slavs', the source of shame in their lives . . . Shortly before my departure [from Tomsk] I saw some of the Slavic rank-and-file doing their school work, learning German . . . in their childish, clumsy handwriting, I saw the most precious autograph of the Austro-Hungarian fatherland.[53]

Revertera's loyalty rankings had nothing to do with the actions and thoughts of the prisoners, but rather with who they were and how the Russians treated them. Her perception of what a loyal Slav is – one who wants to shed his Slavic identity – is firmly rooted in late nineteenth century colonialist and racist discourses, which idolized the simple, childlike and loyal 'natives'. Her conflation of German *Kultur* with Austro-Hungarian patriotism left very little room for other forms of dynastic patriotism. Ironically, her own account of conversations with prisoners suggest that POWs were attached to the person of Franz-Joseph. She reported several cases of Slavic POWs expressing their love of the emperor in camps which she considered 'Russian propaganda camps' (Irbit and Tiumen).[54] In Petropavlosk she was approached by three Czech NCOs who asked in the name of other Czech POWs why she takes a greater interest in the fate of non-Slav prisoners. She replied that all prisoners were dear to her, that she herself was half Russian and that Franz-Joseph cares for POWs regardless of nationality. 'Upon hearing this [the Czech rank-and-file] were deeply touched; the greetings of their old emperor were received with tears and joyful outbursts.'[55]

Using her excellent personal contacts in Russia, Anna Revertera managed to extend her stay to five months instead of the pre-arranged eight weeks. She thus was able to visit more Siberian camps than originally planned, returning to Petrograd only on 5 May 1916. Staying in Petrograd ten days, Revertera conducted a series of meetings with top Russian officials and dignitaries including the Empress-mother and the Chief of Staff Belaev. Upon arriving in Vienna in the beginning of June, she was informed that Franz-Joseph would like to see her immediately. Arriving in Schönbrunn in the midst of the Brusilov offensive catastrophe, Revertera expected a broken old man. She found Franz-Joseph however in sharp wits, and he questioned her attentively about the condition of the prisoners in Russia, complaining that he never seems to get straight answers from bureaucrats. He was particularly interested in the condition of his officers in captivity. Revertera informed him that officers could enjoy walks outside camp if he would allow them to give their word of honor not to escape. Franz-Joseph thought that to give one's word of honor to the enemy 'was unmilitary and most of all contrary to the Austrian tradition'.[56] The issue that was most on his mind was the loyalty of the officers: 'is it true,' he asked according to Revertera, 'that a few of my officers are fighting against me'. She answered briefly in the affirmative, 'without giving names and details. Every word burnt my lips . . . and he cried with the unspeakable tears of old age. The tears flowed over the wrinkled cheeks and could not be stopped. They poured with mightier strength as I told him about the heroism of the faithful, their misery in Siberian prisons and their never failing loyalty.'[57]

The first round of visits was considered a success in all three belligerent countries.[58] The Austro-Hungarian and German nurses visited altogether 123 camps, which contained according to official count 272,919 Austro-Hungarians and 47,953 Germans.[59] At the request of the Russian Empress-Mother, the Red Cross societies of the three belligerents proceeded to negotiate a second round of visitations, which was to begin in April 1916 and include six nurses from each country.[60] However, the sinking of the Russian hospital ship 'Portugal' by a German submarine in the Black Sea resulted in a suspension of the negotiations. The Russian demand for a formal apology for the 115 people killed was accepted by Austria-Hungary but not by Germany, resulting in a suspension of visits until July 1916. Only after the intercession of Prince Carl of Sweden did the Russian government agree to allow a second round of visitations. This incident illustrates very well how the Great War challenged the distinction between 'legitimate' and 'illegitimate' targets, which was at the heart of every international convention since the Geneva Convention of 1864. It illustrates also how a transgression (or conversely a perceived transgression since Germany claimed that the hospital ship was not marked well with the Red Cross sign) in one area may very quickly affect other areas. It is important however to emphasize that despite the temporary suspension of the visits, a way was found to continue and even broaden the program. This in turn exemplifies once more the fact that in certain important aspects World War One was a nineteenth-century conflict.

The Austro-Hungarian nurses sent to Russia during the second tour were all new faces. Although Anna Revertera's re-appointment was at first approved by the Austro-Hungarian *Kriegsministerium*, the overwhelmingly negative feedback to her mission from POWs resulted in her removal.[61] As with the first round of visits, the women chosen were all of prominent background: the doyenne of the second round, Princess Kunigunde von Croy-Dülmen, was related to the Russian Benckendorff and her cousin Count Alexander von Benckendorff served as the Russian ambassador in London. Like Anna Revertera before her, she was expected to use her extensive Russian contacts to cut through red tape. Two additional members of the Habsburg aristocracy were the Hungarian countess, Pauline von Stubenberg-Palffy and her Bohemian niece, Countess Nora Kinsky. Although chosen already in March 1916 on account of her language skills and work among wounded Austro-Hungarian soldiers, the twenty-six year old Kinsky became even deeper involved in the fate of the prisoners when her brother Zdenko and her fiancé Count Ferdinand Wilczek were captured during the Brusilov Offensive (June 1916). Her posthumously published diary, written during what unforeseeably became a two year stay in Russia, remains still to a large extent a hidden jewel among World War I personal journals.[62] Alongside Croy-Dülmen, Stubenberg-Palffy and Kinsky two additional nurses were added as representatives of the Hungarian Red Cross Society: Countess Magda Cebrian and Sister Andorine von Huszár. In comparison to the first tour, the nurses received relatively smaller areas to cover; Croy-Dülmen was assigned the Moscow-Yaroslavl-Tver areas as well as a few large camps along the Trans-Siberian line (Omsk, Tomsk Novo-Nikolaevsk), Stubenberg-Palffy received the problematic Ufa, Kazan and Orenburg regions, Kinsky received the east-Siberian region and the two Hungarian nurses, Cebrian and von Huszár, divided between them respectively west and central Siberia (except the camps which were allocated to Croy-Dülmen). Conspicuously absent were Turkestan, where recruitment riots among the local population put the entire region off-limits to the nurses, and north European Russia, which became highly sensitive because of the Murman line strife.[63]

Leaving Austria-Hungary in late June 1916, the nurses traveled again via Berlin and Stockholm arriving in Petrograd on 7 July 1916.[64] Like their predecessors they were bogged down in the capital due to disagreements on routes and jurisdictions. Once again the time was used for an extensive briefing by Swedish, Danish and American officials. Their stay was also used to re-spark old contacts with Russian dignitaries and visit the Russian Tsarina in Tsarkoe Selo on 27 July. The Empress and her daughter, Grand Duchess Olga, received the two delegations separately (first the German and then the Austro-Hungarian), wearing nurses' uniforms.[65] Nora Kinsky commented briefly in her diary about 'how sad Her Majesty appeared', but was nonetheless impressed by the magnificence of the palace gardens. The visit did apparently result in a telegraph from the Empress to her protégé Prime Minister Stürmer, urging him to let the nurses finally leave Petrograd.

In certain respects the task of the second mission was an easier one. The dreadful shortages in clothing and medications had already been partly relieved before their arrival, and the most severe outbreaks of typhus and other epidemics were luckily behind them. Moreover, the Austro-Hungarian nurses brought with them more money and medical equipment than their predecessors. This time they came with 15,500,000 Austrian crowns for distribution as personal gifts, loans and collective projects, as well as with six truck-loads of medical supplies.[66] The delegations began departing gradually from Petrograd in early August 1916, but four of the nurses – two German and two Austro-Hungarian – had to wait until early September for their permission. They received however authorization to inspect hospitals and internment facilities in the Petrograd area and obtained a first glimpse of what their mission would be like. Nora Kinsky, who was one of the Austro-Hungarian nurses left in the capital (alongside Andorine von Huszár), wrote in her diary about her 'thrill to see finally our compatriots!'[67] On August 13, 1916 she met 125 wounded and sick POWs, feeling excited and overwhelmed: 'A Rumanian Honvéd captain was moved to tears because he could speak Rumanian with me, he could not speak a word in any other language.'[68] She encountered many tuberculosis cases and a number of moribund prisoners, and experienced for the first time the close monitoring of her activities by the Russian authorities: 'a disgusting Russian individual stood behind me all the time and listened to every word I said to them [the wounded POWs]. He was not amused when I used Hungarian or Rumanian.'[69]

On 5 September 1916, Nora Kinsky and Andorine von Huszár finally left Petrograd, the last nurses to do so. Kinsky, who was assigned east Siberia and the Russian pacific maritime region (*Primorskaia*), took with her fifty tightly hand-written pages about her mission and her diary, which she would scrupulously fill throughout her mission. Writing primarily in French, Kinsky inscribed certain sections of her diary in Czech, German and Hungarian to confuse snoops and Russian agents. From the beginning of her mission it is clear that Kinsky did not encounter the same grievous conditions her predecessors discovered in some POW camps. Although she was often critical of medical facilities and Russian disciplinary procedures, she nonetheless considered many of the camps decent and unproblematic. One does not find in her account any camp even remotely approximating Mihalotzy's and Revertera's respective descriptions of Totskoe and Yekatrinburg. What bothered Kinsky most is the lack of discipline she perceived among all ranks of Austro-Hungarian POWs, and the apparent sloth and demoralization among officers and intellectuals:

> We passed the day with the officers in Skotovo. Neither order nor discipline. That is sad. The camp is not far from the [Pacific] ocean, the view is pretty, but the barracks are too small and there is not enough room for the officers . . . I have found the moral condition of the officers much worse than that of the rank-and-file. It is quite understandable that they suffer more in captivity than the rank-and-file. The scarcity of work is terrible for them.[70]

The next day – 23 September 1916 – she visited both the officer and rank-and-file camp in Rasdolnoe, 'finding many "intellectuals" extremely stupid and without any discipline to speak of'.[71] Four days later the delegation visits the camp of Spasskoe, where she discovers to her dismay that one year volunteers and intellectuals were given separate quarters by the commandant. 'They were unpleasantly surprised when I did not give them more money than regular soldiers.'[72] Nonetheless, Kinsky commented, the intellectuals treated her well and they all drank miserable coffee together.

Kinsky's insistence on discipline was rooted in her belief that the personal and the mental health of the prisoner, as well as his attachment to the Habsburg monarchy, were dependent on retaining as much of a military structure as possible. She was alarmed to discover that a POW orchestra from the camp of Khabarovsk performed in concerts organized on the outside by the Russian Red Cross society. The fact that the proceedings of the concerts went to support wounded Russian soldiers meant that Austro-Hungarian POWs were not taking the distinction of friend/foe very seriously.[73] She criticized in many cases Austro-Hungarian officers as incompetent disciplinarians, especially in comparison to German officers, and thought they had significant problems bridging national lines. Visiting the camp of Peshchenka [Chita, east Siberia] she commented that 'Magyar [POWs] want to Magyarize everybody which causes problems now and then.'[74] She noticed that Czech POWs keep to themselves, but were always overjoyed to meet her and chat in Czech.

Six weeks into her inspection tour, Nora Kinsky ran out of money. Money that was supposed to be telegraphed by the Danes from Petrograd did not arrive, and the delegation had to visit camps empty-handed. 'So much trouble and efforts were made to reach these areas and now nothing can be done to help these unhappy people. This is so stupid. Curse these Danish institutions in Petrograd!'[75] Kinsky's exasperation further grew upon encountering logistical problems, bureaucratic annoyances and unpleasant individuals. Caustic remarks and portrayals increasingly pepper her account; after meeting the Cossack Ataman of the Transbaikalia she commented: 'He is a small, black, horrible man; I believe [he is] a completely evil individual.'[76] Regarding various Russians who monitored her actions Kinsky complained: 'we are constantly surrounded by spies, male and often also female. These latter are even dumber and more incompetent than their colleagues.'[77] She found it humiliating that some POWs would rather talk to the Russian member of the delegation, Prince Boris Kochakidze, than presumably confide in a woman, and declined an invitation to dinner with an American delegate because she did not want stories circulating that she runs around with crowds of men.[78]

The death of Franz-Joseph on 21 November 1916 seems to have changed the tone of Nora Kinsky's mission. Hearing the news first from the Danish member of the delegation she refused to believe it until receiving confirmation from home. Kinsky immediately submitted a petition to the Russian governor requesting to hold a requiem for Franz-Joseph 'with as many POWs as possible'.[79] The request was approved on Thursday 7 December and the requiem was held the following day in a big church in the town of Chita. 'It was very solemn . . . the soldiers sang somewhat off-key but with enthusiasm.'[80] Following the requiem and approaching the last three weeks of her mission, Kinsky's attention focuses more and more on the chances of meeting her brother and fiancé – whom she revealingly calls in her diary 'the brothers' – in the camp of Omsk. After being allowed to be with 'the brothers' in Omsk for a week, Kinsky decided to seek permission to stay in Russia as a simple nurse and to be close to the two. Waiting in Petrograd for authorization, Kinsky experienced first hand the March 1917 Revolution and the changing of government. On 20 March 1917, Kinsky was notified that her request had been approved by the Provisional Government and that she would be permitted to go to Astrakhan where her brother and fiancé had been sent. Kinsky remained in Astrakhan until March 1918, encountering and describing the political upheaval in Russia. She returned back home considerably weakened and spent the greater part of the next two years attempting to recuperate. In a bittersweet ending, taken out almost from a fairy tale, Nora Kinsky married her fiancé Ferdinand Wilczek in January 1921, gave birth to one daughter (the future Princess Gina von Liechtenstein) and died on 26 March 1923. Before her death she translated the various sections of her diary into French and typed it. For more than fifty years her diary lay in Vaduz, inaccessible to the public; finally her husband decided to have it translated into German and published it in 1976.

Figure 5.5: Nora Kinsky in nurse's uniform.
'I caught a terrible cold. The last image these poor POWs would have is of a pale puffed-up monkey with inflamed eyes.' Diary 8 December 1916

Source: Kinsky, Russisches Tagebuch.

Figure 5.6: Nora Kinsky distributing money.

Source: Kinsky, Russisches Tagebuch.

The Austro-Hungarian relief effort continued until May 1918. In addition to material relief distributed by the Swedish Red Cross, a permanent Austro-Hungarian delegation was established in August 1917 in Moscow headed by Andorine von Huszár. Her ability to function was increasingly limited following the Bolshevik revolution in November 1917, and she found herself under arrest following the German army's advances in February and March 1918. By then the opportunities for visits and inspection had ceased to exist and the repatriation of POWs begun. What did the Austro-Hungarian relief effort accomplish during its three years of existence?

First, it helped to relieve the most severe shortages and undoubtedly saved thousands of lives. Still, it was not a generous relief effort and paled in comparison to what Germany had done for its captive soldiers. In other words, the Habsburg monarchy could have saved more lives if its military elite was not so negatively predisposed towards the POWs. Second, as Elsa Brändström pointed out, the appearance of enemy nurses in some of the remotest places in Russia, demonstrated to camp personnel that there was outside interest in the fate of prisoners of war and that they cannot be 'looked upon as creatures whom everyone might ill-treat with impunity'.[81] Third, the willingness of Austria-Hungary, Germany and Russia to agree on a program of relief and visitation showed that the spirit of Hague was still very much alive on the eastern front of World War I.

However, it is far less clear whether the material aid and the nurses' visits convinced Austro-Hungarian POWs that their home state truly cared about their well being. The prisoners' letters analyzed in the next chapter show the answer was far from a clear 'yes' or 'no'.

Notes

1. Nora Gräfin Kinsky, *Russisches Tagebuch 1916–1918*, Stuttgart: Seewald Verlag, 1976, caption between pp. 112–13.
2. Hague Convention, Article 4.
3. See above Chapter 3.
4. Sil Vara [Geza Silberer], *Briefe aus der Gefangenschaft: zugunsten der Oestereichischen Gesellschaft vom Roten Kreuze (für die österreichischen Kriegsgefangenen in Rußland und Sibirien) und des Kriegshilfsbüro des k.k. Ministerium des Innern*, Vienna, 1917, Introduction.

5. For some of these images See Peter Paret, Beth Irwin Lewis, Paul Paret (eds) *Persuasive Images: Posters of War and Revolution*, Princeton: Princeton University Press, 1992, Chapter 1, The First World War.

6. Regarding the 'mood of 1914' there is still no study about Austria-Hungary comparable to Jean-Jacques Becker's work about France. Still, most historians agree that the failures of 1914 coupled with the growing dependence on Germany (who in turn was stuck in the western front quagmire) shattered the hopes for a short and decisive war. See Norman Stone, *The Eastern Front 1914–1917*, New York: Charles Scribner's Sons, 1975, Chapter 6; Manfried Rauchensteiner, *Der Tod des Doppeladlers: Österreich-Ungarn und der erste Weltkrieg*, Böhlau: Graz, Wien, Köln, 1993, Chapters 6–11; István Deák, *Beyond Nationalism: A Social and Political History of the Habsburg Officer Corps 1848–1918*, New York: Oxford University Press, 1992, Chapter 11.

7. Although memoirs written after the war tend to emphasize that both conditions and treatment in captivity were bad from the very beginning, letters written by POWs during the first months of the war paint a very different picture. From a censorship report sent to the Ministry of War on 2 November 1914: 'The analysis of POW correspondence since the last report (20 October 1914) gave the following results: the positive to very positive reports from Russia and Siberia continue to predominate. A few even talk about emigrating to the latter place.' AOK (1914/1915), GZNB:Karton 3726, Akt 12.

A month later: 'The reports coming here from Russia are still positive to a large extent.' Ibid, akt 44. A comparison of Siberian POW camps done by the Austro-Hungarian censorship in December 1914 found that out of thirty-one places of internment examined, conditions in only one could be considered as 'bad'. Conditions in thirteen could be considered as 'good' and conditions in three could be considered as 'very good'. The remaining fourteen places of internment had reasonable conditions although they deteriorated since the previous report. Ibid., Akt: 427 pp. 5–6. For an extensive discussion of the question whether POWs were treated according to what the then-existing international law prescribed see above Chapters 2, 3 and epilogue.

8. According to Brändström, 4,500 POWs out of 8,600 brought to Novo-Nikolaevsk in the Winter of 1914–1915 died from typhus and other diseases.

9. 'Grüsse aus Sibirien: Lebenszeichen eines Kriegsgefangenen 1914–1919', Hrsg. und mit einem Nachwort versehen von Margot Lutze. Manuscript in BA/MA (Freiburg, Germany) Msg 200/1194. p. 3. November 1914:

Wir hatten von den ersten Stunden an eine gute Behandlung. Das Essen war besser als ich dachte. Wir bekamen Speck, Suppe, Fleisch, Eier, Tee, Cigaretten . . . überall wurde uns durch Zeichen bedeutet, daß es sehr kalt sei und jedem einzelnen schien unsere Uniform sehr dünn. Wohl 20 Mann lagen im Kreis um uns herum, stets bemüht, daß unsere nassen Füsse mit Heu bedeckt waren. Übermüdet schliefen wir ein. Als wir am anderen Morgen erwachten, sah nur noch der Kopf aus dem Heu, so hatten uns die Soldaten mit Heu zugedeckt, damit wir die Nacht nicht erfroren.

10. *Schreib das auf, Kisch!: Das Kriegstagebuch von Egon Erwin Kisch*, Berlin, 1930. Kisch did not want to take a third pair of underwear to the front although his mother implored him. 'Do you think I am going to the Thirty Years War?!', p. 12.

11. Brändström, Among Prisoners of War, p. 73.

12. Heinrich Freiherr von Raabl-Werner, 'Österreich-Ungarns offizielle Kriegsgefangenenfürsorge', in Hans Weiland and Leopold Kern (eds) *In Feindeshand: Die Gefangenschaft im Weltkriege in Einzeldarstellungen*, pp. 324–31.

13. Ibid., pp. 326–7; Magdalene von Walsleben, *Die deutsche Schwester in Sibirien*, Berlin: Furche Verlag, 1919, p. 6; Alexandrine von Üxküll, *Aus einem Schwesterleben*, 2. Auflage, Stuttgart, 1956.

14. Nachtigal, op.cit, p.255.

15. Heinrich Freiherr von Raabl-Werner, 'Österreich-Ungarns offizielle Kriegsgefangenenfürsorge', in *In Feindeshand* , pp. 325–6.

16. Nora Gräfin Kinsky, *Russisches Tagebuch 1916–1918*.

17. To a lesser extent it also included independent neutral inspections by delegates of the American State Department and the Swedish Red Cross organization. American delegates inspected camps in their capacity as official representative of Austria-Hungary and Germany in Russia until April 1917.

18. This is based on Elsa Brändström's data in *Among Prisoners of War in Russia and Siberia*, p. 173.

19. There is a significant discrepancy in the sums provided by Elsa Brändström in *Among Prisoners of War in Russia and Siberia* and in the *In Feindeshand* article 'Das Rote Kreuz in Rußland'. The former lists 85,572,990 Austrian Crowns while the latter lists 361,306,300 Austrian Crowns. The article also discusses money sent to cover the costs of neutral delegations, so I interpret the discrepancy to mean the difference between net transfers to POWs and total costs of the relief operation. Thus, according to this calculation, only 23 per cent of the funds actually reached the POWs. See Brändström *Among Prisoners of War in Russia and Siberia*, pp. 173–4 and , 'Das Rote Kreuz in Rußland' in *In Feindeshand*, vol. 2, pp. 286–7 .

20. Heinrich Freiherr von Raabl-Werner, 'Österreich-Ungarns offizielle Kriegsgefangenenfürsorge', in *In Feindeshand*, p. 326.

21. Figures are taken from Holger Herwig, *The First World War: Germany and Austria-Hungary 1914–1918*, pp. 230–1.

22. Johann von der Wülbecke, 'Meine Erlebnisse in russischer Kriegsge-fangenschaft', Bundesarchiv Militärarchiv, Freiburg im Breisgau, Germany, Msg 200/932, pp. 15–17.

23. John Hutchinson, *Champions of Charity: War and the Rise of the Red Cross*, Boulder CO: Westview Press, 1996, pp. 24–30.

24. See Chapter 2.
25. Brändström, *Among Prisoners of War in Russia and Siberia*, p. 177.
26. Ibid, pp.177–8.
27. Hans Weiland, 'Elsa Brändström: Caritas inter arma', *In Feindeshand*, vol. 2, p. 238.
28. *In Feindeshand*, vol. 2, p. 238. The translation from the original German text is mine. The original text is the following:

> Ein kleines Wort im Vorübergehn
> Ein Gruß, ein Dank, ein freundlich Lachen
> Wie uns so lang nicht mehr geschehn . . .
> Sonne! Wie kannst du uns glücklich machen
> Wenn wir nach dunkler Nacht dich sehn.
>
> Uns ist der ganze Tag geweiht,
> Da wir am Morgen dich getroffen
> Die Not wird lind, verklärt das Leid,
> du bringst uns neues, seliges Hoffen . . .
> Komm wieder! Komm in harter Zeit!

29. Elsa von Hanneken, 'Die Tientsiner Hilfsaktion: Eine Hilfsaktion für Kriegs- und Zivilgefangene in Tientsin', *In Feindeshand*, vol. 2, p. 267.
30. Brändström, *Among Prisoners of War in Russia and Siberia*, pp. 192–3; 'Die YMCA der Verein christlicher junger Männer der Vereinigten Staaten von Nordamerika und seine Hilfe für die Kriegsgefangenen', *In Feindeshand*, pp. 318–23.
31. Elsa Brändström argues that the YMCA used its own funds. However, the American Embassy in Petrograd received 17,500,000 Austrian crown between August and February of 1917 and Department of State documents suggests a link between the YMCA and the American Embassy. See Brändström, *Among Prisoners of War in Russia and Siberia*, pp. 192–3; 'Das Rote Kreuz in Rußland' in *In Feindeshand*, vol. 2, pp. 286–7; United States National Archives, Department of State, 763.72114.
32. Reinhard Nachtigal, 'Die dänisch-österreichisch-ungarischen Rotkreuzdelegierten in Rußland 1915–1918: Die Visitation der Kriegsgefangenen der Mittelmächte durch Fürsorgeschwestern des österreichischen und ungarischen Roten Kreuzes', *Zeitgeschichte*, 25 (1998), pp. 367–8.
33. Käthe von Mihalotzy, 'Eine Reise durch Kriegsgefangenenlager in Rußland und Turkestan. Aus dem Tagebuch einer delegierten des österreichischen Roten Kreuzes', *In Feindeshand*, vol. 2, p. 251.
34. Ibid.
35. Gräfin Anna Revertera, 'Als österreichische Rotkreuzschwester in Rußland', *Süddeutsche Monatshefte*, September 1923, p. 271.
36. Käthe von Mihalotzy, 'Eine Reise durch Kriegsgefangenenlager in Rußland und Turkestan', *In Feindeshand*, vol. 2, p. 251.

37. Ibid, p. 252.

38. Ibid.

39. Revertera, 'Als Rotkreuzschwester in Rußland und Sibirien', *In Feindeshand*, vol. 2, p. 245; Mihalotzy, p. 252; Nachtigal 'Die dänisch-österreichisch-ungarischen Rotkreuzdelegierten in Rußland 1915–1918', p. 368.

40. Revertera, 'Als Rotkreuzschwester in Rußland und Sibirien', p. 245.

41. Ibid.

42. Brändström, *Among Prisoners of War in Russia and Siberia*, p. 166.

43. Mihalotzy, p. 255.

44. Mihalotzy, p. 255.

45. Ibid.

46. Brändström, *Among Prisoners of War in Russia and Siberia*, p. 167.

47. Mihalotzy, p. 256.

48. Ibid., p. 255.

49. Ibid., p. 256.

50. Revertera, 'Als österreichische Rotkreuzschwester in Rußland', *Süddeutsche Monatshefte*, September 1923, p. 258.

51. Nachtigal 'Die dänisch-österreichisch-ungarischen Rotkreuzdelegierten in Rußland 1915–1918', p. 369.

52. Revertera, *Süddeutsche Monatshefte*, p. 261.

53. Ibid., p. 267.

54. Ibid., pp. 260–1.

55. Ibid., p. 276.

56. Ibid., p. 280; Franz Joseph did however relent and promise to think this request over.

57. Ibid., p. 281.

58. Raabl-Werner, 'Österreich-Ungarns offizielle Kriegsgefangenenfürsorge', in *In Feindeshand* p. 327.

59. Brändström, *Among Prisoners of War in Russia and Siberia*, p. 165; Nachtigal, 'Die dänisch-österreichisch-ungarischen Rotkreuzdelegierten in Rußland 1915–1918', p. 369.

60. Ibid., p. 369.

61. Ibid., p. 369.

62. Nora Gräfin Kinsky, *Russisches Tagebuch 1916–1918*, Stuttgart: Seewald Verlag, 1976.

63. See above chapters 2, 3 and Nachtigal, 'Die dänisch-österreichisch-ungarischen Rotkreuzdelegierten in Rußland 1915–1918', p. 369.

64. This time both the German and Austro-Hungarian nurses traveled together. Thus eleven foreign nurses arrived simultaneously in Petrograd in early July 1916.

65. Kinsky, p. 23.

66. Brändström, *Among Prisoners of War in Russia and Siberia*, p. 169.

67. Kinsky, p. 29.

68. Ibid., p. 30.

69. Ibid., p. 30.

70. Ibid., p. 44.

71. Ibid., p. 45

72. Ibid., p. 47.

73. Ibid., p. 51.

74. Ibid., p. 63.

75. Ibid., p. 62.

76. Ibid., p. 64.

77. Ibid., p. 56.

78. Ibid., pp. 55, 62.

79. He is the same Cossack Ataman who she characterized as 'an evil person' and a 'total bastard'. Ibid., p. 64.

80. Ibid., pp. 64–5.

81. Brändström, *Among Prisoners of War in Russia and Siberia*, p. 168.

6

Imperial Identities and Personal Concerns: The Perspective of the Prisoners[1]

In the past I heard much about the Red Cross, their duties etc. We, the rank-and-file, don't know anything about this. I had the opportunity to speak with POWs from various districts, but I haven't found even one who could tell me that someone from our ranks has been visited by the [Austrian] Red Cross. Higher ranks, yes, that I read in a St. Pölten newspaper that found its way here by accident. Concerning the men it's just: hold out, endure, pay taxes and shut up! [hinhalten, aushalten, fest Steuer Zahl'n und Maul Halten!][2]

POW Landsturmmann, Franz Kotter
Kharkov, 31 January 1917

Repatriation and the Repatriation System (Heimkehrwesen)

Austro-Hungarian POWs began returning in significant numbers from Russia in the winter of 1917–18. Before that only 22,123 severely wounded Austro-Hungarian POWs – 'whose disablement prevented their military service either permanently or for a considerable time' – were exchanged for Russian POWs through Swedish mediation.[3] In addition, 1,226 partially disabled Austro-Hungarian prisoners were released in 1916–17 to Danish and Norwegian custody and interned there for the duration of the war.[4] However, the advance of the German army into Ukraine and the Baltic area (December 1917–February 1918), coupled with the disintegration of the Russian military, meant that a larger number of POWs could now trek back home. The journey was by no means an easy one: POW Captain Gottfried von Scotti decided with a friend on 17 December 1917 to leave his camp near Lake Baikal. After making elaborate and time-consuming preparations, they traveled thousands of miles westward via Ufa, Moscow and Smolensk before finally arriving on Palm Sunday 1918 at the small town of Orsha (White Russia), which had been captured by the German army two days earlier.[5] This uncoordinated movement of POWs westward was taking place while Russia, Germany and Austria-Hungary were negotiating an orderly exchange mechanism. Like many other issues discussed in Brest-Litovsk, Bolshevik Russia and the Central Powers could not find an acceptable formula regarding POW repatriation. The disparity between the number of Russian POWs in Germany (1,434,000) and the number of Germans in Russia (167,000) was the main impediment: whereas Bolshevik negotiators called for an 'all for all' exchange, German representatives insisted on a 'head for head' exchange, primarily in order to retain as many POW laborers as possible on Junker estates.[6] Thus, the Brest-Litovsk treaty signed on 3 March 1918 did not contain procedures for an orderly exchange of war prisoners. A supplemental agreement added to the main document did call for the establishment of commissions to hammer out the details of POW exchange and to facilitate repatriation after an agreement had been reached. The first Austro-Hungarian repatriation commission was sent at the end of March 1918 to Ukraine – which had been recognized as an independent state in the Brest-Litovsk treaty – and attempted to coordinate the orderly return of POWs there. The second, more important commission to Russia, had to wait until June 1918 before being sent to Moscow because Germany, Russian and Austria-Hungary could not agree on the details of repatriation.[7] The final agreement between the Central Powers and Bolshevik Russia which accepted the German 'head for head formula' – was signed on 24 June 1918 in Berlin, six months after POWs had actually begun returning from captivity.[8] Subsequently, the Austro-Hungarian repatriation commission to Russia functioned just three months before the collapse of Dual Monarchy in October–November 1918. Moreover, the escalating civil war in Russia during the summer and fall of 1918 increasingly hindered the ability of the Central Powers' commissions to assist returning POWs. Thus, the opportunity for complete repatriation of prisoners, which had been created in the chaotic aftermath of the Bolshevik Revolution, was to a large degree squandered.

Notwithstanding, no fewer than 670,508 Austro-Hungarian POWs did manage to return from Russia by 18 October 1918 according to the official figures of the k.u.k. *Kriegsministerium*.[9] Ernst von Streeruwitz, the head of the political section of Department 10.Kgf, wrote a memo in January 1918 arguing that '[I]t is the prediction of

10.Kgf.-Abteilung that the thoroughly systematic exchange in the intended form is not feasible, and in any case [repatriation] has already begun. The POWs stream back in masses over the eastern front without any means of transportation and supplies.'[10] Overall, only 27.6 per cent (or 185,680 POWs) returned from Russia 'in an orderly fashion' – with the aid and agreement of the Austro-Hungarian commissions in Kiev and Moscow.[11] The uncontrolled westward movement of POWs became especially strong during the months of April-May 1918 with a daily average of slightly more than four thousand returning prisoners (*Heimkehrer*).[12] In one day alone – 12 May 1918 – 10,653 rank-and-file POWs and nineteen officers returned to Austria-Hungary.[13]

Upon crossing the demarcation lines, the *Heimkehrer* encountered considerable distrust from the Austro-Hungarian military authorities. This distrust found expression in a bureaucratic and cumbersome 'repatriation system' (*Heimkehrwesen*) which was strong on restrictions and short on compassion. As General (*General-oberst*) Max Ronge, head of the Intelligence Bureau in the General Staff, explained: 'what awaits [the returnees] is not a jubilant welcome but a thorough examination of heart and conscience.'[14] Ernst von Streeruwitz advised KM officials: 'we have now the duty to take measures to ensure the adjustment of this disorderly mass, as frictionless as possible, to military order and discipline.'[15]

Beyond the very real concern regarding the spread of contagious diseases to the Austrian and Hungarian hinterlands, there were other factors involved in setting up this restrictive repatriation system: First, as discussed above in Chapter 1, it was widely suspected in the AOK that many POWs had either allowed themselves to be captured by the Russians or deserted outright into enemy hands.[16] Second, Austro-Hungarian POWs of Slavic and Italian origin received in captivity preferential treatment (over Austro-German, Magyar and Jewish POWs) and efforts were made by successive Russian governments to recruit them to anti-Habsburg military formations.[17] Thus, the repatriation system was intended to weed out those who had become ideologically anti-Habsburg in captivity. Third, there was an extraordinary fear that many returning POWs had been influenced in Russia by Bolshevik agitation (or to use the epidemiological language of the AOK 'infected by the Bolshevik bacillus') and were more than likely to aggravate the volatile social situation within the Dual Monarchy. In January 1918, Austria-Hungary experienced a wave of strikes that encompassed hundred of thousands of workers in most of its major industrial areas. As the chronicler of the collapse of Habsburg Monarchy, Z. A. B. Zeman, had noted: 'into such a situation . . . prisoners of war started returning from Russia . . . The Austro-Hungarian authorities, both civil and military, began making their last effort to prevent the spread of revolutionary doctrines, Bolshevik in particular.'[18]

Consequently, the repatriation policy prescribed by the AOK was a combination of precautionary (a 'prophylactic political device'), punitive, investigative and didactic measures. It reflected a deep distrust vis-à-vis the *Heimkehrer* and a belief that captivity significantly eroded imperial loyalties while strengthening identities inimical to the very existence of the state.[19] Thus, before being granted a four-week leave, returning POWs (*Heimkehrer*) were required to undergo a sorting out process in 'reception stations' (*Heimkehrer-übernahmestationen*), spend at least a fortnight in medical quarantines, complete successfully ten days of 'disciplinary re-education' (*disziplinäre Nachschulung*), report for duty at their reserve units and most importantly account (*rechtfertigen*) for their behavior in captivity in 'justification proceedings'. Only then, and only after their conduct in captivity had been cleared, did the prisoners receive their furlough. POW officer Gottfried von Scotti reported a sense of humiliation by this reception and told the interrogating officer: 'I feel the fatherland had let me down.'[20] To which the officer answered in an irritated manner that 'personally he cannot do a thing about it'.[21] Another POW Eduard Stoss wrote:

> We were overjoyed to be again in the fatherland after so many difficult experiences. The unbelievable suspicion with which we were greeted struck us as very peculiar. The manner of the reception prepared everywhere for the *Heimkehrer*, who had risked their lives hundreds of times by daring to escape, made us sick and embittered.[22]

The idea that during their captivity in Russia POWs became disaffected and often ideologically anti-Austrian also permeates much of the historical literature on the subject. Studies on captivity have traditionally focused on the activities of anti-Habsburg military units such as the Czech or the South Slav legions, the creation and exploits of the Bolshevik internationalist units, the propaganda efforts among the prisoners. Many of these studies had their own ideological axe to grind (for example works glorifying or respectively vilifying the Czech Legion and studies originating in the former Soviet bloc) and were thus more inclined to depict POWs as taking sides and making

clear-cut choices.[23] Holger Herwig's most recent study of the Habsburg military is reflective of this thesis, arguing that 'it was well
known that many of the [returning] soldiers had embraced revolutionary philosophy while in Russia.'[24]

Yet, there are reasons to believe that the number of Austro-
Hungarian POWs that had actually made an unequivocal ideological
commitment was much smaller than usually portrayed: out of an
estimated 250,000-300,000 Czech and Slovak POWs in Russian
captivity no more than 50,000 joined the Czech Legion at the height
of its influence, and similarly less than 10 per cent of the estimated
200,000 South Slav POWs volunteered to fight in an anti-Habsburg
formation.[25] Even the data of the Austro-Hungarian War Ministry
regarding the loyalty of the returnees suggests that relatively few
committed themselves to an openly anti-Austrian course: out of the
120,272 POWs who were screened by May 1918, the behavior of
only 1,620 could not be 'justified'; 514 *Heimkehrer* were labeled
'suspect of disloyal activity' (no conclusive proof was found), and
603 returnees deserted from their reserve units before their investigations could be completed (and of course may have deserted for a
variety of reasons).[26]

Thus, if a fundamental shift occurred in the loyalties of Austro-
Hungarian prisoners, it did not translate into manifest political
patterns.[27] If war and captivity did indeed 'heighten self awareness
. . . and sort out loyalties', as cultural historian Hubertus Jahn argued,
then it was discernible more in what the prisoners thought and felt
than in what they did.[28] In other words, to find out whether Habsburg
loyalties were significantly eroded during captivity while national
and class identities were strengthened one should try and pay
attention both to what POWs were thinking and writing during
captivity rather than their overt actions.

One way to gain access to contemporaneous sources is to tap into
a very large collection of letters written by POWs and preserved in
the Austrian *Kriegsarchiv*. The late Hungarian historian Péter Hanák
was the first to suggest using correspondence, and his work had been
extensively quoted in Eric Hobsbawm's influential work *Nations
and Nationalism since 1870*. While acknowledging Hanák's significant contribution, I propose here a different methodology and
different conclusions.[29] At the heart of this chapter is an analysis of
a defined body of 1,476 letters written by Austro-Hungarian POWs
in the period November 1916-March 1918, primarily – but not
exclusively – in the German, Czech and Polish languages.[30] These

letters fulfil a dual role within this study: first, they enable us to see how the relief effort was viewed from the perspective of prisoners themselves, since all of them discuss the activities of the Austro-Hungarian Red Cross and its agents. Second, they provide a unique sample to look at how POWs viewed their home state and what kind of terminology they used for that purpose. Based on this sample of letters, this chapter argues that Austro-Hungarian POWs in Russia did indeed become increasingly critical of their home state in the years 1916–18. However, contrary to what has been assumed so far, this critique did not manifest itself in socialist or nationalist terms, but, rather in what might be termed a 'civic spirit' i.e. direct criticism of specific practices and specific policies of the Habsburg state.

Prisoner-of-War Letters and their Usefulness as a Historical Source

The huge number of letters and postcards handled during the war by the POW Censorship (*Gemeinsames Zentralnachweisbureau des Roten Kreuzes* or GZNB) provided the Austro-Hungarian military authorities with a unique tool to evaluate what the POWs were doing and thinking.[31] The POW censorship grew into an organization of substantial size, which not only produced a plethora of reports and assessments, but also amassed many of the original letters or their German translations (see Chapter 3). Today there are still many tens of thousands of these letters and postcards preserved in the *Kriegsarchiv* in Vienna.[32]

Prisoners' letters and postcards provide an excellent source for historians attempting – in E. P. Thompson's often used phrase – to examine 'history from below'.[33] They were written during the events and before the final outcome of the war was known, they were more direct and less constructed than captivity literature (memoirs, novels and reworked diaries) and perhaps most importantly they were reflective of a broad social base because to compose them did not require a high degree of literacy. Nevertheless, as German historian Bernd Ulrich has stated regarding soldiers' field correspondence, letters pose a few methodological problems that make it rather difficult to use them.[34]

First, as Hungarian historian Péter Hanák had pointed out, letters are for the most part personal documents.[35] They talk about everyday issues and everyday concerns and do not usually provide a full context to what they are saying. Only seldom does one find letters that deal directly with questions of collective identity, loyalty and political convictions, and the background information on the writer is usually scarce. Thus, POWs' letters offer copious information on many aspects of life in captivity but piecing them together into a meaningful narrative is exceedingly difficult. Second, the letters that are available to us today were predominantly letters that the Austro-Hungarian censorship found 'objectionable' (on a monthly basis these letters constituted roughly between 1.5–5 per cent of the entire volume of correspondence). Therefore, it is plausible that, although the censored letters reflected a broad social base they represented nonetheless only a vocal minority among the POW population.

To deal with these methodological problems I approached the censorship material looking for a body of letters that had two important characteristics: first, it did not contain exclusively 'impermissible' information, and, second, it did not deal strictly with personal issues. This search was helped by the fact that from 1916 there was a noticeable increase in the number of information-gathering assignments handled by the censorship in Vienna. Among these assignments were fifteen Red Cross Reports that attempted to assess the effectiveness of the Austro-Hungarian relief effort in Russia by looking at what the prisoners themselves had to say about this undertaking. Included in the appendices to these reports were some of the letters upon which these reports were based; altogether 1,476 letters written by POWs in the period of November 1916–March 1918.[36] Since the primary goal of these reports was to find out which camps had been well attended to by the Austro-Hungarian Red Cross and its delegates and which camps were of greater need, the main criterion for selecting the letters was geographic location and not permissible or impermissible content. Thus, the appendices to the Red Cross reports provide an excellent opportunity to analyze both correspondence that would normally be intercepted and correspondence that the censors had no problem in approving. Moreover, since the Austro-Hungarian state was the protagonist in most of these letters, the Red Cross reports constitute an excellent source for examining both the content and the manner in which POWs discussed their home state.[37]

The Relief Effort: The Prisoners' Perspective

When Péter Hanák examined World War I correspondence (civilian and military) in the late 1960s he relied primarily on quantitative methods. From the sample of correspondence Hanák collected in the military archives in Vienna and Budapest he concluded that the 1917 revolutions in Russia had profound effect on the civilian population of Austria-Hungary, and that class identities and concerns were more important at that juncture of time than national identities. Twenty years later his research received considerable exposure in Eric Hobsbawm's *Nations and Nationalism* because it fit very well in Hobsbawm's argument regarding the frailty and artificiality of national identities.[38]

The main advantage of Hanák's quantitative approach was that it provided both an overview and a clear indication of change. However, as mentioned above, the Austro-Hungarian censorship material does not easily lend itself to representative sampling and some of Hanák's research methods raised questions about the validity of his conclusions: First, Hanák went over 1,511 letters that had been written in the winter of 1917–18 and chose 502 which he regarded as 'historically relevant', ignoring letters with no explicit political content as irrelevant. Second, Hanák's analysis included letters written by POWs, by their families and friends in the civilian sector of Austria-Hungary and by soldiers.[39] These groups were able, to a certain extent, to exchange opinions and ideas throughout the war, however it was not until POWs began returning home in the spring of 1918 that they truly belonged to the same public. During most of the war POWs lived in a radically different environment and were exposed to different political influences. Thus, talking about 'public opinion' (*Volksmeinung*) as Hanák did is rather problematic. Finally, Hanák relied solely on quantitative analysis. In doing so he ran the risk of glossing over important differences in motivation, narrative style and political imagination. Writers can express the same idea for strikingly different reasons, in a thoroughly different manner and with completely different personal and collective implications. The historian dealing with the GZNB material in quantitative methods is faced with the dilemma of either adhering to rigid categories and disregarding important differences, or creating a plethora of additional categories that make coherent general conclusions almost impossible. Therefore, the fundamental question is whether the correspondence in the GZNB files could be used at all to make valid generalizations, or whether historians should accept the limitations of this material and analyze the letters individually without claiming that they represent wider trends?

Dealing with censorship material requires adjusting expectations to what the sources can offer. We still can learn a great deal about collective identities and about how Austro-Hungarian POWs perceived their home state if we approach the material not as social scientists looking for precise answers but rather as observers in a public meeting. Although we have no control as to who attended this imaginary meeting we nonetheless possess four distinct criteria by which to sort out the public: rank (officers, cadets, rank-and-file), language (primarily German, Czech and Polish), when did the speaker express his opinion and what attitude did he take vis-à-vis the issue under discussion (negative/positive/neutral). In other words, although the material does not allow us to choose who attended the meeting (to choose a representative sample based on the Habsburg monarchy's population) we nevertheless can divide our body of sources into meaningful categories and examine how each group approached the issue at hand. We can look at what is said explicitly, the conceptual environment in each letter and what was meant when the collective pronoun 'us' was used (and who were 'them'?). In short, to combine textual and quantitative analysis.

Approaching the Red Cross material my first question was whether Austro-Hungarian POWs had anything at all positive to say about their state's relief effort. There were severe organizational problems from the very beginning of the relief effort in 1915 and the entire operation suffered from an acute shortage of funds and a lack of qualified personnel.[40] Nevertheless, officials in the Austro-Hungarian War Ministry expected POWs to show gratitude toward the state and showed disappointment when it seemed that 'expressions of gratitude and recognition are less prevalent . . . than accusations and complaints'.[41]

However, a closer examination of the Red Cross letters reveals that disappointment was not the only mood expressed in them. An analysis of the first five months sufficiently covered by the reports (December 1916–April 1917) shows that the percentage of 'positive' letters was about the same as the negative letters, both constituting roughly one third of the correspondence (see Table 6.1). The rest of the letters were descriptive laconic statements ('neutral' letters) which informed the addressee what the writer had received. Thus, a preliminary quantitative analysis of the correspondence suggests – perhaps surprisingly – that more POWs had been satisfied with the relief effort than the censorship's own reading of the material had suggested.

The key to understanding this apparent incongruity is the word 'satisfied'. One very rarely finds examples of exuberance or happiness

Table 6.1: POWs Attitude Toward the Relief Effort: December 1916–
November 1917

Month	Number of letters	Positive		Neutral		Negative	
		Number	Per cent	Number	Pert cent	Number	Per cent
Dec. 1916	103	17	16.5	68	56.0	18	17.4
Jan. 1917	187	41	21.9	109	58.2	37	19.7
Feb. 1917	182	34	18.6	98	53.8	50	27.4
Mar. 1917	158	47	29.7	65	41.1	46	29.1
Apr. 1917	141	45	31.9	53	37.5	43	30.4
May 1917	89	22	24.7	36	40.4	31	34.8
Jun. 1917	92	15	16.3	35	38.0	42	45.6
Jul. 1917	98	12	12.2	33	33.6	53	54.1
Aug. 1917	85	10	11.8	33	38.8	42	49.4
Sep. 1917	97	7	7.2	49	50.5	41	42.3
Oct. 1917	109	12	11.0	44	40.4	53	46.6
Nov. 1917	54	2	3.7	18	33.3	34	63.0
Total	**1395**	**264**	**18.9**	**641**	**46**	**490**	**35.1**

even in those letters who had taken a favorable attitude vis-à-vis the
Austro-Hungarian relief effort. The tone in most cases is reserved and
the emphasis is on the usefulness of certain items to the writers. POW
Martin Marx, for example, writing to Hungary from a camp near the
city of Saratov (southern European Russia): 'we experienced some
joy, having received from the Red Cross uniforms, boots and a warm
blanket. We received also underwear and winter underwear.'[42]
Another prisoner, Rudolf Suchel, told his family in Lower Austria that
'presents from Austria were distributed here. I received a tunic,
underwear and socks, all of which came very handy to me.'[43] Ladislav
Pravenec writing to Bohemia from Kiev informed his family that 'this
winter I am much better supplied than last winter. We received new
padded clothes, new underwear and new shoe soles.'[44]

Furthermore, satisfaction on a personal level did not translate in
most cases to favorable comments about the Habsburg monarchy.
Only one third of the positive letters written between November
1916 and April 1917 were explicitly thankful to those whom the
writer thought were responsible for the relief action;[45] and those
were not always Austria–Hungary or the Austro-Hungarian Red Cross.

The Czech speaking POW Vaclav Panenka writing on 9 January 1917 from a camp near Tomsk thanked warmly 'a certain Countess from Germany, who came and purchased for the prisoners musical instruments, giving each for Christmas three rubles; she organized in Tomsk concerts and theater for the prisoners. So now we go to the theater and to concerts. Someone has compassion and feelings for us after all.'[46] Another Czech speaking POW, writing from Samara three days later, described in detail the things he and his fellow prisoners received and concluded by saying: 'thank those who sent us the uniforms. We were almost completely naked before that, like beggars, now we are again like soldiers.'[47]

It is interesting to note that among those who indeed were thankful to their state, only about one-third referred specifically to 'Austria-Hungary' (or any other variation of the name) or to 'our Red Cross' ('Austrian'/'Austro-Hungarian'). The rest preferred formulations such as 'we thank our beloved fatherland' or singled out the emperor as the one personally responsible for the relief action. Two things are to be said about this preference: first, both the terms 'fatherland' or 'homeland' (*Vaterland* or *Heimat* in the letters written in German)[48] as well as the notion of a caring emperor conjure up images of familial bond. It is not a faceless bureaucracy that is responsible for the relief action but rather someone like a father who aids a family member in an hour of need. In a few of the letters, Red Cross nurses were described as 'loving mothers' and one of the prisoners, Josef Holecek from the POW camp in Minsk, compared his feelings upon receiving new uniforms to the joy he had once felt when his mother came home from the annual fair. As we shall see below, family imagery also figured prominently in POWs' letters of complaints with prisoners often describing their lot as that of 'poor children' or 'step sons'. The second thing to be said about the usage of 'fatherland' and 'emperor', is that it reflected formulas utilized by the Habsburg army to motivate its own soldiers. As Richard Plaschka has shown, from the very beginning of the war until the spring of 1918, Austro-Hungarian soldiers had been told by the Army's High Command (AOK) that they were fighting in the name of God for their Emperor (King in Hungary) and their Fatherland. Even when it became clear that these formulas had only marginal effect on the fighting spirit of soldiers, the AOK stuck to them almost until the very end.[49] Thus, when POWs thanked the emperor or the fatherland for the things sent to Russia, they were accepting (either consciously or unconsciously) the official version of what Austria-

Hungary was all about (monarchical and unified). Conspicuous, however, is that this group was small even among the POWs who were satisfied with the relief effort, and that after April 1917 one is hard pressed to find prisoners like Jan Pekar who wished 'to thank his majesty most respectfully for the uniforms'.[50] Therefore, if the relief effort was organized in part to demonstrate to the prisoners that their home state was a caring place (strengthening thus their imperial loyalties) then it had been unsuccessful.

From May 1917 and onwards there was a significant decrease in the percentage of POWs expressing contentment with the Austro-Hungarian relief effort (Table 6.1). The percentage of letters expressing satisfaction dropped from one out of every three letters to one out of every ten letters. In contrast the number of negative letters shot up and constituted about half of all the correspondence. It is clear that a growing section of the POW population was expressing unhappiness with the relief effort. The question is whether these complaints were more than what Austrians usually characterize as *raunzen* (to grumble) whether they reflected a more fundamental shift in POWs expectations from their state. Whether, for example, we see an increasing tendency to look at the relief effort through the prism of social conflict (as Péter Hanák had thought)? Whether a growing number of POWs pushed the national issue into the forefront of their critique and accused Austria-Hungary of national discrimination?

To deal with these question I divided the letters of complaint into four broad groups based on the dominant conceptual environment of each letter:

1 Letters which accused the Austro-Hungarian state (or the Red Cross) of maltreating certain ranks or certain social classes. The underlying argument here was that because distribution criteria were deliberately unequal a section of the POW population suffered more than it should have. Letters which accused the Austro-Hungarian state or its agents of maltreating certain ranks or certain social classes. An anonymous letter from the camp in Samarkand complained that plain infantry soldiers did not receive anything, 'whereas the One Year Volunteers each received from Nurse Horn twenty rubles. When I asked her for the reasons she just shrugged her shoulders and said that these were her instructions (and this is because the One Year Volunteers have already proved themselves as very useful to the state and the general public).'[51] Another POW, Officer Dr

Friedrich [Bedřich] Zenisek, writing in Czech from the officers' camp in Ufa (Ufa district; eastern European Russia) thought that it was the Austro-Hungarian officers who were receiving the short end of the stick: 'Our government thinks that we can live here like gentlemen officers [*Herren*] with the fifty rubles that are paid to us. We fare worse than each and every man, because we are locked up and unable to work even without pay.'[52]

2 Letters complaining about national discrimination. 'It is only the Hungarians and Germans that the underwear, shoes and uniforms go to', protested one letter in Czech, 'we Slavs must settle for prayer books. I am convinced that the Red Cross is supported by us a hundred times more than in the German areas and in Hungary. This is why I ask you to be indifferent to the whole thing. The other nationalities have already received many gifts.'[53]

3 Letters accusing the state of either forgetting or not caring about its captive soldiers, a critique which I termed 'state indifference'. The argument in most of these letters was that had Austria-Hungary (or the Red Cross) cared more about the prisoners they would not be in such miserable state. Officer Viktor Furlan, for example, writing in German from the camp of Dubovka (Saratov district) accused the Red Cross of deliberately allowing the rank-and-file to die: 'If our exalted Red Cross would see the misery of the men, how more and more of them die [*krepieren*] daily like dirty dogs and in what conditions the sons of the Austrian fatherland find themselves, perhaps some help would indeed come. About the suffering of the officers, who have become hunger pros [*Hungerkünstler*], one does not need to worry at all, they are not dying yet.'[54]

4 Letters that criticized how the relief effort was administered, but did not view the state or its agents as acting in bad faith. This line of critique, which I labeled 'mismanagement', reiterated in one way or another the claim regarding the notorious Austro-Hungarian *Schlamperei* (sloppiness). For example, an anonymous letter, written in German and sent to central offices of Red Cross in Vienna, complained bitterly about the fact that shoes and uniforms had arrived already countless times in Tashkent, while the entire area of Alatyr (Simbirsk district, Eastern European Russia) has been completely ignored. Some prisoners thought that the quality of things sent to Russia was not as good as it should be, and others reprimanded the state for not sending enough support for everyone. The important

thing to remember about these letters is that although the state and the Red Cross are often accused of incompetence and corruption, they are not perceived as indifferent to the fate of POWs or maliciously disposed towards a particular group among them.

Regarding the letters of complaint, I first sought to examine whether indeed many letters were written in the spirit of social opposition. As mentioned above, most Austro-Hungarian POWs shunned formal political commitments that might get them in trouble. Yet, it was entirely plausible that increased contact with the Russian population during the revolutionary year of 1917 heightened the prisoners' awareness of social issues. Moreover, since the Austro-Hungarian relief effort significantly favored officers over rank-and-file POWs (and since over 80 per cent of the letters were from enlisted prisoners), I expected issues of military hierarchy to figure prominently in the letters of complaint.

This however is not what seems to have happened. The percentage of letters of complaint reflecting social opposition did not increase in the course of 1917. Rather, it stayed constant throughout that year, fluctuating on a level between 10–20 per cent (see Table 6.2). If we take into account also the positive and neutral letters we see that indeed only a very small number of POWs discussed the relief effort in terms of social and military hierarchies. In March 1917 immediately after the first revolution only five out of 158 letters (3.1 per cent) referred to social or military stratification. In June 1917, six out of ninety-two (6.5 per cent) and in September 1917, three out of ninety-seven (3.1 per cent). Moreover, the letters contained in the Red Cross reports showed almost no penetration of socialist terminology: among 1,476 letters I found one mention of 'capitalist war', one case of addressees being greeted as 'comrades' and one reference to 'class differences'.

Even those who complained about inequality between different ranks did so in a rather mild and reserved tone. What exasperated rank-and-file POWs was not different treatment per se but its extent. 'I received just two rubles in twenty six months', complained Czech speaking POW Vladimir Zeman, 'while officers who get each month fifty ruble salary receive on top of it support from Austria.'[55] Another POW, Heinrich Pichl objected to the fact that 'a nurse from the Austrian Red Cross . . . gave each POW three rubles, but the gentlemen officers, who get each month fifty rubles and do nothing, got from her twenty rubles each.'[56]

Table 6.2: Distribution of Complaint Letters: January–November 1917

Month	Number of letters	Rank/Class		Nationalism		Indifference		Mismanagement	
		Number	Per cent	Number	Per cent	Number	Per cent	Number	Per cent
Jan. 17	37	13	35.1	4	10.8	4	10.8	14	37.8
Feb. 17	50	5	10	12	24	10	20	17	34
Mar 17	46	5	10.8	5	10.8	8	17.3	20	43.4
Apr. 17	43	9	20.9	11	25.5	4	9.3	14	32.5
May17	31	5	16.1	3	9.6	4	12.9	14	45.1
Jun. 17	42	6	14.2	9	21.4	6	14.2	16	38
Jul. 17	53	10	18.8	10	18.8	13	24.5	14	26.4
Aug 17	42	9	21.4	6	14.2	6	14.2	14	33.3
Sep. 17	41	3	7.3	8	19.5	15	36.5	13	31.7
Oct. 17	53	5	9.4	5	9.4	13	24.5	22	41.5
Nov 17	34	4	11.7	5	14.7	10	29.4	12	35.3
Total	472	74	15.6	78	16.5	93	19.7	170	36

1. Not all letters of complaints could be sorted out into one of the four main groups. As a result, the total number of complaint letters is slightly higher than the combined total of groups 1–4. The greatest monthly discrepancies were in March 1917 and October 1917 when only around 85 per cent of the letters could be assigned to any of the groups. Letters that could not be assigned included mostly personal expressions of discontent without any attempts to explain it.

2. Not all the months included in Table 6.1 are included in Table 6.2. The reason for this divergence is that there were too few letters of complaint during these months to make any meaningful analysis. Thus, during November 1916 there were eight letters of complaint (three nationalism, three state indifference and two mismanagement). During December 1916 there were eighteen letters of complaint (four Rank/Class, two Nationalism, three State Indifference and four Mismanagement). In December 1917 there were four letters of complaint (one Nationalism, two State Indifference, one Mismanagement).

Thus, based on the Red Cross material there is little to support the claim that a significant part of the POW population had been profoundly affected by socialist ideas. Therefore, the strict political screening process that the AOK subjected returning POWs in the spring and summer of 1918, seems to have been an overkill and a miscalculation. While it did not weed out the relatively few POWs that adopted a revolutionary *credo* (these for the most part either stayed to fight with the Bolsheviks or sneaked back clandestinely to Austria-Hungary), there is sufficient evidence to suggest that the *Heimkehrer* intensely resented the quarantines and the military 're-education' that had been imposed on them.

In the same vein, I expected a high percentage of letters of complaint to refer to national differences. There were two main reasons for this: first, Austro-Hungarian POWs in Russia found themselves interacting on a daily basis with people who were culturally and linguistically different; whether these were their fellow POWs from the Habsburg monarchy, their Russian captors or members of the multitude of different people living in the Russian empire.[57] Close proximity and daily contact with people who are manifestly different often invites self-examination, or as British historian Linda Colley put it: 'men and women decide who they are by reference to who and what they are not, once confronted with an obvious alien "them" an otherwise diverse community can become a reassuring . . . "us".'[58] Second, the period covered by the Red Cross reports (November 1916–December 1917) saw a considerable intensification of the activities of, what Katherine Verdery and Mark von Hagen have termed, the 'agents of nationalism' in Russia.[59] During this period the Central Powers announced the re-establishment of Congress Poland (albeit under German hegemony). Declarations by the Central Soviet and the Provisional Government in support of 'Polish self-determination and complete independence in national and international affairs' and increased efforts to recruit Czech, Slovak, Serb, Croat and Slovene POWs to fight against Austria-Hungary in quasi-national armies.[60] Thus, it seemed reasonable to expect that Austro-Hungarian POWs in Russia would take notice of the national fermentation around them and incorporate nationalist ideas and expressions into their correspondence.

Again, this for the most part did not happen. The share of letters complaining about national discrimination in the distribution of relief fluctuated between 10–20 per cent and actually started to drop towards the end of 1917. If we figure into the calculation also the positive and neutral letters we see that only a minority of POWs were examining the relief effort primarily through the prism of nationalism. Formulating it differently, we see in the Red Cross letters no indication that the concept of 'nation' was becoming the key organizing concept of POWs' narratives.

This conclusion, however, should be qualified in two respects. First, there were two distinct groups of prisoners who did increasingly utilize nationalist terminology in their critique of the state: Czech speakers and Polish speakers. In the Czech case this usage is particularly significant since the Czech-speaking POWs, whose letters wound up in the Red Cross reports were exactly those who did not volunteer to the anti-Habsburg Czech Legion – those who were still loyal Habsburg soldiers. Second, those who complained about ethnic discrimination expressed in most cases a very deep disappointment in the state and/or its agents. 'It pains us to be pushed aside and not to be recognized as Austrian soldiers', wrote the Czech-speaking POW I.B. to the Red Cross offices in Prague, 'we have spilled our blood; many of our brothers and sons cover the battlefield in eternal sleep. We suffer like others for the Aus[trian] cause. This is a very bad sign for our homeland.' Another Czech-speaking POW, officer Josef Polcar, asked: 'who inscribed the mark of Cain on our foreheads?'[61] In contrast to POWs who complained about rank discrimination, POWs who protested national discrimination did so vehemently with a conviction that a grave injustice has been done to them. This feeling encouraged some of them to reassess their allegiance toward Austria-Hungary; a particularly interesting example was provided by a Polish speaking officer, M. Wajda, who had been interned in the city of Tsaritsin:

A salary of fifty rubles a month is not enough for our maintenance. A few camps already sent telegrams to the [War] Ministry, however, with no success. Our regime has forgotten completely the Slavs and should not be surprised, therefore, if many of us will feel obligated to search for a job or in desperation volunteer for the front [i.e. to fight against Austria-Hungary] in order to look for death. Our Cam[p] was totally and completely ignored. In Saratov clothes and underwear had been distributed already in February, yet no delegates from the Red Cross came to visit us.[62]

Thus, although the majority of POWs did not assess the relief effort with a nationalist yardstick, those who did, expressed considerable dissatisfaction and linked their unhappiness with a critique of the state. The fact that this did not happen with rank/class discrimination suggests that national equality was significantly more important to the individuals involved than social inequality (and by extension that national identities were subjectively far more important to POWs than class identities)

However, what mostly bothered POWs was neither rank discrimination nor ethnic discrimination, but rather the question of why Austria-Hungary was not doing a better job with the relief effort. As to why the relief effort fell short of the mark there were two main divisions among the prisoners: those who believed Austria-Hungary simply did not care about the prisoners and those who thought there was something fundamentally wrong with how the operation was administered.

Those who thought Austria-Hungary did not concern itself with its captive soldiers ('State Indifference'), reached this conclusion in many cases by comparing Austria-Hungary's and Germany's relief efforts. Prisoner-of-war Anton Preininger, for example, writing from the camp of Abshevo (Samara Gubernia) sent a letter of complaint to the editor of one of Budapest's newspapers (name missing):

> We take permission to describe to the distinguished editorial board the atmosphere after twenty months in captivity. How our hearts are saddened again and again upon seeing how the Germans from the Reich [i.e. from Imperial Germany] are remembered with gifts and money by their homeland and cities, and how we Hungarians and Austrians stand on the side like poor children. We would be happy to receive for once a sign of life from our homeland.[63]

Another POW, Josef Schwarz from the camp of Alekseievo-Leonovo (Don area), thought that at the very least Austria-Hungary should have made an effort to give the prisoners something for Easter. 'How is it so', he asked, 'that for the holidays Germans from the Reich are given by their Red Cross uniforms, underwear and shoes, while nobody cares that we poor Austrians don't have anything to wear?'[64]

Others, especially POW officers, complained that their government and the Red Cross were unresponsive to what they are trying to communicate. 'A report written on our behalf by the Swedish Red Cross', wrote the Hungarian-speaking POW *Offizieraspirant* Gyula Kisfalu, 'was not acknowledged by our government, not even with a slight movement of the ear.'[65] Similarly, a Danish representative told POW officer Rudolf Bauer that 'it seems that the Austrian regime either knows very little or is misinformed about the POWs.'[66] This sense of abandonment found expression in analogies with the fate of 'poor children', 'stepchildren' and 'castaway children'. By identifying with archetypal examples of pure, defenseless and maltreated family members, POWs were rejecting emphatically any claims the Habsburg state might have had to being benign and paternalistic. Rather, as POW Franz Uebergänger wrote back home to Tyrol, 'it is the great and cruel inhumanity of Austria that allows us prisoners to freeze.'[67]

Although the great majority of the 'state indifference' group used an emotional-pathetic tone to make their point, there was a second, ironic and detached voice, that came up in some of the letters in this group. POW Wolfgang Sedlacek, told, for example, his mother in Austrian Silesia:

> I received again, i.e. for the third time in the course of thirty-two months of captivity, a postcard from the Red Cross worth three Heller. You see my beloved mother, the relief effort has indeed improved since the year [19]14. In the years 1914 and 1915, I received nothing from the Red Cross and in the year 1916, quite accidentally, six rubles from countess Revertera, then again a three Heller postcard. Clothes and such things, not yet.[68]

Irony, it is worth noting, is more subversive than pathos. It belittles and ridicules its target by maliciously exposing the gulf between claims and reality. Literary historian Paul Fussell argued, in his classic *The Great War and Modern Memory*, that ironic recollection was by far the preferred style of western-front memoirists and that since World War I, irony has become 'an inseparable element of the general vision of war in our time'.[69] Irony is most effective when it is understated. When the reader has to halt for a split-second (or longer) and figure out what the writer 'really' means. However, the writer who uses irony never knows for certain whether the reader would actually halt and therefore takes a risk of being understood at face value rather than ironically. Thus, writing ironically is a luxury that can be afforded only by those who do not mind being misunderstood. It could not have been the dominant tone of Austro-Hungarian POWs in Russia, who very much wanted their situation to be known back home, and who felt that their communications so far had not been understood very well.

The perception that the people in charge of the relief effort did not truly grasp the severity of the situation, might also explain why POWs sent letters and petitions directly to the Austrian Red Cross, or in some cases requested their families to intercede on their behalf.

'Go to the Red Cross', instructed POW Spazek, 'and say that they can take better care of their poor prisoners in Russia, so that the prisoners get at least their mail, if no uniforms, shoes and underwear are given. This is why the Red Cross is there, not for the title. It is really true that not a soul cares about us.'[70] The tone of POW Spazek's appeal reflects very clearly his disappointment, anger and frustration with the Austro-Hungarian relief effort. Yet, it also tells us that he thought that those in charge could be pressured to change their priorities, otherwise he would not have sent his family to protest on his behalf. Thus, one could read the accusations regarding state (or Red Cross) indifference as shorthand meaning: 'We are unhappy because our well-being does not seem important to those who could help to alleviate our situation.' 'We could still be placated if the proper actions (distribution of more clothes, money, shoes etc.) would immediately be taken.'

In other words, by using the means at their disposal (petitions and letters to the Red Cross, letters to newspapers and by having families voice discontent), prisoners were engaging in political action aimed at securing more funds.

Letters complaining about how the relief effort was managed were potentially the most useful to the Austrian and Hungarian Red Cross, because they focused on specific shortcomings that needed to be addressed. Nonetheless, due to the paucity of money, the scarcity of on-the-spot personnel and the sheer enormity of this operation, these problems seem not to have been addressed at all. Thus, descriptions of corrupt practices and examples of general disorder figured prominently in POWs' letters of complaint throughout the year 1917 (see table 6.2).

Corruption, it should be noted, was almost never ascribed to representatives of the Red Cross. Except one case, in which a Swedish pastor was accused of selling clothes on the black market and pocketing the money, almost all other complaints about corruption referred to prisoners in positions of responsibility cheating other prisoners, or to corrupt Russian camp personnel.[71] Prisoner-of-war F. Schaflechner, working in a factory near Perm, wrote that '1,200 cans of condensed milk were sent by the Red Cross intended for general distribution. But these fell into such hands . . . that sold [the cans] to the Russians for a lot of money.' Franz Wänke told his mother back in Bohemia that 'I know that you part with the last things you have because you think that your son gets something. But you are badly deceived: all that you give, you give for nothing. We are cheated here by our own people far worse than by the Russians. I don't even have a complete set of uniforms.'[72] Other prisoners complained that favoritism (*Protektion*) was rampant; that 'only *Protektionskinder* are taken into consideration when aid comes from the home country' and that 'the rest have to turn a blind eye'.[73] Letters from forty-one different camps reported incidents of embezzlement, some of which were very serious: clothes and supplies worth 42,000 rubles were reported to have been stolen from the camp of Omsk, while in Tula clothes and uniforms were reported as being sold to the rank-and-file POWs for thirty rubles instead of being given to the most needy. Thus, families in Austria-Hungary were consistently receiving the impression that the Red Cross was not doing its utmost to ensure fair and orderly distribution. 'The Red Cross just doesn't want to function', wrote POW Lieutenant Gustav Pröglhof from Totskoe (Samara), 'although it had sufficient time for learning because of the length of the war . . . Therefore be a little stand-offish with your contributions to the Red Cross. Relatives of POWs are never stingy with their contributions because they expect their loved-ones in far away places to get a share. If they hear how things are really settled, there could only be anger.'[74]

Another major source of irritation to POWs was the fact that distribution among the various camps was seldom even. Small camps and camps that were far from a railroad track received fewer visitations and less support than the larger and the more conveniently located camps. On a few occasions relief seems to have failed to reach fairly large regions such as the Don area in southern European Russia and the Viatka province north of Kazan. Prisoners from the district of Alatyr (Simbirsk province) sent a collective letter to the offices of the Austrian Red Cross in Vienna complaining that other regions received support whereas they did not get anything: 'the people in Tashkent have so much that they have enough to sell and here we go around naked. This is certainly a great *Schweinerei*! War you know how to wage. This is your scandalous management in Austria!'[75]

On other occasions uneven distribution was the result of where a specific camp was on a nurse's itinerary. Nora Kinsky's delegation, for example, expected to receive a transfer of money halfway through its assignment, when it left the Priamur district and entered the province of Transbaiklia (see above Chapter 5). This, however, did not happen and the delegation found itself very short on cash. Thus, Nora Kinsky could not give as much money in the second part of her mission and had to deal with prisoners' frustration:

We are very happy to learn of a planned visit of a Red Cross nurse. During the waiting days before the visit everybody was in a festive mood, however what disappointment and bitterness after the visit. This person did not seem to know why she was here. Perhaps it is now a sport to travel and visit POW camps, perhaps it is fashionable to see how POWs live and fare.[76]

Finally, two additional prevalent complaints should be briefly mentioned; one which was voiced by POWs of all ranks and one which appeared almost only in officers' letters. First, some of the items sent to Russia were apparently of very poor quality, unsuitable for local climatic conditions or on a few occasions completely useless. Uniforms were reported to disintegrate after a few days, shoes were said to lack proper insulation material and things sent from Austria were described as being 'old junk' (*alte Sachen*). In letters reminiscent of a scene in Jean Renoir's *Grand Illusion*, prisoners from seven different camps complained that the aid sent by the Red Cross consisted only of prayer books and pictures of saints: 'the honorable Austrian Red Cross sent us on the above-written date [29 May 1917] holy books and holy pictures instead of something to wear, shirts or something of the sort. We all were in the [battle]field and we are not children anymore.'[77]

Second, many officers were infuriated by the fact that a share of the money given to them by the Red Cross was said to be a loan and that their families in Austria-Hungary were often asked to return this loan immediately. 'The nurse broke her promise as a countess', wrote POW officer O. Ledvina to his wife in Bohemia, 'she said that we need to pay the sum only after the war.'[78] Another POW, officer Dr Bohus Kynych told his parents that 'the ten rubles the Red Cross committee gave each and every POW were said to be gift. Now, news arrive via my friends that the Red Cross demanded outrageous sums from their parents. If anyone demands money from you, tell them that I never took a loan. These ten rubles that we are talking about were a gift not a loan.'[79]

Examining the language and content of the 1,476 letters contained in the Red Cross reports suggests two important conclusions about the prisoners' loyalties and collective identities:

First, in the period between December 1916 and December 1917, Austro-Hungarian POWs in Russia became increasingly critical of their state. However, contrary to expectations, this increased critique did not express itself primarily by reference to social or national oppositions, but rather as direct critique, aimed at specific policies and specific practices of the Austro-Hungarian state and its representatives. In other words, POWs were increasingly willing to speak up (or ask their relatives and friends to speak up on their behalf), but in most cases they were doing so not as members of specific nationalities or social groups, but rather as Austro-Hungarian POWs. Moreover, even in letters written in the spirit of class opposition (in most cases opposition between the ranks), the critique was specific and constructive. Only seldom can one detect any desire for revolutionary upheavals or any major restructuring of the Austro-Hungarian state.

Second, the critique (and to a lesser degree also the praise) articulated in the Red Cross letters, indicated clearly that Austro-Hungarian prisoners expected their state to do whatever it could for their well-being. They expected that Austria-Hungary would care about their fate and that their opinions would receive a serious and respectful hearing by those in charge of the relief effort. By this Austro-Hungarian POWs were not very different from French, British and German soldiers on the Western front, who often engaged in subversive tactics when their opinions seemed to be ignored by their armies' command.[80] In other words, Austro-Hungarian POWs in Russia were making their government aware that if modern warfare required an extraordinary degree of commitment and sacrifice, then commitment and sacrifice should be reciprocal. For Austro-Hungarian captured soldiers it was clearly the Habsburg state that had abandoned them rather than the other way around.

Notes

1. Two shorter versions of this chapter appeared in German in the journal *Zeitgeschichte* 25 (1998), pp. 348–56 and in English in Austrian History Yearbook 31 (2000), pp. 87–105.

2. Österreichisches Staatsarchiv (öStA)/Kriegsarchiv (KA)/Armeeoberkommando (AOK) 1917 Gemeinsames Zentralnachweisbureau des Roten Kreuzes-Auskunftstelle für Kriegsgefangene (GZNB) Kart. 3751, Akt 4664, letter 35.

3. Brändström, *Among Prisoners of War in Russia and Siberia*, pp. 180–4.

4. Ibid., p. 203; specifically in Denmark there were 272 Austro-Hungarian POW officers and 622 rank-and-file. In Norway there were 128 officers and 204 rank-and-file. Thus, officers made up almost one third of these very privileged prisoners, although they made up less than 3 per cent of the number of Austro-Hungarian POWs in Russia.

5. Von Scotti was seized by a friend from a hospital near Lake Baikal – where he had been recovering from dysentery – and was told 'let's go'. After obtaining clothes, money and food for the ride, the two left their camp in east Siberia on 13 February 1918 and boarded the Trans-Siberian train in the direction of Moscow. After a thirteen day trip, severe snow storms, inspections by Bolshevik patrols and an onslaught of hungry people, who assumed these lucky Siberians had bread on them, they arrived in Moscow. Everywhere they saw evidence of the severe fighting during Bolshevik Revolution and encountered Austro-Hungarian POWs begging in the streets for money and food. They continued via Borodino and Smolensk, arriving finally in the town of Orsha (White Russia) where rumors located the German army. Scotti and a group of Austro-Hungarian POW officers sneaked across cease fire lines and reached a German outpost and freedom. 'Aufzeich-nungen von Obst. Gottfried von Scotti über der Kriegsgefangenschaft in Rußland', *Kriegsarchiv, Nachlaß Mühlhofer*, B/231:16, pp. 14–21.

6. Gerald H. Davis, 'The Life of Prisoners of War in Russia 1914–1921', in Samuel R. Williamson and Peter Pastor (eds) *Essays on World War I: Origins and Prisoners of War*, pp. 182.

7. Ibid., pp. 182–3; Hannes Leidinger and Verena Moritz, 'Österreich-Ungarn und die Heimkehrer aus russischer Kriegsgefangenschaft im Jahr 1918', *Osterreich in Geschichte und Literatur*, (1997), pp. 390–1.

8. A provision though was added that after all the German POWs had been repatriated, Germany would release Russian POWs according to the same pace. Davis, 'The Life of Prisoners of War in Russia 1914–1921', p. 182.

9. The number of returnees (*Heimkehrer*) could be – and most probably was – higher than that, since the various categories do not add up: the number of POWs stuck in Russia during the Civil War is usually assessed at 450,000–500,000 and the deaths at 385,000 (of which some had died after October 1918). Thus, depending on the total estimate of the number Austro-Hungarian POWs in Russia, there are between 50,000 and 500,000 unaccounted POWs (see chapter 1).

10. Quoted from Inge Przybilovszki, *Die Rückführung der österreich-ungarischen Kriegsgefangenen aus dem Osten in den letzten Monaten der k.u.k Monarchie*, Ph.D. Dissertation, University of Vienna, 1965, p. 38.

11. Ibid., p. 336; Hannes Leidinger and Verena Moritz, 'Österreich-Ungarn und die Heimkehrer aus russischer Kriegsgefangenschaft im Jahr 1918', pp. 390-1.

12. In April 1918 the daily number of returnees averaged 4025 POWs (of them twenty officers) and in May 1918, 4288 POWs (thirty-five officers). I

calculated the averages based on the information contained in Inge Przybilovszki's dissertation, pp. 336-7.

13. Inge Przybilovszki, *Die Rückführung der österreich-ungarischen Kriegsgefangenen aus dem Osten in den letzten Monaten der k.u.k Monarchie*, p. 337.

14. On repatriation see Hannes Leidinger and Verena Moritz, 'Österreich-Ungarn und die Heimkehrer aus russischer Kriegsgefangenschaft im Jahr 1918', *Osterreich in Geschichte und Literatur*, 6 (1997), pp. 385-403; Richard Plaschka, Arnold Suppan and Horst Haselsteiner, *Innere Front. Militärassistenz, Widerstand und Umsturz in der Donaumonarchie*, Vienna– Verlag für Geschichte und Politik, 1974, vol. 2; Otto Wassermair, *Die Meutereien der Heimkehrer aus russischer Kriegsgefangenschaft bei den Ersatzkörpern der k.u.k. Armee im Jahre* 1918, Ph.D. Dissertation, University of Vienna, 1968; Inge Przybilovszki, *Die Rückführung der österreich-ungarischen Kriegsgefangenen aus dem Osten in den letzten Monaten der k.u.k Monarchie*, (Ph.D. Dissertation, University of Vienna, 1965); On the possible exception of the Hungarian POWs see: Ivan Völgyes, 'Hungarian Prisoners of War in Russia', *Cahiers du monde russe et Soviétique*, 14 (1973). The quotation is from: Hannes Leidinger and Verena Moritz, p. 394.

15. Inge Przybilovszki, *Die Rückführung der österreich-ungarischen Kriegsgefangenen aus dem Osten in den letzten Monaten der k.u.k Monarchie*, p. 38.

16. See above Chapter 1 and also Chapter 3.

17. See above Chapter 3.

18. Z. A. B. Zeman, *The Break-Up of the Habsburg Empire 1914–1918, A Study in National and Social Revolution*, London: Oxford University Press, 1961, p. 142.

19. As to confirm this view a series of large-scale mutinies broke out among Austro-Hungarian reserve units in the spring and summer of 1918 that were organized and led in many cases by returning POWs.

20. Scotti, p. 21.

21. Ibid.

22. Eduard Stoss, in In Feindeshand.

23. See above Chapters 1 and 3.

24. Holger Herwig, The First World War: Germany and Austria-Hungary 1914-1918, p. 358.

25. Until the arrival of Masaryk in Russia in the spring of 1917 only 3,000 Czech POWs volunteered to the Legion. It is not exactly clear how many volunteered during the next year when a recruiting drive was launched. The figure of 100,000 proposed by the Czech nationalist historians in the 1920s and 1930s is very exaggerated. See Vavra and also Kalvoda. Regarding the South Slavs see Banac, op.cit.

26. Wassermair, pp. 87-8.

27. There were strong reasons for not making such a commitment including the knowledge that eventually they would be required to give account of their behavior in Russia. The Austrian military chaplain, Karl Drexel, described how officers captured together put together an agreed version of the circumstances surrounding their capture. Karl Drexel, *Feldkurat in Sibirien*, Innsbruck, 1940; in another example, a Czech recruiting officer attempted in the summer of 1917 to enlist POW volunteers in the labor camp of *Kamenskii Zavod*, he found according to a letter written by one of the prisoners only 'three fools who are willing to support the continuation of the war', this despite of four days of propaganda activity among many Czech, Romanian, Croat and Slovene prisoners.

28. Hubertus Jahn, *Patriotic Culture in Russia During World War I*, Ithaca, 1995, p. 3.

29. Péter Hanák, 'Die Volksmeinung während des letzten Kriegsjahres in Österreich-Ungarn', *Die Auflösung des Habsburgerreiches. Zusammenbruch und Neuorientierung im Donauraum*, Vienna, 1970, pp. 58–66; Eric Hobsbawm, *Nations and Nationalism since 1780: Programme, Myth, Reality*, pp. 126–30.

30. See note 36 for the full language distribution.

31. See above, Chapter 4.

32. Heinrich Freiherr v. Raabl-Werner, 'Österreich-Ungarns offizielle Kriegsgefangenenfürsorge', *In Feindeshand*, vol. 2, p. 325. On the function of the Austro-Hungarian censorship during World War I, see Gustav Spann, *Zensur in Österreich während des I. Weltkrieges 1914–1918*, Ph.D. Dissertation University of Vienna, 1972.

33. On history from below, on the related approach of *Alltagsgeschichte* and on military history from below see: Samuel Hynes, *The Soldiers' Tale: Bearing Witness to Modern War*, New York: Penguin 1997; Alf Lüdtke (ed.) *The History of Everyday Life: Reconstructing Historical Experience and Ways of Life*, translated by William Templer, Princeton: Princeton University Press, 1995; Wolfram Wette (ed.) *Der Krieg des kleinen Mannes*, Munich, 1992; Jim Sharpe, 'History from Below', in Peter Burke (ed.) *New Perspectives on Historical Writing*, University Park, PA, 1989, pp. 24–41; Richard Holmes, *Acts of War: The Behavior of Men in Battle*, New York, 1986; John Keegan, *The Face of Battle: A Study of Agincourt, Waterloo and the Somme*, London, 1976; E. P. Thompson 'History from Below', *Times Literary Supplement*, 7 April 1966.

34. On the difficulties of analyzing letters see Bernd Ulrich, 'Feldpostbriefe des ersten Weltkrieges: Möglichkeiten und Grenzen einer alltagsgeschichtlichen Quelle', *Militärgeschichtliche Mitteilungen*, 53 (1994), pp. 73–83; see also Aribert Heim, 'Die heile Welt im Stahlgewitter: deutsche und englische Feldpost aus dem ersten Weltkrieg', in Gerhard Hirschfeld, Gerd Krumeich, Dieter Langwiesche, Hans Peter Ullman (eds) *Kriegserfahrungen: Studien zur Sozial- und Mentalitätsgeschichte des ersten Weltkrieges*, Essen Klartext, 1997, pp. 129–45; Manfred Hettling and Michael Jeismann, 'Der

Weltkrieg als Epos. Philipp Witkops, Kriegsbriefe gefallener Studenten', in Gerhard Hirschfeld, Gerd Krumeich and Irina Renz (eds) *Keiner fühlte sich mehr als Mensch . . . Erlebnis und Wirkung des ersten Weltkrieges*, Essen: Klartext, 1993, pp. 175-98.

35. Péter Hanák, 'Die Volksmeinung während des letzten Kriegsjahres in Österreich-Ungarn', *Die Auflösung des Habsburgerreiches: Zusammenbruch und Neuorientierung im Donauraum*, pp. 58-66.

36. The language distribution of the letters was the following: German 818, Czech 351, Polish 149, Ukrainian sixty-one, Slovak thirty-six, Slovene twenty-seven, Hungarian fourteen, Italian seven, Romanian five, Croat four, Serb two, German translation without an indication of the original language two. The rank distribution was the following: rank-and-file 1099, officers 237, one year volunteers fifty, cadets forty-two, ensigns thirty-four, chaplains two, unclear twleve.

37. On the Austro-Hungarian relief effort see: Reinhard Nachtigal, 'Kriegs- gefangene der Habsburgermonarchie in Russland', *Österreich in Geschichte und Literatur*, 4-5a, (1996), pp. 248-62; Gerald H. Davis, 'National Red Cross Societies and Prisoners of War in Russia, 1914-1918', *Journal of Contemporary History*, 28 (1993), pp. 31-52; Nora Kinsky, *Russisches Tagebuch 1916-1918*, Stuttgart, 1976; Alexandrine von Üxküll, *Aus einem Schwesterleben*, Stuttgart, 1956; Elsa Brändström, *Among Prisoners of War in Russia and Siberia*; Heinrich Freiherr von Raabl-Werner, 'Österreich- Ungarns offizielle Kriegsgefangenenfürsorge', in *In Feindeshand*, pp. 324- 31; Magdalene von Walsleben, *Die deutsche Schwester in Sibirien*, Berlin: Furche Verlag, 1919.

38. Ibid.; Eric Hobsbawm, *Nations and Nationalism since 1780: Pro- gramme, Myth, Reality*, pp. 126-30.

39. Contrary to what Hobsbawm asserts, only a few letters came from soldiers in the field.

40. See above Chapter 5.

41. Friedrich Spitzer, 'Unsere Kriegsgefangenen und Internierten in Rußland und Rumänien N.2', Chapter 1 'Besuche der österreichischen u. deutschen Schwestern vom Roten Kreuz', pp. XIV–XV, öStA/KA/AOK 1917/ GZNB Kart:3750 Akt:4600.

42. Bericht 4, kart:3751 letter 129.

43. Ibid., letter 131.

44. Bericht 2, kart 3750 letter 60.

45. Fifty-seven out of 188 letters.

46. Kart 3751, Akt 4664, letter 7.

47. Ibid., letter 32.

48. In languages other than German I am referring to what had been translated by the censors as *Vaterland* or *Heimat* .

49. Part of the reason why the AOK stubbornly insisted on 'emperor' and 'fatherland' was because more precise formulations of war aims (for example those which would take into account social or national factors) were not only

objectionable to the AOK but could also alienate large sections of the population. From the perspective of the AOK, 'emperor' and 'fatherland' were broad enough rallying calls that on the one hand placed political questions on hold, while on the other hand emphasized unity and the monarchical character of the state. Richard G. Plaschka. 'Contradicting Ideologies: the Pressure of Ideological Conflicts in the Austro-Hungarian Army of World War I', in R. Kann, B. Kiraly and P. Fichtner (eds), *The Habsburg Army in World War I: Essays on the Intellectual, Military and Economic Aspects of the Habsburg War Effort*, New York: East European Quarterly distributed by Columbia University Press, 1977, pp. 105–19. Only in the spring of 1918 was a propaganda unit established within the framework of the army, ostensibly only to counter enemy propaganda. The Enemy Propaganda Defense Agency (*Feindespropaganda-Abwehrstelle FA*) produced brochures on such topics as 'the Industrial and Social Reconstruction after the War' and trained a cadre of about 150 education officers. According to Mark Cornwall the *FA* failed because it could not seriously delve into political issues and because by the summer of 1918 shortages in food and nationalist agitation had made 'the troops less receptive to Austrian propaganda'. Mark Cornwall, 'Morale and Discipline in the Austro-Hungarian Army', Lecture delivered in the conference: Mobilizing for Total War: Society and State in Europe 1914–1918, Trinity College Dublin, 23–25 June 1993.

50. Platovka (Orenburg), Jan Pekar March 4, 1917. (Letter originally written in Slovak) KA/AOK 1917/ Kart 3752/Akt 4759/letter # 70.

51. 'Samarkand an Oberlehrer Brunner, Stockau, Böhmen 28 March, 1917'. (Letter written originally in German) Kart 3752/Akt 4759/letter # 76.1.

52. Kart:3754/Akt:4843/letter#124.

53. 'Verchoturye (Perm) an Frau Anna Riha, Unter Sarka, Böhmen, February 28, 1917'. (Letter written originally in Czech), Kart:3754/Akt:4843/letter #100.

54. 'Offizier Viktor Furlan nach Stmk [Styria] 24 July, 1917'. AOK (1917)/GZNB/Kart:3754/Akt:4843/ letter # 33.

55. 'Omsk (Omsk), Vladimir Zeman nach Wallachitsch-Meseritsch, Mähren' without date, KA/AOK 1917/ Kart 3750/Akt 4600/letter # 111d.

56. Kart 3750, Akt 4660, letter 111.d; Ibid, letter 149.b.

57. Even people who had lived in nationally heterogeneous areas before the war did not have the level of daily contact with 'others' that POWs had. If one were to conduct a mental experiment, trying to experience the first couple of hours in a typical morning of Austro-Hungarian POWs in Russia, it would most probably involve waking up in a room with 300–500 other men, many of them speaking (perhaps too loudly) a language one does not understand. One would need to negotiate the usage of the latrines and washing facilities with other prisoners (again in a multitude of languages), whose hygienic norms might very well seem repulsive. One would then be counted by the Russian guards and given daily instructions in a foreign language. Breakfast would then be offered, most often 'Russian style' – ten

men sharing a large bowl of cereal, each dipping a large wooden spoon into the collective bowl. For detailed description of the everyday in captivity, see above Chapter 2.

58. Linda Colley, *The Britons: Forging of the Nation 1707–1837*, New Haven and London: Yale University Press, 1992, p. 6.

59. The three most significant agents are national political organizations, nationally oriented publications and proto-national armies.

60. Fritz Fischer, Germany's Aims in The First World War, New York: W. W. Norton, 1967, Chapter 16–19.

61. 'Balashov (Gov. Saratov) Kgf. I.B an das Rote Kreuz in Prag', 2 April 1917, AOK (1917)/ GZNB/Kart:3751/Akt:4700/letter #15; 'Saratov Josef Polcar nach Böhmen, March 22, 1917', AOK (1917)/ Kart 3752/Akt 4759/ letter # 76.b.

62. 'Zaritzyn (Government Saratov) Offizier M. Wajda nach Galizien, 21 September1917', AOK (1917)/GZNB/ Kart:3755/akt:4909/letter #20.

63. 'Abschewo (Samara), Anton Preininger nach Budapest: 19 February, 1917' (written originally in German), AOK (1917)/GZNB/ Kart:3751/ akt:4664/letter #1.

64. 'Aleksjejewo-Leonowo (Dongebiet), Josef Schwarz nach Böhmen, 14 April, 1917' (written originally in German), AOK (1917)/GZNB/ Kart:3752/ akt:4759/letter #1.

65. 'Stretensk , (Transbaikalien), Offiz. Asp. Gyula Kisfalu nach Ungarn, 20 October', 1917, (letter written originally in Hungarian), AOK (1917/ 1918)/GZNB/ Kart:3756/Akt: 4932/letter #119. They were told this by the Swedish delegation itself.

66. 'Krasnojarsk (Janissesjk), Lt. Rudolf Bauer nach Böhmen, 22 September 1917', (letter written originally in German), letter # 90.

67. 'Agrys (Wjatka), Franz Uebergänger nach Tirol, March 11, 1917' (letter written originally in German), AOK (1917)/GZNB/ Kart:3751/Akt: 4700/ letter #1.

68. 'Petropawlowsk (Akmolinsk), Wolfgang Sedlacek nach Troppau, 12 February 1917', (letter written originally in German), AOK (1917)/GZNB/ Kart:3751/akt:4664/letter #128.

69. Paul Fussel, *The Great War and Modern Memory*, Oxford: Oxford University Press, 1975, p. 33.

70. 'Morschansk (Tambov) Kgf. Spazek nach Wien ohne datum' (letter written originally in German), AOK (1917)/GZNB/ Kart:3755/akt:4909/letter #291.

71. There were three letters discussing Russian corruption. In one case a Swedish delegate was reprimanded for entrusting distribution to the Russian commander, who proceeded then to steal the money.

72. 'Bairnovka (Irkutsk), Franz Wänke nach Böhmen, April 4, 1917' (letter written originally in German), Kart 3751, Akt 4700 , letter 12

73. 'Atschinsk (Jenissejsk) Alois Grandegger nach Tirol, October 5 1917', (letter originally written in German), Kart: 3756/Akt: 4980/letter # 198.

74. 'Totzkoje (Samara), Lt. Gustav Pröglhof nach Nied. Oest [Lower Austria]', 21 October 1917, (letter written originally in German), Kart: 3756/Akt: 4980/letter # 261.

75. This is an undated petition sent to Vienna Kart: 3752/Akt: 4759/letter # 10.

76. 'Beresowka (Transbaikalien), Iwan Ssamatowka nach Galizien, January 15, 1917', (letter written originally in Ukrainian), Kart: 3751/Akt: 4664/letter # 21.

77. 'Schtscheglowskoje (Tomsk), an Frau Elise Kneissl, Karlsbad, May 29, 1917', (letter written originally in German), Kart: 3754/Akt: 4843/letter # 108.

78. 'Chwalinsk (Saratow), Offiz. O.Ledvina nach Böhmen, October, 12, 1917' (letter written originally in Czech), Kart: 3756/Akt: 4980/letter # 246.

79. 'Galitsch (Kostroma), Offiz. Dr. Bohus Kynych nach Böhm, August 7, 1917' (letter written originally in Czech), Kart: 3755/Akt: 4909/letter # 270.

80. On this see: Leonard Smith, *Between Mutiny and Obedience: The case of the French Fifth Infantry Division during World War I*, Princeton: Princeton University Press, 1994; Wilhlem Deist: 'Verdeckter Militärstreik im Kriegsjahr 1918', in Wolfram Wette (ed.), *Der Krieg des kleinen Mannes*, Munich: Piper, 1992; Richard Holmes, *Acts of War: The Behavior of Men in Battle*, New York: The Free Press, 1986; Allan Wildeman, *The End of the Russian Imperial Army: The Old Army and the Soldiers' Revolt (March–April 1917)*, Princeton: Princeton University Press, 1980; Tony Ashworth, *Trench Warfare: the Live and Let Live System*, New York: Holmes & Meier, 1980.

Epilogue. Captivity in the Collective Remembrance of the Great War – The Emergence of a Commemorative Pecking Order

The story of Austro-Hungarian POWs in Russia did not end in the autumn of 1918 when the Dual Monarchy disintegrated. Those POWs who did not or could not return before November 1918 became citizens of new states that were immersed in their own labor pains. The political leadership of these emerging states – composed usually of bourgeois and/or moderate socialist elements – did not look forward to the return of their captive citizenry. The fears regarding the spread of Bolshevik ideas, which had preoccupied the Austro-Hungarian military leadership in the spring and summer of 1918, did not subside in the immediate aftermath of the war. Thus, in the winter of 1918–1919 the successor states sought to restrict repatriation from Russia while placing those who had managed to escape in special quarantine camps.[1] Preparations for the final repatriation of approximately 425,000–430,000 prisoners of war did not begin in earnest until the spring of 1920. On 11 April 1920 the Council of the League of Nations appointed the Norwegian polar explorer, Fridtjof Nansen, as high commissioner for POW repatriation and allocated the successor states a loan of 600,000 pound sterling to finance the operation. Simultaneously, a series of agreements between Soviet Russia and the states of central and eastern Europe were negotiated through the mediation of the International Red Cross Society – the first on 19 April 1920 with Germany the last in July 1921 with Hungary – clearing the way for full scale repatriation.[2] In March 1922 Nansen reported that 427,386 prisoners had been repatriated from Russia with only 4,000 remaining, some of which did not want to return.[3]

Like other World War I veterans, ex-POWs formed and joined veteran associations after their arrival. The Austrian Federal Association of Former POWs (B.e.ö.K.) grew from mutual assistance groups established during captivity in the camp of Krasnoyarsk, including among its honorary members a chancellor and the head of the Red Cross Society. The B.e.ö.K established an archive and a museum for captivity, and held ceremonies to commemorate those who had died in captivity. Elsa Brändström raised money for orphanages and for the children of POWs, and opened two sanatoria for crippled prisoners of war in Germany. Like other veterans, ex-POWs sought to bestow meaning through word, stone and ritual: they published scores of memoirs, erected monuments for the dead and arranged periodic ceremonies. Nonetheless, despite the ubiquity of ex-prisoners in post World War I Europe (and it is worth mentioning yet again that one out of every eight veterans to re-enter civilian society after the war had been a POW) and despite their commemorative activity, the story of captivity never became part of what has been termed the Memory of the Great War.[4] As a conclusion to this work, I would like to reflect on why an abundance of individual memories left no stamp on the collective remembrance of the war. I will focus on what was perhaps the most important medium through which prisoners attempted to tell the story of war captivity: the POW memoir.

In his analysis of soldiers' narratives from World War I, literary historian Samuel Hynes pointed to the extraordinary attention given to Western Front accounts. In his view, more than any other major war this century, World War I has been viewed both in public memory and in history through the prism of 'the Big Show' i.e. the Western Front. The tale of soldiers 'fighting along a narrow band of earth that stretched across northern France from the Channel to the Swiss border . . . created our own war-in-our-heads in which the Western Front is the entire war.'[5] Other fronts and other battles became neglected 'side-shows' with no place 'in our collective memory of the First War'.[6]

To a certain extent this imbalance occurred because the Western Front was where the – economically, politically and culturally – dominant belligerents deployed the majority of their soldiers. The fact that war accounts of German, French and British soldiers were received with great interest in Berlin, Paris and London, meant that they were also read in places that looked up to western Europe for cultural models. In mandatory Palestine, for example, Erich Maria Remarque's *All Quiet on the Western Front* was commissioned for Hebrew translation a mere three months after its first publication in Germany, and progress reports were issued regularly in local newspapers (it took six months to translate).[7]

However, it was not only cultural hegemony that accounted for the focus on the Western Front. There was something intrinsically compelling about the stories that Western Front soldiers were telling. First, there was the prevalence of death and its absolutely ghastly details. Trench warfare resulted in a spatial and a temporal concentration of killing, which, in the words of Antoine Prost, 'was a transgression of the limits of the human condition'.[8] Moreover, Western Front soldiers inhabited a strange and different landscape ('the troglodyte world' in Paul Fussell's phrase): craters, tree stumps, barbed wire, mud, rats, protruding bones. As Hynes points out 'it was life lived in conditions of terrible absolute *difference*. That is surely part of its appeal to us, one reason we go on reading about it.'[9] Finally, the people who produced these war narratives were for the most part recruited civilians of educated and middle class backgrounds. These were principally literate men with authentic war credentials who appealed to an educated reading public. The fact that the producers of these war narratives actually partook in the worst aspects of trench warfare lent them a moral authority, which I would like to argue 'side-show' memoirists often lacked.

One of the most overlooked 'side-shows' of World War I has been the eastern front. Although it would be hard to explain the Russian revolutions, the collapse of Austria-Hungary or the dramatic political developments in Germany in 1917–1918 without recourse to the eastern front, there are nonetheless few scholarly or popular treatments of the subjects. Captivity it is worth pointing out once more was a predominantly eastern front phenomenon. In contrast to the stalemate in the west, warfare in the east was a mobile affair with the front shifting back and forth hundreds of miles. Thus, approximately two thirds of the soldiers captured during World War I had been taken captive on the Eastern Front, many of them during a few 'big catches' in the first two years of the war. Still, the mere fact that captivity occurred mainly in the east does not fully explain why POW memoirs were not received with interest. After all, many of these narratives contain gruesome portrayals of death and misery that competed in shock value with the 'battlefield gothic' of the Western Front.[10] One POW memoirist even found it necessary to include on the first page of his recollections the following warning: 'If there is still a boy in this world who craves for the sparkle of swords, let him crave also for lice, scurvy, whips and such a hunger as to eat half-roasted disease-stricken rats.'[11] In short, as with Western Front memoirs, POW narratives from World War I contained at times dreadful descriptions of human misery. Why were they not found equally compelling by the reading public?

There are five primary reasons, I would like to suggest, for the general disinterest in POW accounts from World War I: the 'relativity' of POW suffering vis-à-vis other soldiers as well as civilians, the seemingly 'familiar' nature of POW misery, the social background of the POW memoirists, the apologetic nature of many POW narratives and finally the political discontinuities in central and eastern Europe.

1 Relativity of POW Suffering. There was much in World War I captivity to tax human endurance (especially for the rank-and-file POWs): material deprivation, diseases, separation from one's family, complete lack of privacy, sexual frustrations and the uncertainty regarding the date of repatriation. In addition, there was the real possibility of not surviving captivity at all as happened to an estimated 8.7 per cent (751,000) of prisoners. Many of those who did survive had trouble reintegrating into civilian life. The Swiss physician, A. L. Vischer, who had treated POWs in several countries during the war, and who interviewed several hundreds of them in the years 1918–1919 concluded that many were suffering from 'barbed wire disease' (*Stacheldrahtkrankheit; psychose du fil de fer*). According to Vischer, a person suffering from the disease exhibits mood swings, irritability, failure of memory and extreme difficulty in concentrating, symptoms that today would probably fall under the broad category of post-traumatic stress disorder (PTSD). 'Europe', warned Vischer, 'will thus be infiltrated with individuals of abnormal psychical tendencies, who will not presumably be without influence on the collective psychology of the community.'[12]

Nevertheless, in comparison with the concentration of death on the western front, the suffering of prisoners appeared to be relatively unsubstantial. In the battle of the Somme there were over a million casualties in five months, in Verdun close to a million and in Passchendaele an estimated 470,000 casualties. During the first hour of the Somme alone an estimated 21,000 British soldiers had been killed, the great majority during the first few minutes. Therefore it is hardly surprising that there was a greater interest in exploring questions of 'war neurosis' (shell shock) than in examining the effects of captivity.

2 The 'familiar' nature of POW misery. POWs had the misfortune
to suffer from 'ordinary' adversity during the World War I. Hunger,
disease, hard labor, overcrowding, were mainstays of human misery
for thousands of years. Aspects of captivity that are usually underscored in other twentieth century wars (such as intentional mistreatment and ideological oppression) were quite rare in World War I,
and the absence of any mention of torture in POW narratives is very
striking. In sharp contrast, there was something new, different and
gruesome about the anguish of soldiers on the western front. Gas
attacks, machine guns and flame-throwers were relatively newcomers, whose enormous capacity to do harm were amplified in the
conditions of western front. Moreover, the combination of trenches
and bombardments created crater-like landscapes that came to
symbolize the war more than any other visual image.[13] In comparison, the landscapes, in which POW narratives took place, were
'foreign' and 'different' only in the traditional way – they took place
in a different country. Prisoners of war who had been interned in
Siberia, for example, devoted considerable space to describe the land
and its peoples, and were almost invariably enchanted by Siberian
nature and impressed by the modernity of its towns. The rank-and-
file prisoners who labored in agriculture and industry inhabited yet
again a familiar peace-time landscape. Even the camps themselves
with their filth and overcrowding resembled in many cases the
peace-time barracks of rank-and-file soldiers.

3 The social background of POW memoirists. As in the case of
western front accounts, the great majority of those who wrote about
captivity were officers of an educated background. Out of the 477
contributions in *In Feindeshand,* probably less than thirty were
written by rank and file POWs. The preponderance of officers among
the POW memoirists stands in sharp contrast to their actual share
among the prisoners: according to *In Feindeshand* 128,473 officers
were taken captive during the World War I, a mere 1.5 per cent of
the total number POWs.

However, the important point here is not that POW officers
monopolized captivity literature, but that their experience in
captivity was so radically different from that of the majority of the
prisoners. The Hague Conventions of 1899 and 1907 prescribed a
decent standard of living for POW officers, which as a rule was
respected by the belligerent countries.[14] Prisoner-of-war officers
were exempt from work, paid monthly salaries by the captor state,

granted the option of going out of camp (by giving their word of honor), allocated decent lodgings and allowed the service of order-lies. When families of captive German officers in Russia printed in their newsletters detailed information about menus in camp canteens, about the extensive self improvement programs organized by the officers and about the various sporting activities, they were rebuked by the Prussian War Ministry and ordered to stop.[15] In short, POW officers could claim only very tenuously that they themselves had been victims.

Consequently, POW memoirs focused usually on one (or more) of the following three themes: the plight of the rank-and-file prison-ers, the efforts of officers to maintain physical and mental health (thus fighting degeneration and demonstrating cultural superiority vis-à-vis the enemy) and escape attempts. Focusing on these themes limited the appeal of POW narratives and created an interest and authenticity chasm between them and western front memoirists. When relating, for example, the suffering of the men, POW officers seem often emotionally removed and lacking the moral authority of an actual participant.[16] It is not coincidental in my opinion that the POW memoirs that enjoyed success among the reading public during the interwar period (for example Dwinger's *Armee hinter Stachel-draht* and Hameiri's *Be-Gehenom shel Mata* (Hell on Earth)) were written by officers who had lived in rank-and-file camps for extensive periods of time. Memoirs that focused primarily on the daily routines of POW officers could generate only a modest amount of interest. These first-hand accounts were probably the most truthful as far as describing what most officers had actually experienced but, as one World War II POW confessed, 'to follow this procedure would amount to imposing on the reader a boredom unbearable as that suffered by the captive himself.'[17] As a result many POW officer memoirs – and most cinematic depictions of captivity including Jean Renoir's masterful *Grand Illusion* – dwell on plans of escape. Reading about escapes is much more riveting than reading about daily routines, and it is a part of a long tradition of war narratives that explore the adventurous, exciting and glorious aspects of fighting. Nevertheless, this was very much out of tune with what western front narratives were saying about modern warfare (espec-ially the narratives written after the years 1914–15).

4 The apologetic quality of World War I POW narratives. In his study of the American POW narrative, Robert Doyle identified a sequence of seven stages which usually structure POW memoirs.[18]

The second of these seven stages, 'capture', is a detailed depiction of the moment of being taken prisoner, usually presented in such a way as to diminish the personal responsibility of the narrator. The Austrian military chaplain, Karl Drexel, described how his regiment commander did not heed the advice of Russian prisoners, and ordered his troops to march directly to where a division and a half of the Russian army was positioned. Hans Baumgartner depicted the cold weather and the difficult terrain of the Carpathian Mountains, and emphasized the fact that his unit was outnumbered and that other units retreated without notifying them.[19] The need of prisoners to justify themselves went in many cases beyond the fear of punishment. The whole ordeal of captivity was frequently presented in POW memoirs as a test of character. Moral dilemmas (for example, to steal or not, to abandon friends for self preservation, how to deal with sexual drives) recur often in these narratives, and the reader is the one who judges the narrator's explanations. Thus, a World War I POW memoir has the character of an apologia that appealed for understanding from the reading public. In contrast, western front memoirs tended to look critically at their own societies, demanding accountability and recognition. Prisoner-of-war memoirs lacked this edge and urgency and seemed to accept an inferior place in the commemorative pecking order.

5 Political discontinuities in central and eastern Europe.
Memory, in the words of Jay Winter and Emmanuel Sivan, is limited by a 'shelf life' – it is kept for a certain span of time through consistent rehearsal.[20] Once societies (or rather individuals and groups within a certain society) cease to rehearse a particular memory it is not renewed, and the process of remembrance eventually comes to an end. Remembrance of a specific memory can also come to a halt when the 'social framework' itself radically changes.[21] In the case of World War I prisoners of war this is in part what seems to have happened. As mentioned above, captivity's 'Big Show' during World War I had been on the eastern front. This is where the majority of the soldiers had been taken captive, and this is where the worst treatment and the highest mortality rates occurred. However, when the repatriation of prisoners on the eastern front had been completed it was a radically different patria that awaited most returning POWs. The various crownlands and provinces of the former Habsburg monarchy had been reconfigured as independent (and self-proclaimed) nation states, while Russia re-emerged from a devastating civil war with a regime that rejected any continuity with the former Tsarist

state. Expecting public recognition in such a social context was quite
problematic: there was very little 'debt' owed to returning POWs and
their contribution to the new political order seemed marginal. Even
in states such as Czechoslovakia and Yugoslavia, that mythologized
the activities of POW-based legions (the Czechoslovak Legion and
the South Slav Legion), it was not captivity that was being remembered
but rather what had happened after POWs left the camps. The fact
that the great majority of Czech, Slovak, Serb, Croat and Slovene
POWs preferred to languish in camps rather than volunteer was
seldom mentioned.

Despite the efforts of the editors of *In Feindeshand* the story of
POWs during World War I remained a marginal component in narratives about the war. Hans Weiland hoped that presenting the story
of POWs would serve as an example for Europeans about the ability
of people to live together.[22] Thus, the cover of *In Feindeshand*
portrayed a circular chain whose links contained miniature portraits
representing various nationalities; the German POW connected to
the Russian, the Austro-Hungarian to the Italian etc. This was obviously
wishful thinking; one could not have seriously accepted the claim
that captivity exemplified typical co-existence of peoples. Nevertheless, this idealized picture did contain a grain of truth regarding
World War I captivity: perhaps it was not brotherly love but definitely
it was not the Somme; perhaps we are not dealing with the absence
of misery but we are certainly not dealing with the most shocking
sights of the war; perhaps captivity did not demonstrate the complete
efficacy the Hague Convention but nonetheless it did provide a
valuable example of where it did do some good. In short, captivity
in World War I does not fit neatly within a grand narrative of World
War I as our century's *Urkatastrophe*.[23] Therefore, 'when we want
World War I to be the worst cautionary example of war', then captivity
at best has a marginal place.[24]

Notes

1. Gerald H. Davis, 'The Life of Prisoners of War in Russia, 1914-1921',
in Samuel Williamson and Peter Pastor (eds) *Essays on World War I: Origins
and Prisoners of War,* pp. 186-7.

Epilogue

2. It is important to remember that Germany held to 190,000 Russian POWs and that repatriation was a reciprocal affair.

3. Davis, 'The Life of Prisoners of War in Russia, 1914-1921', p. 189.

4. George Mosse uses the term 'Memory' alongside the term 'Myth'. In Mosse's terminology the 'Myth of the War Experience' is designed to mask the reality of war in the service of nationalist forces; Paul Fussel uses both 'memory' and 'Idea' as synonyms. To confuse things even further Samuel Hynes uses the term 'myth' but without the pejorative connotations of Mosse. For Hynes a myth is just a simplified version of what had actually happened designed to highlight a certain meaning. George Mosse, *Fallen Soldiers: Reshaping the Memory of the World Wars,* Oxford: Oxford Univerity Press, 1990; Paul Fussell, *The Great War and Modern Memory*, Oxford: Oxford University Press, 1975; Samuel Hynes, *The Soldiers's Tale: Bearing Witness to Modern War*, New York: Penguin Books, 1997; Jay Winter, *Sites of Memory, Sites of Mourning: The Great War in European Cultural History*, Cambridge: Cambridge University Press, 1995.

5. Hynes, *The Soldiers' Tale*, p. 74.

6. Ibid., pp. 74 and 80.

7. Avner Holtzman, *Avigdor Hameiri ve-Sifrut ha-Milchama* (Avigdor Hemeiri and War Literature), in Hebrew, Tel Aviv: Merkaz Koved, 1986, pp. 43-8.

8. Quoted from Jay Winter, *The Experience of World War I*, p.141; see also John Keegan, *The Face of Battle,* Chapter 4.

9. Hynes, *The Soldiers' Tale*, p. 53.

10. The term 'battlefield gothic' is Hynes's. See , *The Soldiers' Tale*, p. 26.

11. Hameiri, p. 1.

12. A. L. Vischer, *The Barbed Wire Disease: A Psychological Study of the Prisoners of War*, London: Oxford House, 1919, p. 25.

13. See, for example, the recently published *Oxford History of the Twentieth Century*, Oxford: Oxford University Press, 1998). There are two visual representations of World War I in the book: Passchendaele after bombardment on p. VII and Otto Dix's famous triptych pp. 74-5. Dix's painting is also used on the cover of the latest synthesis about the Central Powers in World War I: Holger Herwig's *The First World War: Germany and Austria-Hungary 1914-1918*, London: Arnold, 1997.

14. See above, Chapter 3.

15. The following warning was found in newsletters from the year 1917:

The Royal Prussian War Ministry wishes to inform families [of German POW officers in Russia] that previous newsletters contained the misconception that the situation among POWs was not exceptionally bad. This may cause bitterness among the prisoners. Newsletters [written by families of POWs] cannot and should not present a definitive picture of life in captivity because they are based on excerpts of letters from this

229

or that writer. Many writers paint a rosy picture because of censorship or because they do not want to burden the addressee. If POWs will continue to receive letters from home underestimating their difficulties, we will have to terminate these newsletters.

See for example, in 'Bericht Nr.7 über das Offizierslager OMSK (nur für den Privatgebrauch der Angehörigen)', Bundesarchiv (BA), Militärarchiv Freiburg (MA), N 448/3.

16. See for example the following description in the memoir of Battalion Commander Walter Lade (Lade, p. 11):

In the winter of 1914/1915 there were 8600 POWs here out of which 4600 died. Now [i.e. March 1915] 6000 prisoners are here, of which there are 800 Germans from the Reich. Some of the prisoners live in stone buildings some in Earth Barracks [commonly used dugout structures of Central Siberia], cold, poorly-lit and damp. One is not allowed to drink un-boiled water but Hungarian troops often do so. Consequences: apathy, typhus (both kinds). In the beginning of April there were a few cases of dementia and suicide. Communication with the rank-and-file barracks is forbidden for us.

17. Pierre Boulle, *My Own River Kwai*, trans. Xan Fielding, New York: Vanguard, 1966, p. 166; quoted from Doyle, Robert C. Doyle, *Visions from Captivity: Interpreting the American POW Narrative*, Lawrence Kansas: University Press of Kansas, 1994, p .85.

18. Robert C. Doyle, *Visions from Captivity: Interpreting the American POW Narrative*, Lawrence Kansas: University Press of Kansas, 1994, Chapter 4 and appendix 1.

19. See above Chapters 1, 3 and 4.

20. Jay Winter and Emmanuel Sivan (eds) *War and Remembrance in the Twentieth Century*, Cambridge: Cambridge University Press, 1999, pp. 16-17.

21. Maurice Halbwachs, *On Collective Memory*, conclusion.

22. In Feindeshand, p. 17.

23. Thomas Nipperdey, *Deutsche Geschichte*, Band 2, p. 758.

24. Samuel Hynes, *The Soldiers's Tale: Bearing Witness to Modern War*, p. 55.

Bibliography

Archival Collections

Austrian State Archives
(Österreichisches Staatsarchiv-ÖstA)

(a) Archiv der Republik: Kgf. (Inneres) Gruppe 04/16.2: Box 6B, Box 112, Boxes 172–176.

(b) Kriegsarchiv:
1) Armeeoberkommando (AOK) 1914–1918/ Gemeinsames Zentralnachweisbureau des Roten Kreuzes-Auskunftstelle für Kriegsgefangene (GZNB). Boxes number 3726–3759.
2) Nachlässe B/231, B/247, B/268, B/312, B/578, B/597, B/671, B/744, B/763, B/785, B/854, B/863, B/917, B/919, B/961.
3) Kriegsministerium (KM)/Akt 1916 14.A 63-13.

Military Museum-Vienna (Heeresegeschichtliches Museum)

Streeruwitz, Ernst Ritter von, *Kriegsgefangene im Weltkrieg 1914–1918*, unpublished manuscript. Compiled during the war and deposited in 1928.

German Federal Archives (Bundesarchiv)

Msg. 1/2725. Rey, Josef, *Meine Erlebnisse während und nach der Kriegsgefangenschaft in Russland in der Zeit von 1915–1920*, Bundesarchiv/Militärarchiv, Freiburg im Breisgau, pp. 51–4.

Militärarchiv (BA/MA) Freiburg im Breisgau: 'Elsa Brändström Gedächtnis Archiv' Msg.200. Especially Msg.200/20, Msg.200/36, Msg.200/131, Msg.200/132, Msg.200/270, Msg.200/310, Msg.200/932, Msg.200/1060, collection N/448-3.

Russian State Military Historical Archive *(Rossiiskii Gosudarstvennyi Voenno-Istoricheskii Arkhiv-RGVIA)*

*Fond [f.].1396/Opis[op.]2/*Delo [d.] 1931, d.1933, d.1936, d.1937, d.1942, .1943, d. 1948, d.1952, d.1954-5, d.1957,d.1958, d.1959, d.1965-6, d.1969, d.1971. d.1977, d.1978, d.1982, d.1992-3, d.1995., d.2000, d.2002, d.2010, d.2011, d.2018, d.2019.

*F.1396/op.3/*d.32, d.176, d.538.

*F.1396/op.4/*d.69-73.

*F.1396/op.5/*d.18-19, d.24, d.31, d.48, d.55.

*F.1558/op.9/*d.1, d.2, d.6, d.11, d.15, d.19-20, d.27, d.33, d.37, d.52, d.56.

*F.1606/op.2/*d. 614-15, d.1061, d.1062, d.1063, d.1070, d.1071, d.1074.

*F.1759/op.3/*d.432, d.434, d.435, d.437, d.438, d.439, d.440, d.441, d.445, d.449, d.450, d.453, d.457, d.468, d.471, d.473, d.480.

*F.2000/op.9/*d.6, d.7, d.15, d.18, d.20,22, d.25, d.30, d.36, d.49,52, d.53, d.61, d.72.

F.2000/op.11/ d.3, d.4, d.6, d.19, d.25, d.30, d.40, d.54, d.55, d.226, d.385.

F.2003/op.1/d.1125, d.1464, d.1467.

F.2003/op.2/ d.323-6, d.328, d.331, d.333, d.334, d.341, d.342, d.345.

*F.12651/op.11/*d.114, d.115.

*F.16275/op.1/*d.78.

The National Archives of the United States *(NA)*

Records of the Department of State Relating to World War I and its Termination, 1914-1929. Record Group 59; Microfilm number M367. Department of State/ File Number 763.72114 (European War, Prisoners of War).

Suffixes: suffix 367 (Burr Report), suffix 547 (Ogilvie and Lewis Report), suffix 580 (Peirce Report), suffix 622 (Burr Report), suffix 818 (Cresson Report), suffix 820 (Peirce Report), suffix 1084 (reports on Kharkov, Kursk, Kiev), suffix 1088 (Warfield Report about Irkutsk), suffix 1148 Sterling Report (Troizk and Orenburg), suffix 1158 (distribtion of clothes) suffix 1167 (epidemic in Stretensk), suffix 1167 (Warfield Report on the epidemic in Stretensk), suffix 1176 (conditions in western Siberia), suffix 1261 and 1262 (reports on Nizhni Novgorod and Turkestan), Suffixes 1277-8 (Warfield Report on conditions in Siberia), suffix 1391 (Warfield Report on

Rasdolnoe), suffix 1394 (interview with Russian Foreign Minister Sazonov about POW work), suffix 1513 (Priamur district), suffix 1629 (conditions in Totskoe), suffixes 2547-8 (Turkestan and Kazan), suffix 2793 (Irbit and Perm), suffix 3898 (final report, June 1917).

Published Primary Sources

Blond, Kasper, *Ein Unbekannter Krieg: Erlebnisse eines Arztes während des Weltkrieges*, Leipzig, 1931.

Brändström, Elsa, *Unter Kriegsgefangenen in Russland und Sibirien 1914-1920*, Berlin, 1920; The revised English edition appeared in 1929 under the title *Among Prisoners of War in Russia and Siberia*, London: Hutchinson Publishers, 1929. All quotes in this dissertation are from this edition.

Breitner, Burghard, *Unverwundet Gefangen: Aus meinem sibirischen Tagebuch*, Vienna: Rikola Verlag, 1921.

Drexel, Karl, *Feldkurat in Sibirien 1914-1920*, Innsbruck and Leipzig: F. Rauch, 1940.

Dwinger Edwin Erich, *Between White and Red*, translated by Marion Saunders, New York: Charles Scribner's Sons, 1932.

Dwinger, Edwin Erich, *Die Armee hinter Stacheldraht*, Berlin, Jena: E. Diederichs, 1929 (appeared in English under the title: *The Army behind Barbed Wire: A Sibirian Diary*, translated by Ian Morrow, London: George Allen & Unwin, 1930).

Dworsky, Alexander, 'Im Lager', in Hans Weiland and Leopold Kern (eds) *In Feindeshand : Die Gefangenschaft im Weltkriege in Einzeldarstellungen*, two vols, Vienna: Bundesvereinigung der ehemaligen österreichischen Kriegsgefangen, 1931, p. 106.

Dyboski, Roman, *Seven Years in Russia and Siberia 1914-1921*, Cheshire CT: Cherry Hill Books, 1971, Translated by Marion Moore Coleman, originally published in Polish in 1922 under the title *Siedem lat w rosji i na syberji*, (1922).

Hahn, Georg, *Kriegsgefangenen in Russland*, Mainz: Verlag der Volkszeitung, 1926.

Hameiri, Avigdor, *Begehenom shel Mata* (Hell on Earth), third edition, Tel Aviv: Dvir, 1989.

Hanneken, Elsa von, 'Die Tientsiner Hilfsaktion: Eine Hilfsaktion für Kriegs- und Zivilgefangene in Tientsin', in Hans Weiland and Leopold Kern (eds) *In Feindeshand: Die Gefangenschaft im Weltkriege in Einzeldarstellungen*, two vols, Vienna: Bundesvereinigung der ehmatigen österreichischen Kriegsgefangen, 1931, vol. 2, p. 267.

Hašek, Jaroslav, *The Good Soldier Švejk*, London: Penguin Books, 1922.

Jungabauer, Gustav, 'Auf Transport', in Hans Weiland and Leopold Kern (eds) *In Feindeshand: Die Gefangenschaft im Weltkriege in Einzeldarstellungen*, two vols, Vienna: Bundesvereinigung der ehemaligen österreichischen Kriegsgefangen, 1931, vol. 1, p. 86.

Kindall, Sylvain G., *American Soldiers in Siberia*, New York: Richard R. Smith, 1945.

Kinsky, Nora Gräfin, *Russisches Tagebuch 1916–1918*, Stuttgart: Seewald Verlag, 1976.

Kisch, Egon Erwin, *'Schreib das auf Kisch': Das Kriegstagebuch von Egon Erwin Kisch*, Berlin: E. Reiss, 1930.

Knöbl, Hans, 'Im Duklapaß gefangen', in Hans Weiland and Leopold Kern (eds) *In Feindeshand : Die Gefangenschaft im Weltkriege in Einzeldarstellungen*, two vols, Vienna: Bundesvereinigung der ehemaligen österreichischen Kriegsgefangen, 1931, vol. 1, p. 64–5.

Kohn, Hans, *Living in a World Revolution: My Encounters with History*, New York: Trident Press, 1964.

Mihalotzy, Käthe von, 'Eine Reise durch Kriegsgefangenenlager in Rußland und Turkestan. Aus dem Tagebuch einer Delegierten des österreichischen Roten Kreuzes', in Hans Weiland and Leopold Kern (eds) *In Feindeshand : Die Gefangenschaft im Weltkriege in Einzeldarstellungen*, two vols, Vienna: Bundesvereinigung der ehemaligen österreichischen Kriegsgefangen, 1931, vol. 2, pp. 249–58.

Montandon, Georges, *Im Schmeltztiegel des fernen Osten: Geschichte der sibirischen Mission des Internationalen Komitees vom Roten Kruez zu Gunsten der österreichischen und ungarischen Kriegsgefangenen*, Vienna: Manzsche Verlags-und Universitäts-Buchhandlung, 1923.

Ölçen, Mehmet Arif, *Vetluga Memoir: A Turkish Prisoner of War in Russia, 1916–1918*, translated and edited by Gary Leiser, Gainesville: University Press of Florida, 1995.

Pörzgen, Hermann, *Theater ohne Frau: Das Bühnenleben der Kriegsgefangenen Deutschen 1914–1920*, Königsberg and Berlin: Ost-Europa Verlag, 1933.

Price, Hereward T., *Boche and Bolshevik: Experiences of an Englishman in the German Army and in Russian Prisons*, London: John Murray, 1919.

Raabl-Werner, Heinrich Freiherr v., 'Der Einfluß der Propaganda unter den Kriegsgefangenen in Rußland auf den Zusammenbruch

Österreich-Ungarns', *Militärwissenschaftliche und-technische Mitteilungen*, 59, (1928), p. 782.

Raabl-Werner, Heinrich Freiherr von 'Österreich-Ungarns offizielle Kriegsgefangenenfürsorge', in Hans Weiland and Leopold Kern (eds) *In Feindeshand: Die Gefangenschaft im Weltkriege in Einzeldarstellungen*, Wien, 1931, pp. 324-31.

Revertera, Anna Gräfin, 'Als österreichische Rotkreuzschwester in Rußland', *Süddeutsche Monatshefte*, September (1923), pp. 251-81.

Revertera, Anna Gräfin, 'Als Rotkreuzschwester in Rußland und Sibirien', in Hans Weiland and Leopold Kern (eds) *In Feindeshand: Die Gefangenschaft im Weltkriege in Einzeldarstellungen*, two vols, Vienna, 1931, vol. 2, pp. 244-51.

Ronge, Max, *Kriegs-und Industriespionage: 12 Jahre Kundschaftdienst*, Zürich: Amalthen-Verlag, 1933.

Streeruwitz, Ernst Ritter von, *Springflut über Österreich: Erinnerungen, Erlebnisse und Gedanken aus bewegter Zeit 1914-1929*, Vienna and Leipzig: Bernina Verlag, 1937.

Streeruwitz, Ernst Ritter von, 'Der Umsturz in Rußland und die Kriegsgefangenen', in Hans Weiland and Leopold Kern (eds) *In Feindeshand: Die Gefangenschaft im Weltkriege in Einzeldarstellungen*, Vienna: Bundesvereinigung der ehemaligen österreichischen Kriegsgefangen, 1931, pp. 268-9.

US Legation Russia, *Reports of the Delegates of the Embassy of the United States of America in St Petersburg on the Situation of the German Prisoners of War and Civil Persons in Russia*, Zurich: Art. Institut Orell Füssli, 1917.

Üxküll, Alexandrine von, *Aus einem Schwesterleben*, 2. Auflage, Stuttgart, 1956.

Vara, Sil [Geza Silberer], *Briefe aus der Gefangenschaft: zugunsten der Oestereichischen Gesellschaft vom Roten Kreuze (für die österreichischen Kriegsgefangenen in Rußland und Sibirien) und des Kriegshilfsbüros des k.k. Ministerium des Innern*, Vienna, 1917.

Vischer, A. L. *The Barbed Wire Disease: A Psychological Study of the Prisoners of War*, London: Oxford House, 1919.

Volck, Herbert, *Die Wölfe: 33,000 Kilometer Kriegsabenteuer in Asien*, Berlin: Ullstein & Co, 1918.

Walsleben, Magdalene von, *Die deutsche Schwester in Sibirien*, Berlin: Furche Verlag, 1919.

Weiland, Hans, 'Kriegsgefangenenlager Krasnojarsk', in Hans Weiland and Leopold Kern (eds) *In Feindeshand : Die Gefangenschaft im*

Weltkriege in Einzeldarstellungen, two vols, Vienna: Bundesver-
einigung der ehemaligen österreichischen Kriegsgefangen, 1931.
Weiland, Hans and Kern, Leopold (eds), *In Feindeshand : Die
Gefangenschaft im Weltkriege in Einzeldarstellungen*, two vols,
Vienna, 1931.
Wenzel, Anne-Marie, *Deutsche Kraft in Fesseln: Fünf Jahre Schwest-
erdienst in Sibirien*, Potsdam: Ernte, 1931.
Willfort, Fritz, *Turkestanisches Tagebuch: Sechs Jahre in Russische-
Zentralasien*, Vienna: W. Braumüller, 1930.
Winkler, Wilhelm, *Berufsstatistik der Kriegstoten der öst.-ung.
Monarchie*, (Vienna: L. W. Seidel & Sohn, 1919).
*Za svobodu: obrázková Kronika Československého hnutí na Rusi
1914–1920*, four vols. Prague: Nákl. Památníku odboje (1922–
9), 1924.
Zweig, Arnold, *The Case of Sergeant Grischa*, originally published
London: Penguin Books, 1927.

Secondary Works

Anderson, Bendict, *Imagined Communities: Reflections on the
Origins and Spread of Nationalism*, revised edition, London and
New York: Cornell University Press, 1991, originally published in
1983.
Antal, Józsa, *Háboru hadifogság forradalom: Magyar internacion-
alista hadifoglyok az 1917-es oroszországi forradalmakban*,
(War, Captivity, Revolution: Hungarian Internationalist Prisoners
of War in the Russian Revolution of 1917), Budapest, 1970.
Applegate, Celia, *A Nation of Provincials: The German Idea of
Heimat*, Berkeley: University of California Press, 1990.
Aron, Raymond, *The Century of Total War*, New York: Doubleday,
1954.
Ashworth, Tony, *Trench Warfare: the Live and Let Live System*, New
York: Holmes &Meier, 1980.
Banac, Ivo, 'South Slav Prisoners of War in Revolutionary Russia', in
Samual Williamson and Peter Pastor (eds) *Essays on World War
I: Origins and Prisoners of War*, New York: Columbia University
Press, 1983, p. 121–48.
Bartov, Omer, *Murder in our Midst: The Holocaust, Industrial
Killing and Representation*, New York: Oxford University Press,
1996.
Beaumont, Joan, 'Rank, Privilege and Prisoners of War', *War and
Society*, (1983), pp. 67–94.

Bibliography

Becker, Jean-Jacques, *The Great War and the French People*, Leamington Spa: Berg, 1985.

Berghahn, Volker, *Germany and the Approach of War in 1914*, (London, 1973).

Berghahn, Volker, *Modern Germany: Society, Economics and Politics in the Twentieth Century*, second edition, Cambridge: Cambridge University Press, 1987.

Bernd, Ulrich, 'Feldpostbriefe des ersten Weltkrieges: Möglichkeiten und Grenzen einer alltagsgeschichtlichen Quelle', *Militärgeschichtliche Mitteilungen*, 53 (1994), pp. 73-83.

Birman, M. (ed.), *Internatsionalisty v boiakh za vlast' Sovietov*, Moscow, 1965.

Bradley, J. F. N., *La Legion tchecoslovaque en Russie 1914-1920*, Paris, 1968, appeared in English in the Eastern European Monographs series: *The Czechoslovak Legion in Russia 1914-1920*, Eastern European Monographs CCCXXI, Boulder and New York, 1991.

Breuilly, John, *Nationalism and the State*, 2nd edition, Chicago, 1992, originally published in 1982.

Brubaker, Rogers, *Nationalism Reframed: Nationhood and the National Question in the New Europe*, Cambridge: Cambridge University Press, 1996.

Burdick, Charles, and Moesnner Ursula, *The German POWs in Japan, 1914-1920*, Lanham, New York and London: the University Press of America, 1984.

Carr, E. H., *The Bolshevik Revolution, 1917-1923*, three vols, London: Macmillan, 1950.

Chatterjee, Partha, *The Nation and its Fragments: Colonial and post-Colonial Histories*, Princeton: Princeton University Press, 1993.

Chickering, Roger, *Imperial Germany and the Great War, 1914-1918*, Cambridge: Cambridge University Press, 1998.

Cohen, Gary, *The Politics of Ethnic Survival: Germans in Prague 1861-1914*, Princeton: Princeton University Press, 1981.

Colley, Linda, *The Britons: Forging of the Nation 1707-1837*, New Haven and London: Yale University Press, 1992.

Confino, Alon, *The Nation as a Local Metaphor: Württemberg, Imperial Germany and National Memory 1871-1918*, Chapel Hill: University of North Carolina, 1997.

Cornwall, Mark (ed.), *The Last Years of Austria-Hungary: Essay in Political and Military History 1908-1918*, Exeter Studies in History No.27, Exeter:University of Exeter Press, 1990.

Cornwall, Mark, 'Morale and Discipline in the Austro-Hungarian Army', Lecture delivered in the conference: Mobilizing for Total War: Society and State in Europe 1914-1918, Trinity College Dublin, 23-25 June 1993.

Craig, Gordon, *Germany 1866-1945*, New York and Oxford: Oxford University Press, 1978.

Daniel, Ute, *The War from Within: German Working-Class Women in the First World War*, trans. Margaret Ries, Oxford and New York: Berg Publishers, 1997.

Davies, Norman, *God's Playground: A History of Poland*, two vols, New York: Columbia University Press, 1982.

Davis, Gerald H., 'Deutsche Kriegsgefangene im Ersten Weltkrieg in Rußland', *Militärgeschichtliche Mitteilungen*, (1982), pp. 37-49.

Davis, Gerald H., 'National Red Cross Societies and Prisoners of War in Russia, 1914-1918', *Journal of Contemporary History*,.28 (1993), pp. 31-52.

Davis, Gerald H., 'Prisoner of War Camps as Social Communities: Krasnoyarsk 1914-1921', *Eastern European Quarterly*, 21 (1987), pp. 147-63.

Davis,Gerald H., 'The Life of Prisoners of War in Russia, 1914-1921', in Samuel Williamson and Peter Pastor (eds) *Essays on World War I: Origins and Prisoners of War*, New York, 1983, pp. 162-96.

Deák, István, *Beyond Nationalism: A Social and Political History of the Habsburg Officer Corps 1848-1918*, New York and Oxford: Oxford University Press, 1990.

Deist, Wilhlem, 'Verdeckter Militärstreik im Kriegsjahr 1918', in Wolfram Wette (ed.) *Der Krieg des kleinen Mannes*, Munich: Piper, 1992.

Dix, Rudolf, *Deutsche Internationalisten in der Großen Sozialistischen Oktoberrevolution*, East Berlin: Dietz, 1987.

Doyle, Robert C., *Voices from Captivity: Interpreting the American POW Narrative*, Lawrence Kansas: University Press of Kansas, 1994.

Eksteins, Modris, *Rites of Spring: The Great War and the Birth of the Modern Age*, London: Houghton Miffton, 1989.

Ezerov, Robert, 'Die Sowjetische Historiographie und die deutschen und österreichischen Kriegsgefangenen-Internationalisten', *Zeitgeschichte*, 25 (1998), pp. 343-7.

Ferguson, Niall, *The Pity of War: Explaining World War I* New York: Basic Books, 1998.

Figes, Orlando, *A People's Tragedy: a History of the Russian Revolution*, New York: Viking, 1996.

Fischer, Fritz, *Germany's Aims in The First World War*, New York: W. W. Norton, 1967.

Fischer-Galati, Stephen and Béla K. Király, *War and Society in East Central Europe*, vol. 22, Eastern European Monographs No. CCXXXIII, Boulder CO, Columbia University Press, 1987.

Fitzpatrick, Sheila, *Stalin's Peasants: Resistance and Survival in the Russian Village after Collectivization*, New York and Oxford: Oxford University Press, 1994.

Foucault, Michel, *Discipline and Punish: The Birth of the Prison*, New York: Vintage Books, 1979.

Fritzsche, Peter, *Germans into Nazis*, Cambridge MA: Harvard University Press, 1998.

Fussell, Paul, *The Great War and Modern Memory*, Oxford: Oxford University Press, 1975.

Garber, Marjorie, *Vested Interests: Cross Dressing and Cultural Anxiety* New York: HarperCollins, 1992.

Gattrell, Peter, *A Whole Empire Walking: Refugees in Russia during World War I*, Bloomington: Indiana University Press, 1999.

Geertz, Clifford, *The Interpretations of Cultures: Selected Essays*, New York: Basic Books, 1973.

Gellner, Ernst, *Nations and Nationalism*, Ithaca and New York: Cornell University Press, 1983.

Gilbert, Martin, *The First World War: A Complete History*, New York: Henry Holt & Company, 1994.

Gillis, John, (ed.), *Commemorations: The Politics of National Identity*, Princeton: Princeton University Press, 1994.

Gergory, Adrian, *The Silence of Memory: Armistice Day 1919–1946*, Berg: Oxford and Providence, 1994.

Grieves, Keith, *The Politics of Manpower, 1914–1918*, Manchester UK: Manchester University Press, 1988.

Hagen, Mark von and Barkey, Karen, (eds), *After Empire: Multiethnic Societies and Nation Building: The Soviet-Union and the Russian, Ottoman and Habsburg Empires*, New York: Westview Press, 1997.

Hagen, Mark von, 'The Great War and the Mobilization of Ethnicity in the Russian Empire', in Jack Snyder and Barnett Rubin (eds) *Post Soviet Political Order: Conflict and State Building*, New York: Routledge, 1998, pp. 34–57.

Hagen, Mark von, *Soldiers in the Proletarian Dictatorship: The Red Army and the Soviet Socialist State, 1917–1930*, Ithaca and London: Cornell University Press, 1990.

Halbwachs, Maurice, *On Collective Memory*, edited and translated by Lewis A. Coser Chicago: The University Of Chicago Press, 1992.

Hanák, Péter, 'Die Volksmeinung während des letzten Kriegsjahres in Österreich-Ungarn', *Die Auflösung des Habsburgerreiches. Zusammenbruch und Neuorientierung im Donauraum*, Munich: R. Oldenbourg, 1970, pp. 58–66.

Hayes Carlton, *Essays on Nationalism*, New York: Macmillan, 1937.

Heim, Aribert, 'Die heile Welt im Stahlgewitter: deutsche und englische Feldpost aus dem ersten Weltkrieg', in Gerhard Hirschfeld, Gerd Krumeich, Dieter Langwiesche, Hans Peter Ullman (eds) *Kriegserfahrungen: Studien zur Sozial- und Mentalitätsgeschichte des ersten Weltkrieges*, Essen: Klartext, 1997, pp. 129–45.

Herwig, Holger, *The First World War: Germany and Austria-Hungary 1914–1918* London: Arnold, 1997.

Hettling, Manfred and Jeismann, Michael, 'Der Weltkrieg als Epos. Philipp Witkops, Kriegsbriefe gefallener Studenten', in Gerhard Hirschfeld, Gerd Krumeich and Irina Renz (eds) *Keiner fühlte sich mehr als Mensch . . . Erlebnis und Wirkung des ersten Weltkrieges*, Essen: Klartext, 1993, pp. 175–98.

Hobsbawm, Eric, *Nations and Nationalism since 1780: Programme, Myth Reality*, Cambridge: Cambridge University Press, 1990.

Holls, Frederick W., *The Peace Conference at the Hague and its bearings on International Law and Policy*, New York: Macmillan, 1900.

Holmes, Richard, *Acts of War: The Behavior of Men in Battle*, New York: Free Press, 1989.

Holtzman, Avner, *Avigdor Hameiri ve-Sifrut ha-Milchama* (Avigdor Hemeiri and War Literature), in Hebrew, Tel Aviv: Merkaz Koved, 1986.

Holquist, Peter, 'Information is the Alpha and the Omega of Our Work: Bolshevik Surveillance in Its Pan-European Context', *Journal of Modern History*, 69 (September, 1997), pp. 415–50.

Howard, Michael 'Constraints on Warfare', in Michael Howard, George Andreopolous and Mark Shulman (eds) *The Laws of War: Constraints on Warfare in the Western World*, New Haven: Yale University Press, 1994, ch. 1.

Howard, Michael and Louis, Roger Wm. (eds), *Oxford History of the Twentieth Century*, Oxford: Oxford University Press, 1998.

Bibliography

Howard, Michael, *War in European History*, Oxford, 1975.

Hroch, Miroslav, *Social Preconditions of National Revival in Europe*, Cambridge: Cambridge University Press, 1985.

Hutchinson, John, *Champions of Charity: War and the Rise of the Red Cross*, Westview Press: Boulder Colorado, 1996.

Hynes, Samuel, *The Soldiers's Tale: Bearing Witness to Modern War*, New York: Penguin Books, 1997.

Jahn, Hubertus, *Patriotic Culture in Russia during World War I*, Ithaca and London: Cornell University Press, 1995.

Janos, Andrew, *The Politics of Backwardness in Hungary, 1825–1945*, Princeton: Princeton University Press, 1986.

Jaszi, Oscar, *The Dissolution of the Habsburg Monarchy*, Chicago: University of Chicago Press, 1929.

Jelavich, Barabara, *Modern Austria: Empire and Republic 1815–1986*, Cambridge: Cambridge University Press, 1987.

Jeřábek, Rudolph, 'The Eastern Front 1914–1918', in Mark Cornwall (ed.), *The Last Years of Austria-Hungary: Essays in Political and Military History 1908–1918*, Exeter: University of Exeter Press, 1990, pp. 101–16.

Joll, James, *The Origins of the First World War*, Longman: London and New York, 1984.

Kalvoda, Josef, 'Czech and Slovak Prisoners of War in Russia during the War and Revolution', in Samuel Williamson and Peter Pastor (eds) *Essays on World War I: Origins and Prisoners of War*, New York: Columbia University Press, 1983, pp. 215–38.

Kann, R., Kiraly B. and P. Fichtner (eds), *The Habsburg Army in World War I: Essays on the Intellectual, Military and Economic Aspects of the Habsburg War Effort*, New York: East European Quarterly distributed by Columbia University Press, 1977.

Kann, Robert, *A History of the Habsburg Empire 1526–1918*, Berkeley: University of California Press, 1974.

Kedourie, Elie, *Nationalism*, 4th edition, Oxford and Cambridge: Blackwell, 1993.

Keegan, John, *A History of Warfare*, New York: Vintage Books, 1993.

Keegan, John, *The Face of Battle: A Study of Agincourt, Waterloo and the Somme*, London: Penguin Books, 1976.

Keegan, John, *The First World War*, New York: Alfred Knopf, 1999.

Kennedy, Paul, 'Military Effectiveness in the First World War', in Allan Millet, Murray Williamson and Kenneth Watman (eds) *Military Effectiveness*, vol. 1, Boston: Unwing Hyman, 1988, pp. 329–50.

Kieval, Hillel, *The Making of Czech Jewry: National Conflict and Jewish Society in Bohemia 1870–1918*, Oxford: Oxford University Press, 1988.

Klante, Margarete, *Die Geschichte der Tschechischen Legion in Rußland*, Königsberg: Ost-Europa Verlag, 1929.

Klante, Margarete, *Von Wolga bis Amur: Die Tschechische Legion und der russische Bürgerkrieg*, Königsberg and Berlin: Ost-Europa Verlag, 1931.

Kocka, Jürgen, *Facing Total War: German Society, 1914–1918*, Leamington Spa: Harvard University Press, 1984.

Kohn, Hans, *The Idea of Nationalism*, New York: Collier Books, 1944.

Kondrat'ev, V. A., 'Iz istorii bor'by nemetskich voennoplennykh-internatsionalistov za ustanovlenie sovetskoi vlasti v Sibiri i na Dal'nem Vostoke v 1917–1920 gg', *Noyabr'skaia revolyutsia v Germania*, Moscow, 1960.

Krammer, Arnold, 'Soviet Propaganda among German and Austro-Hungarian Prisoners of War in Russia, 1917–1921', in Samuel Williamson and Peter Pastor (eds) *Essays on World War I: Origins and Prisoners of War*, Boulder CO: East European Monographs, 1983, pp. 239–64.

Krivoguz, I. M., and Polyanskii, I. S., *Germanskie i avstriyskie voennoplennye-internatsionalisty*, Moscow, 1967.

Kudela, Josef, *Přehled vývoje čsl. revolučního hnutí na Rusi*, Prague, 1923.

Kudrina, Yulia, 'Das Dänische Rote Kreuz in den Jahren des Ersten Weltkrieges', *Zeitgeschichte*, 25 (1998), pp. 375–9.

Lehmann, Albrecht, *Gefangenschaft und Heimkehr: Deutsche Kriegsgefangene in der Sowjetunion*, Munich: C.H. Beck Verlag, 1986.

Leidinger, Hannes and Moritz, Verena, 'Österreich-Ungarn und die Heimkehrer aus russischer Kriegsgefangenschaft im Jahr 1918', *Österreich in Geschichte und Literatur*, 6 (1997), pp. 385–403.

Leidinger, Hannes, 'Gefangenschaft und Heimkehr: Gedanken zu Voraussetzungen und Perspektiven eines neuen Forschungsbereiches', *Zeitgeschichte*, 25 (1998), pp. 333–42.

Lévai, Jenö, *Fehér cártol-vörös Leninig: Magyar hadifoglyok szerepe a nagy orosz átalakulásban* (From White Tsar to Red Lenin: The Role of Hungarian Prisoners of War in the Great Transformation), Budapest 1932.

Bibliography

Liddell Hart, B. H. *The Revolution in Warfare*, London: Faber & Faber, 1946.

Lieblich, Amia, *Seasons of Captivity: The Inner World of POWs*, New York: New York University Press, 1994.

Lieven, Dominic, *Russia and the Origins of the First World War*, Oxford: St Martin's Press, 1983.

Liulivicius, Vejas Gabriel, *War Land on the Eastern Front: Culture, National Identity and German Occupation in World War I*, Cambridge: Cambridge University Press, 2000.

Lüdtke, Alf (ed.), *The History of Everyday Life: Reconstructing Historical Experience and Ways of Life*, translated by William Templer, Princeton: Princeton University Press, 1995.

Macartney, C.A., *The Habsburg Empire 1790–1918*, New York: Macmillan, 1969.

Martin, Wallace, *Recent Theories of the Narrative*, Ithaca and London: Cornell University Press, 1986.

McFall, Kelly, 'Pledging Allegiance: Perceptions of Patriotism in the Habsburg Officer Corps, 1914–1918' paper presented at the American Association for the Advancement of Slavic Studies (AAASS) 1998.

Magenschab, Hans, *Der Krieg der Großväter, 1914–1918: Die Vergessenen einer großen Armee*, Vienna: Edition S, 1993.

Melman, Billie (ed.), *Borderlines: Genders and Identities in War and Peace 1870–1930*, Routledge: New York and London, 1998.

Molenda, Jan, 'The Formation of National Consciousness among Peasants and the Part they Played in Regaining Independence', *Acta Polonica Historica*, 63-4 (1991) pp. 121–48.

Moritz, Verena, 'Die österreichische-ungarischen Kriegsgefangenen in der russischen Wirtschaft 1914 bis Oktober 1917', *Zeitgeschichte*, 25 (1998), pp. 380-9.

Mosse, George, *Fallen Soldiers: Reshaping the Memory of the World Wars*, Oxford: Oxford University Press, 1990.

Nachtigal, Reinhard 'Kriegsgefangene der Habsburgermonarchie in Russland', *Österreich in Geschichte und Literatur*, Heft 4-5a, (1996), pp. 248-62.

Nachtigal, Reinhard, 'Die dänisch österreichisch ungarischen Rotkreuzdelegierten in Rußland 1915-1918: Die Visitation der Kriegsgefangenen der Mittelmächte durch Fürsorgeschwestern des österreichischen und ungarischen Roten Kreuzes', *Zeitgeschichte*, 25 (1998), pp. 366-74.

Nachtigal, Reinhard, 'Seuchen unter miltärischer Aufsicht in Rußland Das Lager Tockoe als Beispiel für die Behandlung der Kriegsgefangenen 1915-1916', *Jahrbücher für Geschichte Osteuropas*, 48 (2000), pp. 363-87.

Nipperdey, Thomas, *Deutsche Geschichte, 1866-1918*, 2 vols, *Machtstaat vor der Demokratie*, Munich: C. H. Beck, 1992.

Nolte, Claire, 'Ambivalent Patriots: Czech Culture in the Great War', in Aviel Roshwald and Richard Stites (eds) *European Culture in the Great War: The Arts, Entertainment and Propaganda, 1914-1918*, Cambridge: Cambridge University Press, 1999, pp. 162-75.

Nolte, Claire, 'The New Central Europe of Thomas Garrigue Masaryk', *Wilsonian Central Europe Current Perspectives*, New York: Pilsudski Institute, 1995.

Nora, Pierre, *Realms Of Memory: Rethinking The French Past*, English edition, Lawrence D. Kritzman (ed.), Arthur Goldhammer (trans.), Columbia University Press, 1996.

Očak, Ivan, 'O Jugoslavenima u bjeolgardeskim jedinicama u Rusiji 1918-1920', (About Yugoslav and White Guard Units in Russia 1918-1920), *Časopis za suvremenu povijest*, 1 (1974), pp. 39-56.

Očak, Ivan, *Jugosloveni u Oktobru* (Yugoslavs in October), Belgrade, 1967.

Pach, Zsigmond Pál, and Okladnikov, A. P., *Magyar Internacionalisták Szibériában és a Távol-Keleten*, (Hungarian Internationalists in Siberia and in the Far East), Budapest, 1978.

Pardon, Inge and Schrawiljov, Waleri, (eds.), *Lager, Front oder Heimat. Deutsche Kriegsgefangene in Sovietrußland 1917-1920*, 2 vols, Berlin: S. K. Saur, 1994.

Paret, Peter, Irwin Lewis, Beth and Paret Paul, *Persuasive Images: Posters of War and Revolution*, Princeton: Princeton University Press, 1992.

Pastor, Peter, 'Hungarian POWs in Russia during the Revolution and Civil War', in Samuel Williamson and Peter Pastor, *Essays on World War I: Origins and Prisoners of War*, Boulder CO: Columbia University Press, 1983, pp. 149-62.

Pastor, Peter, 'Introduction' in Samuel Williamson and Peter Pastor (eds) *Essays on World War I: Origins and Prisoners of War*, Boulder CO: Columbia University Press, 1983, pp. 113-17.

Paulová, Milada, *Jugoslavenski odbor: Povijest jugoslavenske emigracije za svjetskog rata od 1914-1918*, Zagreb: Izdala Prosvjetna nakladna zadraga, 1925.

Pichlík, Karel, Vávra Vlastimil, and Křížek Jaroslav, *Červenobílá a rudá: vojáci ve válce a revoluci 1914–1918*, Prague: Našé vojsko, 1967.

Pichlík, Karel, *Zahraniční odboj, 1914–1918, bez legend*, Prague, 1968.

Plaschka, Richard, 'Zur Vorgeschichte des Überganges von Einheiten des Infantrieregiments Nr. 28 an der russischen Front 1915', *Österreich und Europa: Festschrift für Hugo Hantsch zum 70, Geburtstag*, Graz, 1965, pp. 455–64.

Plaschka, Richard, Suppan, Arnold and Haselsteiner, Horst, *Innere Front. Militärassistenz, Widerstand und Umsturz in der Donaumonarchie*, 2 vols, Vienna: Verlag für Geschichte und Politik, 1974.

Popovič, Nikola, *Jugoslovenski dobrovoljci u Rusiji, 1914–1918*, (Yugoslav Volunteers in Russia 1914–1918), Belgrade: Udruzenje dobrovoljaca, 1977.

Przybilovski, Inge, *Die Rückführung der österreich-ungarischen Kriegsgefangenen aus dem Osten in den letzten Monaten der k.u.k Monarchie*, Ph.D. Dissertation, University of Vienna, 1965.

Rachamimov, Alon, 'Alltagssorgen und politische Erwartungen: Eine Analyse von Kriegsgefangenenkorrespondenzen in den Beständen des Österreichischen Staatsarchiv', *Zeitgeschichte*, 25 (1998), pp. 348–56.

Rachamimov, Alon, 'Diaspora Nationalism's Pyrrhic Victory: The Controversy Regarding the Electoral Reform of 1909 in Bukovina', in John Micgiel (ed.), *State and Nation Building in East Central Europe: Contemporary Perspectives*, New York: Columbia University Institute on East Central Europe, 1996.

Rachamimov, Alon, 'Imperial Loyalties and Private Concerns: Nation, Class and State in the Correspondence of Austro-Hungarian POWs in Russia 1916–1918', *Austrian History Yearbook*, 31 (2000), pp. 87–105.

Rachamimov, Alon, 'The Czech Legion', 'The Eastern Front', and 'Elsa Brändström' in Jonathan Vance (ed.) *Encyclopedia of Prisoners of War and Internment*, Santa Barbara CA: ABC Clio, 2000.

Rachamimov, Alon 'Provincial Compromises and State Patriotism in fin-de-siècle Austria-Hungary', *Tel Aviver Jahrbuch für deutsche Geschichte*, 30 (2001).

Rauchensteiner, Manfried, *Der Tod des Doppeladlers: Österreich-Ungarn und der Erste Weltkrieg*, Graz, Wien, Köln: Verlag Styria, 1993.

Rechter, David, 'Galicia in Vienna: Jewish Refugees in the First World War', *Austrian History Yearbook*, 28 (1997), pp. 113–30.

Roberts, Adam, 'Land Warfare: from Hague to Nuremberg' in Michael Howard, George Andreopolous and Mark Shulman (eds) *The Laws of War: Constraints on Warfare in the Western World*, New Haven: Yale University Press, 1994, p. 121.

Roshwald, Aviel and Stites, Richard (eds), *European Culture in the Great War: The Arts, Entertainment and Propaganda, 1914–1918*, Cambridge: Cambridge University Press, 1999.

Rossi, Marina, *I prigionieri dello Zar: soldati italiani dell'esercito austro-ungarico nei lager della Russia 1914–1918*, Milan: Mursia, 1997.

Rothenberg, Gunther, *The Army of Francis Joseph*, West Lafayette IN: Purdue University Press, 1976.

Rothenberg, Gunther, 'The Nationality Problem in the Habsburg Army, 1740–1920', in Stpehen Fischer-Galati and Béla K. Király (eds) *Essays on War and Society in East Central Europe, 1740–1920*, War and Society in East Central Europe, Vol. 22, Eastern European Monographs No. CCXXXIII, Boulder CO: Columbia University Press, 1987, pp. 47–67.

Rothschild, Joseph, *East Central Europe between the Two World Wars*, Seattle: University of Washington Press, 1974.

Rozenblit, Marsha, *The Jews of Vienna 1867–1914*, Albany: New York, 1983.

Runciman, W.G., *Relative Deprivation and Social Justice*, London: Routledge & Kegan Paul, 1966.

Schudson, Michael, 'Dynamics of Distortion in Collective Memory', in Daniel Schacter, *Memory Distortion: How Minds, Brains and Societies Reconstruct the Past*, Cambridge: Harvard University Press, 1995, p. 348.

Schacter, Daniel, ed., *Memory Distortion: How Minds, Brains and Societies Reconstruct the Past*, Cambridge: Harvard University Press, 1995.

Scott, James Brown, *The Hague Conventions and Declarations of 1899 and 1907*, 2nd edition, New York: Oxford University Press, 1915.

Shanafelt, Gary, *The Secret Enemy: Austria-Hungary and the German Alliance, 1914–1918*, East European Monographs, No. 187, Boulder and New York: Columbia University Press, 1985.

Sharpe, Jim, 'History from Below', in Peter Burke (ed.) *New Perspectives on Historical Writing*, University Park PA: Pennsylvania State University Press, 1989, pp. 24–41.

Showalter, Dennis, *Tannenberg: Clash of Empires*, Hamden CT: Archon Books, 1991.

Sivan, Emmanuel and Winter, Jay (eds), 'Setting the Framework', in *War and Remembrance in the Twentieth-Century*, Cambridge: Cambridge University Press, 1999.

Sivan, Emmanuel, *Dor Tashakh: Mythos. Dyokan ve-Zikaron*, (The 1948 Generation: Myth Profile and Memory) in Hebrew, Tel Aviv: Merkaz Koved, 1991.

Sked, Alan, *The Decline and Fall of the Habsburg Empire, 1815–1918*, London and New York, Longman, 1989.

Smith, Anthony, *The Ethnic Origins of Nations*, Oxford: Blackwell, 1986.

Smith, Leonard, *Between Mutiny and Obedience: The case of the French Fifth Infantry Division during World War I*, Princeton: Princeton University Press, 1994.

Spann, Gustav, *Zensur in Österreich während des I. Welt Krieges 1914–1918*, Dissertation zur Erlangung des Doktorsgrades an der philosophischen Fakultät der Universität Wien, Vienna, 1972. Ph.D.

Speed, Richard, *Prisoners Diplomats and the Great War: A Study in the Diplomacy of Captivity*, New York: Greenwood Press, 1990.

Šteidler, František, *Československé hnutí na Rusi*, Prague: Nákl. Památníku odboje, 1922.

Stone, Norman, *The Eastern Front 1914–1917*, New York: Charles Scribner's Sons, 1975.

Steinmetz, George, 'Reflections on the Role of Social Narrative in Working Class Formation: Narrative Theory in the Social Sciences', *Social Science History*, 16 (1992), pp. 489-516.

Strachan Hew, (ed.), *The Oxford Illustrated History of the First World War*, Oxford: Oxford University Press, 1998.

Striegnitz, Sonja, 'Die aktive Teilnahme ehemaliger deutscher Kriegs-gefangener an der Oktoberrevolution 1917 und an den Kämpfen des Bürgerkrieges 1918-1922', *Zeitschrift für Geschichtwissen-schaft*, 8 (1960).

Striegnitz, Sonja, *Deutsche Internationalisten in Sowjetrußland 1917-1918, proletarische Solidarität im Kampf um die Sowjet-macht*, East Berlin, 1979.

Tökes, Rudolf, *Béla Kun and the Hungarian Soviet Republic: The Origins and Role of the Communist Party of Hungary in the Revolutions of 1918-1919*, New York: Praeger, 1967.

Thompson E. P. 'History from Below', *Times Literary Supplement*, 7 April 1966.

Thunig-Nittner, Gerburg, *Die tschechoslowakische Legion in Rußland: Ihre Geschichte und Bedeutung bei der Entstehung der 1. Tschechoslowakischen Republik*, Wiesbaden: Harrassowitz, 1970.

Trotter, W., *Instincts of the Herd in Peace and War*, New York: Macmillan, 1915.

Tunstall,Graydon, *Planning for War against Russia and Serbia: Austro-Hungarian and German Military Strategies, 1871–1914*, New York: Columbia University Press, 1993.

Vance, Jonathan, *Objects of Concern: Canadian Prisoners of War through the Twentieth Century*, Vancouver: University of British Columbia Press, 1994.

Vance, Jonathan (ed.), *Encyclopdia of Prisoners of War and Internment*, Santa Barbara CA: ABC Clio, 2000.

Vávra, Vlastimil, 'K počátkům intervence čs. legií v Rusku (léto 1918)' ('Regarding the beginnings of the intervention of the Czechoslovak Legion in Russia in the year 1918'), *Historie a vojenství* , (HV; History and Warfare), 1959.

Vávra, Vlastimil, 'Americký imperiliasmus v pozadí čs. intervence na Sibiri', ('American Imperialism in the background of the Czechoslovak Intervention in Sibeřia'), *Historie a vojenství*, (HV; History and Warfare), 1954.

Vávra, Vlastimil, 'Formování České družiny' ('The Formation of the Czech Družina'), *Historie a Vojenství*, 1, 1990, pp. 107–18.

Vávra, Vlastimil, 'Příprava protisovětské intervence na severu Rusko', ('The preparation of the anti-Soviet interventions in northern Russia'), *Historie a vojenství*, (HV; History and Warfare), 1963: 1.

Vávra, Vlastimil, *Klamná cesta: Připrava a vznik protisovětského vystoupení* čs. legií, Prague: Vojenský historický ústav, 1958.

Vávra, Vlastimil,: 'Z Masarykovy kontrarevoluční činnosti v Rusku' ('From Masaryk's Counter-Revolutionary Activity in Russia'), *Historie a vojenství*, (HV; History and Warfare), 1954: 1.

Völgyes, Ivan, 'Hungarian Prisoners of War in Russia', *Cahiers du monde russe et Soviétique*, 14 (1973), pp. 54–85.

Vyšný, Paul, *Neo-Slavism and the Czechs 1898–1914*, Cambridge: Cambridge University Press, 1977.

Wassermair, Otto, *Die Meutereien der Heimkehrer aus russischer Kriegsgefangenschaft bei den Ersatzkörpern der k.u.k. Armee im Jahre 1918*, Dissertation zur Erlangung des Doktorsgrades an der philosophischen Fakultät der Universität Wien, Vienna, 1968.

Weber, Eugen *Peasants into Frenchmen: The Modernization of Rural France, 1870–1914*, Stanford CA: Stanford University Press, 1976.

Wentzlau Lieker, Hanna (ed.), *Elsa Brändström-Dank*, Berlin: Heliand-Verlag, 1938.

Wette, Wolfram, 'Militärgeschichte von unten: Die Perspektive des "kleinen Mannes"', *Der Krieg des kleinen Mannes*, Munich: Piper, 1992, pp. 9–47.

Wette, Wolfram (ed.), *Der Krieg des kleinen Mannes*, Munich: Piper, 1992.

Wheatcroft, Andrew, *The Habsburgs: Embodying Empire*, London and New York: Viking, 1995.

Wildeman, Allan, *The End of the Russian Imperial Army: The Old Army and the Soldiers' Revolt (March–April 1917)*, Princeton: Princeton University Press, 1980.

Williamson, Samuel R., and Pastor, Peter (eds), *Essays on World War I: Origins and Prisoners of War*, East European Monographs CXXVI, (Boulder CO: Columbia University Press, 1983.

Wills, Garry 'A Reader's Guide to the Century', *The New York Review of Books*, 15 July (1999), p. 24.

Wilson, Trevor, 'The Significance of the First World War in Modern History', in R. J. Q. Adams (ed.) *The Great War, 1914–1918: Essays on the Military, Political Social History of the Great War*, College Station: Texas A&M University Press, 1990, pp. 7–27.

Wingfield, Nancy, 'Commemorations of the Battle of Zborov: Gender and Politics in the Construction of Official Historic Memory in Czechoslovakia', unpublished conference paper, 1999.

Winter, Dennis, *Death's Men: Soldiers of the Great War*, London: Penguin Books, 1979.

Winter Jay and Baggett, Blaine, *1914-1918: The Great War and the Shaping of 20th Century*, (London: BBC Books, 1996) this book accompanies the eight part PBS and BBC series.

Winter, Jay, *The Experience of World War I*, London: Macmillan, 1988.

Winter, Jay, *The Great War and the British People*, Cambridge MA: Harvard University Press, 1985.

Winter, Jay, *Sites of Memory, Sites of Mourning: The Great War in European Cultural History*, Cambridge: Cambridge University Press, 1995.

Wistrich, Robert, *The Jews of Vienna in the Age of Franz-Joseph*, Oxford: Oxford University Press, 1990.

Yanikdağ, Yücel, 'Ottoman Prisoners of War in Russia 1914–1922', *Journal of Contemporary History*, 34 (1999), pp. 69–85.

Zeman, Z.A. B., *The Break-Up of the Habsburg Empire 1914–1918, a Study in National and Social Revolution*, London: Oxford University Press, 1961.

Index

American
  delegation to the Hague
    Conference, 71, 83n12
  Embassy in Petrograd, 6, 88,
    128n45,188n31
  Inspectors, 57, 69, 89, 104,
    128n45, 164-5, 175, 187n17
Anti-Bolshevik Forces, 13, 120
Anti-Habsburg forces, 61n9, 81,
  86n55, 124, 151, 195
  historiography, 12, 194
  Russian policy towards, 57, 115,
    118, 124, 193
  See also Czechoslovak Legion,
    South Slav Corps
AOK (Armeeoberkommando-Army
  High Command-Austria-
  Hungary)
  advocating reprisals, 7
  attitude toward repatriation, 152,
    193-4, 206
  attitude toward POW problem,
    31-33, 152
  mobilization blunders, 60
  motivation of soldiers, 201,
    218n49
  understanding of 'loyalty'/
    'disloyalty', 33, 43-4, 134,
    139, 146, 152, 156n25,
    157n41
Armistice, 60, 120
Army High Command see AOK
Artisans see labor
Association of Czechoslovak
  Societies in Russia see Svaz

Associations of Former POWs, 1 ,
  2, 221-2 see also veterans
Astrakhan see camps

Baltic area, 68, 114, 119, 191
Banac, Ivo, 13, 16, 24n40, 79, 118,
  121
Bartov, Omer, 17, 68, 83n4
Battles eastern fron,t 35, 38, 222
Battles western front, 38
  see also western front
Bauer, Otto 3
Baumgartner, Hans, 46, 48, 64n44,
  227
Beaumont, Joan, 73, 83n8, 97
Berezovka see camps
Black and Yellow Offensive, 35, 38
Bolshevik
  influence on POW, 13, 15, 81,
    119-121, 125, 193-4, 206,
    221
  Internationalists, 12, 121, 194
    see also Internationalist
Bolshevik Revolution conditions
  after, 55, 102-3, 114, 135, 185,
    214n5
Bolshevik Russia at Brest-Litovsk,
  192
  military formations, 12
Books see recreation
Brändström, Elsa
  activity after the war, 222
  coordinator of relief effort,
    164-9, 185
  heroine and myth, 167-170

historian of captivity, 5–6,
21n14, 48, 51, 81, 109–112,
126n6
Memorial Archive, 29n59
Breitner, Burghard, 9, 22n22, 146
Brusilov Offensive, 33, 38, 43, 47,
50, 106, 178–180
Burial *see* mortality

Cadets, 56, 99, 175, 217n36
Camp Newspapers, 29, 106
Rasdolnoe, 29, 99
S'vogerl, 191
Camps
Antipikha, 104
Assembly, 34–5, 54–9, 76,
93–94
Darnitsa, 34–5, 54–59 passim
Kuzhukhovo, 35, 54–59
passim
Ugrishkaia, 34–5, 54–59
passim
Astrakhan, 7, 90, 184
Berezovka, 92, 94, 99, 167
Bui, 98
Cheliabinsk, 90
Chita, 90, 177, 182
Commandants, 48, 94–6, 99,
177, 182
Darnitsa *see* camps – assembly
Dauria, 90, 92, 94
Irkutsk, 102
Kamenskii Zavod, 119, 216n27
Khabarovsk, 101, 127n28, 144,
166, 182
Kharkov, 89, 90, 191
Kishinev, 92
Kokand, 93
Krasnaia Rechka, 92, 101
Krasnoyarsk, 16, 82, 90, 92,
99–100, 103, 173–4, 222
Nargin Island, 93
Nikolsk Ussurik, 90, 92
Novo-Nikolaevsk, 90, 95, 103,
163, 180, 186

Omsk, 57–8, 90, 94–7, 101, 103,
110, 131n82, 158n42, 180,
183, 211
Orenburg, 90, 95, 104, 174, 180
Poltava, 96
Rasdolnoe, 29, 92, 99, 106, 135,
182
Samara, 120, 174, 201, 208, 211
Samarkand, 202
Simbirsk, 91, 111, 203, 211
Spasskoe, 91, 94, 182
Stretensk, 92–3, 95, 105, 128n45
The Fortress (gorodok) 95, 163
Tobolsk, 91, 96
Tomsk, 90, 103, 129, 178, 180,
201
Totskoe, 69, 80, 95, 126n18,
175, 182, 211
Troitzki, 91, 95
Ugrishkaia *see* camps – assembly
Voennyi Gorodok *see* camps –
the fortress
Yekaterinburg, 91, 95
Capture
moment of, 9, 34, 37, 44–50, 75,
77, 216n27, 227
mass, 33–4, 44–5
narratives, 9, 59
notification of, 55
wounds, 145–7
Censorship
Censors, 139–140
Criteria, 142–4
GZNB (Gemeinsames
Zentralnachweisbureau des
Roten Kreuzes-Auskunftstelle
für Kriegsgefangene; Austro-
Hungarian POW censorship),
7, 28n58, 50–1, 88–9, 96,
109–110, ch.4 passim, 164,
186n7, 196–199
language groups, 50, 139–142,
144–5, 147–152
legal basis of, 136–137
structure of, 137–140

techniques, 145
Central Asia *see* regions –
  Turkestan
Chaplains, 72, 217n36
Charitable Organizations
  American YMCA, 78, 165,
    169-171, 188n31
  Tientsin Hilfsaktion, 78, 125n2,
    165, 169-171
Clothing
  allocation, 57, 72, 76, 78, 93
  hygiene 53, 104
  preparedness of Russia, 103, 118
  purchase of, 99, 105, 124
  relief, 78, 105, 125n2, 163-5,
    169-171, 175, 181, 200, 207
  stripped of -capture, 47
  theft, 112, 210-1
  unsuitable/shortages, 163, 177,
    209-210
Collective Remembrance, 2, 10,
  18-20, 221-222
Commandants *see* Camps –
  Commandants
Conrad von Hötzendörf, 31-32,
  61n6 *see also* AOK
Conscription, 71, 107, 131n79
Croy-Dülmen, Kunigunde Princess,
  7, 180
Czech Infantry Regiments 28 and
  36 *see* desertions
Czech Brigade *see* Czechoslovak
  Legion
Czech Company (Česká družina),
  23n34, 116-17
Czech Legion *see* Czechoslovak
  Legion
Czech Speaking POWs
  becoming POWs, 44-5, 50,
    61n12, 148-10, 152, 157n41
  flexible identities, 58
  nurses perception of, 177-8,
    181, 183
  percentage among POWs, 44,
    61n6

perception of relief effort,
  201-7, 217n36
volunteers, 116-121, 207,
  215n25, 216n27, 228
Czechoslovak Legion
  after Russian revolution, 115,
    119-121, 124-125,
    130n75-76
  Czech component in, 23n34
  historiography of, 12-15,
    194-195
  memory of, 228
  POW volunteers *see* Czech
    speaking POWs

Darnitsa *see* camps Assembly
Davis, Gerald, 15-16, 26n48, 37-8,
  79, 89
Deák, István, 60, 65n74, 157n35
Death Certificates *see* mortality
Denmark
  as mediator, 78, 114, 164, 174,
    183
  Danish Red Cross *see* Red Cross
    Danish
  Parcels purchased in, 166
  POWs interned in, 191, 214n4
Desertions
  AOK perception of, 32-33,
    p.61n6
  assessment of K-Gruppe, 143
  Czech IR 28 and 36, 12, 32-3,
    61n9, 63n32, 65n74
  Czech national mythology, 12
  Internationalist units, 132n91
  possibility of large scale, 32-7,
    44-9, 59
Doctors *see* health
Doyle, Robert, 9-10, 22n23, 49,
  226
Drexel, Karl, 9, 45, 47-8, 216n27,
  227
Duel *see* honor
Dwinger, Edwin Erich, 10-11,
  23n29, 109, 226

Dyboski, Roman, 9, 92
Dysentery *see* health

Ensigns *see* officers
Epidemics *see* health
Escape, 70-4, 94, 97, 112-13, 149,
     179, 194
Ex-POW Organizations *see*
     Associations of Former POWs
Extra-Curricular Activities *see*
     recreation

Families
     and the authorities, 8, 32, 168,
          173-5, 200-1, 209-212
     correspondence with, 50, 135-6,
          142, 222
     Jewish, 151
     Newsletters, 87-9, 97, 129, 226
     notifying, 55, 70, 75-6
Food *see also* Hunger
     during capture, 44, 48, 50, 54
     international law, 72
     officers, 99, 103, 123, 127n28
     quality of, 110-2, 163, 174-5
     russian 'style', 54
     shortages, 66n82, 105, 121, 141,
          218n49
     slavic pows, 57, 93-4
     supply of, 96, 129n70, 131n82,
          165, 169
Franz-Joseph, Emperor of Austria
     King of Hungary, 74, 148-9,
          178-9, 183, 189n56
Fussell, Paul, 10, 17, 20n5, 123,
     209

Geneva Conventions *see*
     International Law – Geneva
     Conventions
German speakers
     casualties among, 63n35, 146-47
     flexible identities, 57-8
     memoirs of, 10-11,
     nurses perception of, 177-8

percentage among POWs, 1-2,
     19n2, 38-44
perception of relief effort, 195,
     201, 203, 208, 213
treatment of, 57, 80-1, 93-4, 97,
     103, 106-8,120
Germany
     anti-semitism of officers, 56
     forces on the eastern front,
          80n5,
     mortality of pows in, 107
     number of pows and
          repatriation, 31, 40-3,192,
          221-3
     relief, 124, 163, 166-170, 179,
          185, 201, 208
     reprisals, 106, 112, 179
     utilization of POWs, 114-115,
          124, 129n70, 214n8, 229n2
Gulags, 17, 67-9, 79-82, 85n44,
     123
GZNB *see* Censorship-GZNB

Hague Conventions *see*
     International Law-Hague
     Conventions
Hameiri, Avigdor, 9, 11, 31, 47, 55,
     65n74, 226
Hašek, Jaroslav, 3
Health,110, 147, 182, 226
     'barbed-wire disease', 224,
          229n12
     diarrhea, 52, 112
     doctors /physicians, 45-47,
          51-2, 72, 94-5, 105, 128n44,
          168, 176
     dysentery, 52, 78, 214
     epidemics, 69, 73, 80, 95-6,
          103-105, 124, 126n18,
          128n45, 145, 181
     hospitals, 35, 49-51, 103,
          128n45, 168, 173, 181
     hygiene, 76
     lethargy, 103
     lice, 53,104, 118, 223

Index

mosquitoes, 81, 93, 112
scurvy, 81, 112, 223
tuberculosis, 81, 112, 181
typhoid fever, 78
typhus, 53, 69, 73, 78-80,
    95-96, 104-105, 124, 126n18,
    128n,43, 128n45, 162-163,
    176, 181, 186, 230n16
Heimkehrer see repatriation
Herwig, Holger, 3, 18, 61n9, 122,
    166, 195
Holmes, Richard, 5, 33, 43
Homosexuality, 11
Honor, 45, 74, 96-7, 101-2,
    127n24, 146, 179, 226
Hospital *see* health
Howard, Michael, 3, 70
Hunger, 52, 54, 81, 147-8, 177,
    203, 223-225 *see also* food
Hygiene *see* health

In Feindeshand, 1-3, 7, 9-12,
    39-42, 169-170, 225, 228
Industrial Killing *see* Prototype
    thesis
International law
    Efficacy, 67, 79, 87, 97-98, 107,
        115, 123-5, 185, 225-8
    General, 70-71, 173
    Geneva convention, 72, 83n6,
        84n17, 124, 179
    Hague convention, 6-7, 37, 47,
        55, 62n18, 67-80, 87-89, 117
    Stockholm protocol, 76-78, 124
Internationalists, 14-15, 121,
    132n91, 194
Interrogation and Torture, 34, 48,
    225
Irkutsk *see* camps
Italian Army, 31-33, 42, 60n4, 78,
    93, 96, 118, 131n82, 155n12

Jewish POWs, 14, 50, 56, 58, 120,
    125n2, 150-151, 155n11,
    158n43, 193

Jungbauer, Gustav, 52, 54

Keegan, John, 3, 17, 71, 122
Kerensky Alexander, 118-119
Kern, Leopold, 1-2, 10, 19n1,
    39-42, 106-107
Khabarovsk *see* camps
Killing of POWs *see* mortality
Kinsky, Nora Countess, 7, 161,
    164, 180-185, 211-212
Kisch, Egon Erwin, 43, 163,
    187n10
Klevanskii, A., 37
Kohn Hans, 3, 53, 57, 66n75, 143
Kolchak, Admiral, 13, 120
Krammer, Arnold, 16, 79, 121
Krasnaia Rechka *see* camps
Krasnoyarsk *see* camps
KÜA (*Kriegsüberwachungsamt* -
    War Supervisory Office), 34,
    137-139, 142 *see also*
    Censorship
Kun, Bela, 3, 13-14, 121
Kuzhukhovo *see* - Camps
    assembly

Labor
    agriculture, 59, 78, 89, 111, 115,
        124, 225
        farms, 66, 92, 105, 108-110,
            124
        latifundia, 92, 108-110, 192
    artisans, 66, 111
    construction, 80-81, 111-114
    forced, 73, 79, 82, 110-111, 114,
        120, 124
    industry, 108, 111, 115, 225
    mining, 89, 108, 111
    road and rail construction, 69,
        80-81, 108, 111-114
        see also murman railway
    strikes, 113, 193
Leidinger, Hannes, 16, 38
Letters *see* mail
Lice *see* health

Index

Lieblich, Amia, 4, 48
Lodgings
Officers, 55, 57, 90-91, 102
figure 3.3, 100-103, 182, 225
rank-and-file, 55, 57, 90-91,
98-99, 105, 110, 124, 170,
175, 182
regulations concerning, 72-73,
76-77
various nationalities, 93-94

Magyar Speakers
AOK perception of, 32, 43-44
casualties among, 63n35,
146-150, 157n27
in the Red Army, 13-14,
120-121
inability to send letters, 142,
157n27
nurses perception o,f 177, 182
treatment of, 57, 80-81, 93-4,
108, 120, 193
Mail
Alltagsgeschichte, 16, 28n59, 48,
97, 196-213
censorship *see* censorship
communication, 54-55, 110,
135-137, 152, 170, 173-4
international regulations
concerning, 73-77
postage, 73
postcards, 55, 76-77, 135,
142-44, 196, 209
protest, 54, 152, 210-13
various routes, 135-136
volume of, 135-138, 155n13
Marriages with Russian women,
150-152
Martens Clause, 75, 84-85n35,
87
Masaryk, Thomas Garrigue, 12,
118-119, 215n25
Memoirs, 3, 7-11, 14-16, 22n22,
45-48, 69, 97 186n7, 196, 209
MIAs *see* Missing In Action

Mihalotzy, Käthe von, 7, 173-176,
182
Military District Commands, 29,
58, 93-96, 103, 112, 124, 168,
174
Missing In Action, 35, 40, 75, 77
Mobilization, 60, 134
Morale, 33, 164, 172
Moritz, Verena, 16, 38
Mortality
death certificates, 37, 73, 76
killing of POWs, 46-7
burial, 73
rates, 37-42, 80, 104-107, 123,
132n101, 147, 227
Mosse, George, 18, 20n5
Murman Railway, 69, 80-81,
111-114, 124, 161
Mutinies, 118, 153, 215n19

Nachtigal, Reinhard, 16, 38, 69,
80-81, 163
National Distribution, 34, 43-44,
140, 217n36
NCOs, 47, 55, 89, 92, 167, 175,
178
Neutral Delegates *see* American,
Danish and Swedish delegates
Newsletters *see* Families -
newsletters
Newspapers, 99, 117, 137, 173,
191, 208-210
Nikolsk Ussurisk *see* camps
Non Commissioned Officers *see*
NCOs
Norway
POWs interned in, 191, 214 n4
Novo-Nikolaevsk *see* camps
Nurses
Austro-Hungarian, 7, 78,
172-185, 201-4, 211-212
see also Croy-Dülmen, Kinsky,
Mihalotzy, Revertera, Rosty
German, 78, 163-64, 172,
179-181

see also Üxküll, Walsleben
  Passow
memoirs, 6-7
  Russian, 163-64
  Swedish, 78, 164-171
  see also Brändström, Elsa
Officers
  Capture, 45-6
  German Army, 87, 112, 161,
    182
  Memoirs, 9-11, 28n59, 225-226
  numbers in captivity, 38-42,
    65n70
  Officer Corps, 31, 33, 44, 65n74,
    176-179, 182, 203, 208, 212
  Ottoman Army, 16, 38-42, 46,
    93, 103, 106
  regulations regarding treatment
    of, 55, 66n75, 70, 73-78
  treatment of, 48, 51, 54-58,
    90-92, 98-103, 106-107, 123,
    203-4
  See also Lodgings-Officers,
    Pay-Officers
Omsk *see* camps
Orderlies, 47, 51, 72, 78, 101,
  127n33
Orenburg *see* camps

Parole, 70-74, 84n29, 179
Pastor, Peter, 16, 78-82, 88, 121,
  123
  see also "prototype thesis"
Patriotism
  'patriotic letters', 50-51, 110,
    146-149, 157n36
  multi-national state, 50-51,
    133-35, 146-153, 177-178
  literature on, 12, 18, 155n10
Pay
  allocations,112, 131n82,
    163-66,170-75, 181-184,
    187n19, 204, 212

international law, 55, 73, 76
  officers, 97, 99, 102, 123, 203,
    207, 225
  rank-and-file, 50, 54, 66n82, 89,
    96, 101, 105-114, 124,
    129n70, 204
  ransom, 70
Peirce Herbert, *see* American
  Inspectors
Plaschka, Richard, 32, 201
Polish Speakers, 33, 61n12, 66n81,
  111, 125n2, 148-150, 207
Postage *see* mail
Postcards *see* mail
POWs
  associations *see* associations of
    former pows
  correspondence *see* mail
  deaths *see* mortality
  letters *see* censorship, mail,
    families
  officers *see* officers
  places of internment *see* camps,
    lodgings
  regulations *see* international law
  treatment *see* food, health,
    hunger, lodgings, labor,
    mortality, pay
  wages *see* pay
  work *see* labor
Price, Hereward, 53, 105
Primavesi, Theodor, 139, 147-148
  see also Censorship
Primorskaia *see* regions
Princip, Gavrilo, 78
Privacy, 101, 224
Pro-Bolshevik Units *see*
  Internationalists
Propaganda, 81, 115-121,
  177-178, 194, 216n27, 218n49
Prost, Antoine, 18, 223
Prototype thesis, 17, 67, 69, 78-82,
  123-125
Przemyśl, 33, 38, 56, 99

Index

Raabl-Werner, Heinrich von
Austro-Hungarian
Superintendent for POWs
affairs, 34-37, 161, 164
authority captivity, 7-8, 56, 165
Ransom *see* Pay-Ransom
Rasdolnoe *see* camps
Rauchensteiner, Manfried, 3, 18,
20, 32, 65n74, 122
Recreation
books and studies, 66n75,
99-101
sports, 16, 99, 226
theater and concerts, 11-12, 99,
103, 176, 182, 201
Red Army, 10, 12-15, 120-121
Red Cross
American, 169
Austrian and Hungarian, 6, 9, 74,
146, 173, 179-180, 185, 191,
197-213, 225
Central Information Bureau *see*
Censorship GZNB
Danish, 16, 88, 95, 102, 165-7,
174
delegations, 78, 162-3, 177
German, 6, 167, 179
International Society, 37, 54, 87,
162, 167
nurses *see* Nurses and individual
nurses
postcards *see* Mail
reports, 3
Russian, 179, 182
Swedish, 6, 88, 124, 136,
148n45, 165, 167-169, 172
Red Guards *see* Red Army
Regions
European Russia, 58-59, 79,
90-95, 120, 174, 180, 200,
203
Primorskaia, 52, 90-91, 93-4,
103, 170
Regions - Turkestan, 5, 29n59,
53, 58, 80, 91, 93-96, 108,
113, 174, 176, 180
Samara-Orenburg, 90, 174, 180
Siberia, 4-6, 10-13, 53, 58,
78-80, 90-96, 103, 108-111,
180-182, 225
Transbaikalia, 90-91, 94-95, 99,
104-105, 183
Ural, 93, 95, 111, 120, 180, 192,
203
Volga, 98
Release *see* repatriation, parole
Relief effort
distribution of aid, 5-8, 75-77,
105 ch.5passim
prisoners perspective, ch.6
passim
See also Red Cross, nurses
charitable organization
Religion, 10, 50, 73, 151
Repatriation, 4, 8-9, 34, 70-73,
152-153, 185, 191-195, 206,
214n8, 221, 227, 229n2
Revertera, Anna Countess, 7, 74,
172-182, 209
Roberts, Adam, 67, 123
Ronge Max, 7-8, 139, 152, 193
Rosty-Forgách, Ilona Countess, 7,
173-174

S'vogerl *see* camp - newspapers
Salaries *see* Pay
Sazonov, Sergei, 117, 125
Scurvy *see* health
Siberia *see* regions
Sivan, Emmanuel, 18, 20n4, 227
Slovak Speakers, 23n34, 33, 44,
146, 149-150, 195, 206, 228
Solzhenitsyn, Alexander, 67, 79-82
South Slav POWs, 12-13, 15,
23n34, 33, 39-43, 63, 94, 107,
121
South Slav Corps, 13, 118, 194-5,
228

Stalin, Joseph, 81-82
Stavka, 93, 116-117
Sterling A. *see* American Inspectors
Stockholm Protocol *see*
    international law
Stone, Norman, 18, 43
Streeruwitz, Ernst von, 7-8, 80,
    90-91, 108, 113, 129n70,133,
    153n1, 192-193
Stretensk *see* camps
Strikes *see* labor
Stürmer, Boris, 181
Svaz - Association of Czechoslovak
    Societies in Russia, 116-118,
    130n77
Sweden
    Mediator, 76, 78, 81, 136,
        164-66, 191
    Swedish Red Cross *see* Red Cross
    Sweden, Brändtröm Elsa

Teplushka, 52, 53, 59
Theater *see* recreation
Tientsin *see* charitable organizations
Tito, Josip Broz, 3
Torture *see* interrogation
Totskoe *see* camps, health-typhus
Trains and Train Ride, 36, 49,
    52-54, 64n74, 88, 102, 165,
    168
    see also Teplushka
Transbaikalia *see* regions
Trans-Siberian Railroad *see*
    Czechoslovak Legion

Turkestan *see* regions
Typhus *see* health

Ugrishkaia *see* Camps-assembly
Ukrainian Speakers, 33, 61n12,
    66n81, 140, 148
United States *see* American
Üxküll, Alexandrine Countess, 7,
    132n98, 172

Vance, Jonathan, 5, 21n12, 146
Veterans, 1-2, 5, 168, 221-222

War Supervisory Office *see* KÜA
    (*Kriegsüberwachungsamt*)
Warfield William, 105, 128n45
    see also American Inspectors
Weiland, Hans, 1-2, 10, 39-42,
    46-48, 102-103, 169, 228
Western Front, 9, 11, 18, 38, 209,
    213, 222-227
White armies, 23n29, 120
    see also Kolchak
Winter, Jay 18, 20, 227
Wounded POWs, 37, 47-51, 75,
    84n17, 145-148, 167, 177,
    180-182, 191
Wülbecke, Franz von der, 92, 167

YMCA *see* charitable organizations

Zborov battle of, 13, 16, 24n35,
    118-119